In Quest
of the
Great
White Gods

Books by Robert Marx

Historia de la Isla de Cozumel, Mérida, Yucatán
Voyage of the *Niña II*
Following Columbus
The Battle of the Armanda, 1588
The Battle of Lepanto, 1571
They Dared the Deep: A History of Diving
Pirate Port: The History of the Sunken City of Port
    Royal
Always Another Adventure
Treasure Fleets of the Spanish Main
Shipwrecks in Florida Waters
Shipwrecks in Mexican Waters
Shipwrecks of the Western Hemisphere
Sea Fever: Famous Underwater Explorers
Port Royal Rediscovered
The Lure of Sunken Treasure
Underwater Dig: Manual of Underwater
    Archaeology
Secrets Beneath the Sea
Capture of the Spanish Plate Fleet: 1628
Diving for Adventure
Spanish Treasures in Florida Waters
Still More Adventures
Buried Treasures of the United States
Into the Deep: A History of Man's Underwater
    Explorations
Quest for Treasure (Discovery of the Galleon
    Maravillas)
Shipwrecks in Florida Waters—A Billion Dollar
    Graveyard
The History of Underwater Explorations
Sunken Treasure: How To Find It

Books by Jenifer Marx

Pirates of the Caribbean
The Magic of Gold

In Quest
of the
Great
White Gods

Contact Between the Old and New
World from the Dawn of History

Robert F. Marx
with Jenifer G. Marx

CROWN PUBLISHERS, INC.   NEW YORK

Published by Crown Publishers, Inc., 201 East 50th Steet, New
York, New York 10022. Member of the Crown Publishing
Group.

CROWN is a trademark of Crown Publishers, Inc.

Book design by June Bennett-Tantillo

Manufactured in the United States of America

Library of Congress Cataloging-in-Publication Data
Marx, Robert F., 1933–
    In quest of the great white gods : contact between the Old and
  New World from the dawn of history / Robert F. Marx with
  Jenifer G. Marx.
        p.   cm.
      1. America—Discovery and exploration—Pre-Columbian.
    2. Indians—Antiquities.   3. Underwater archaeology.
    4. Underwater exploration.   5. America—Antiquities.
    6. Marx, Robert F., 1932–   . I. Marx, Jenifer. II. Title.
    E103.M367   1992
    970.01′1—dc20   91-22157
                                                              CIP
ISBN 0-517-58270-8

10   9   8   7   6   5   4   3   2   1

First Edition

This book is dedicated to Donald C. Webster and Michael Needham, good friends and business associates, who have been a great source of encouragement in my quest for the Great White Gods.

Contents

In Quest
of the
Great
White Gods

1

Arrival of the Great White Gods

One morning in 1519, natives along the eastern coast of the Yucatán Peninsula spotted what appeared to be "floating towers" silhouetted against the rising sun. Soon the tall tublike vessels with bellying sails were on the beach, spewing forth strange-looking men—men with white faces, white hands, and bristling black beards. To the copper-skinned natives, the men seemed as alien as creatures from space; yet their arrival was not altogether unexpected. Could they not be the "bearded white gods" who according to legend had come to their land many generations before and taught their ancestors many things before departing to the east with a promise to return someday?

This scenario was repeated several weeks later on the other side of the Yucatán Peninsula when Hernán Cortés landed with his men near the present-day city of Veracruz. After an arduous trek across the steep mountains, prolonged by numerous fierce battles with various Indian tribes, the Spaniards reached the fabled city of Tenochtitlán, the capital of the Aztec nation.

They fully expected to be met with hostility and were amazed at the joyous welcome they were accorded. They soon learned why they were greeted with celebration and treated with honor. The ill-starred Montezuma, emperor of the Aztec, received Cortés in his garlanded palace, where, according to a contemporary chronicle, the Spaniards saw "more gold than they believed existed in the entire world." He managed to make Cortés understand that the Aztec believed the seaborne Spaniards were the returning "great white gods" led by Quetzalcoatl, the principal god of the Aztec, represented by a feathered serpent.

According to Aztec legend, Quetzalcoatl had come from the east in a "winged ship" many centuries before. No one knew who he was or where he came from. He was a wise, kindhearted white stranger with blue eyes and a full gray beard, dressed in a long black robe. He preached a new religion of universal peace and brotherhood. After dispensing a vast body of knowledge to Montezuma's ancestors, he disappeared as mysteriously as he had come.

Many historians believe that the event that gave rise to this legend most likely took place sometime in the eleventh century, when the Norsemen were most active and had already penetrated the North American continent. During that time some of the Irish monks who were trying to convert the Norsemen to Christianity were residing in Greenland. There is a brief entry for the year 1121 in the medieval *Icelandic Annals* stating that "Bishop Eric went to visit Vinland"—that is, North America. Danish historians have established that the Icelandic nobleman Eric Gnupson, also known as Bishop Eric, had arrived in Greenland in 1112, after having been consecrated by Pope Pascal II (1098–1118) in Rome earlier the same year as "Bishop of Greenland and Neighboring Regions." Vinland, one of the "neighboring regions," had been discovered by the Norse explorer Leif Ericsson more than a century earlier, and was most certainly a part of Bishop Eric's diocese.

Bishop Eric never returned from his mission to Vinland.

Unheard from for years, he was presumed dead. The converted Norsemen of Greenland requested that the Pope send a replacement, and eventually a new bishop was dispatched to them.

Whether or not Bishop Eric's travels ever took him to Mexico may never be determined, but for the present he is the most likely candidate for Quetzalcoatl, the "bearded white god." Some historians think the sixth-century Atlantic voyages of the seafaring Irish monk Brendan, abbot of Clonfert, make him a more likely candidate for Quetzalcoatl despite the disparity in dates. It is well documented that Brendan had a seven-year absence (565–572 A.D.) during one of his many voyages, and it is possible he may have reached the shores of Mexico. Whether it was Bishop Eric, Brendan, or an unknown Christian teacher who reached Mexico first may never be known, but there is a great deal of evidence that some Catholic missionary did. Later, when the Spaniards made contact with the Indians of Mexico they were amazed to find so many similarities between the indigenous religion and Catholic worship, including veneration of the cross, holy water, rosaries, the confessional, nuns and monastic orders, symbols of the Trinity, and penances and other practices. Over the centuries the religion brought by Quetzalcoatl was adapted by succeeding generations of natives into their religious practices.

The ruined Mayan city of Chichén Itzá in the center of the Yucatán Peninsula was one of the most important religious centers of the advanced Mayan culture. Jutting from corners of stone buildings and carved on columns all over the ruins are carvings of bearded men with sharp features. Who were these men? They could not have been Maya or any of the other New World Indians, who had very little facial hair and never wore beards. Bearded men can be seen in hundreds of stone carvings and wall frescoes at other Mayan sites spanning a large area from Guatemala to the tip of the Yucatán Peninsula. Hundreds of other pre-Columbian ruins throughout Central and South America also have bas-reliefs, frescoes, or sculptures depicting men with beards.

The Maya first settled in the highlands of Guatemala around 1000 B.C., and they had a flourishing civilization by 300 A.D. Sometime between 700 and 1000 they began abandoning their cities and ceremonial sites and reverted to a more primitive mode of living, mainly in the northern sector of the Yucatán Peninsula. Why this occurred is unknown, but we do know a great deal about their origins, and we know they also revered a "bearded great white god" known as both Kukulcán and Votan.

White gods figure in almost every indigenous culture in the Americas. Unfortunately, their origins are shrouded, chiefly because, in their religious zeal, the invading Spaniards destroyed almost every pre-Columbian manuscript of the conquered Indians—records that may have told of the "white gods" and other visitors to their shores. The Spaniards were obsessed with eradicating the past history of the Indians. In one case a Spanish merchant who returned to Spain from Mexico in 1547 was found to be in possession of an Aztec codex or manuscript. The Holy Inquisition burned him at the stake, along with the codex, which they described as "the work of the devil."

Fortunately one book, the *Popol Vuh (Book of Counsel)*, written in the mid-sixteenth century by a Christianized Maya of Guatemala, managed to survive and was discovered around the beginning of the eighteenth century by a Dominican monk, Fray Francisco Ximénez. Written in the Quiché language in characters of Latin script, it was translated into Spanish and later into English. This text is the scholarly world's main source of Mayan history and mythology. How it managed to escape destruction by the fanatical Spaniards is a mystery. Even today the Quiché Maya people of the Guatemala highlands consider the *Popol Vuh* a sacred book, akin to the Bible.

The Mayan author gathered the facts for his book from countless interviews with the oldest people and also, some scholars believe, from one or more old codices about the origins of Mayan civilization that had escaped destruction.

Many other Maya also contributed to this book, telling what they had been told about their ancestors' origins. The stories are all similar. The people started eastward across the Atlantic and came to the Americas. Their kingdom was founded by a great eastern ruler named Votan. Votan was a white man who with his crew of tall, fair-haired, blue-eyed men in dragon-prowed "serpent ships" brought the Mayan people across the sea and settled them in their new land.

Other Indian tribes throughout the Americas have similar legends. In some, the tribe's ancestors were brought across "the great sea by white men"; in others, "white men" later came to dispense valuable knowledge about agriculture, architecture, and other matters. Mayan tradition claims both of these scenarios. Votan brought them to their new land, and later on another "bearded white god," Kukulcán, came and added to their knowledge.

Many scholars believe that Kukulcán and Quetzalcoatl were the same man and that he never returned to his original land but died somewhere in the New World. Countless archaeological discoveries made throughout Latin America lend some credence to this legend. However, it is more likely that a number of white men came across to the New World. From the statues of bearded white men at La Venta, one of the most important sites of the Olmec, an ancient Indian people centered in the present-day Mexican states of Tabasco and Veracruz, to the Nordic-looking stone heads at ancient Tiahuanaco in Bolivia, there are thousands of ancient American images of men with distinctly un-Indian features.

The *Popul Vuh* repeatedly states that the Maya's ancestors "came from the east across the great sea and were brought by strangers from other lands." It also states that "white men came at different times and served as teachers and guides." A few scholars think that if the *Popul Vuh* is a correct history of the ancient Maya, the "great sea" most likely refers to the Caribbean and not the Atlantic Ocean. They base this on the fact that Mayan artifacts have been discovered on various islands around the Caribbean basin. What they fail to consider is that every single Mayan artifact thus discovered dates after 1000 A.D., and the Maya arrived much earlier in the region of Guatemala.

Late in the eighteenth century, another ancient document turned up in Guatemala. It was translated by the Spanish writer Ordóñez y Aguilar and published in Madrid with the title *Probanza de Votan (Evidence of Votan)*. The booklet had a short life. Within days of its publication the Spanish Crown ordered all copies seized and destroyed, and today only one copy is known to exist. The author was jailed for heresy, though later released after paying a substantial fine. This manuscript traces the origins of the Maya to Votan, who, following a divine command, brought his people from across the "eastern sea" around 1000 B.C. and established their first settlement near the Usumacinta River in Guatemala, where some of the earliest traces of the Mayan civilization have actually been found.

Do these legends have any historical basis? Many myths and legends are formed around a germ of historical fact. The Norse sagas, for example, are stories with a core of truth. Unfortunately, it is not easy to find evidence to corroborate them. One of the problems is that few orthodox historians deem it prudent to risk their academic reputations by challenging established theories. Several decades ago, for example, Yale University published a book about the Vinland Chart, a map believed to be from the tenth century, which showed Vinland as a region of present-day New England. This created a storm of controversy, and eventually the Yale professors who had put forth the theory backed away from it. The time factor is another obstacle in proving the factual origin of various myths. Ancient peoples had varying methods of reckoning dates of important events, and historians sometimes invoke the discrepancy in dates to assert that an event could not have taken place.

The Norwegian explorer-archaeologist Thor Heyerdahl has been in trouble most of his life with archaeologists, anthropologists, and other scholars of prehistory. Heyerdahl first antagonized academia in 1947 when he sailed a balsa-log raft across the Pacific. He christened the raft *Kon Tiki* for the Kon Tiki Viracocha, who according to Peruvian legend was a bearded white god who founded the Incan civilization. Scientists scoffed at the idea that such a craft was capable of crossing large bodies of water. The only thing that Heyerdahl proved, remarked one noted archaeologist, apropos of the *Kon Tiki* expedition, "was that Norwegians are good sailors." Heyerdahl speculated that the ancient pre-Inca culture that created the pyramid complex in Peru may be the missing link in a chain of civilizations spreading from Mesopotamia, the Indus Valley, and Egypt to Meso-America. In his much-criticized work *The Bearded Gods* he wrote that the Inca themselves believed they had lived more or less as savages until a light-skinned, bearded foreigner came into their country, taught them the ways of civilization, and then departed. But today the theory that the South American Indians relied on outsiders to achieve an advanced civilization infuriates many people; it seems politically incorrect.

Heyerdahl is one of the best-known of a group of prehistorians called diffusionists, who believe that most ancient civilizations spread from a common source by land and sea around the world. An opposing and much larger group, the isolationists, believe that ancient civilizations developed independent of one another.

Few scholars fail to accept that there are many remarkable similarities between the civilizations of pre-Columbian America and those of the Old World. But the isolationists believe that cultural parallels in widely separated ancient societies— similarities in agriculture, architecture, astronomy, metallurgy, and religion—could have been the result of independent evolution and invention. They hold that the human mind is apt to react inventively in a similar manner to similar environmental challenges in different areas of the world. Consequently, they think that the occurrence of identical tools, weapons, artistic motifs, customs, and other cultural details does not prove that there was contact between the Old and New World.

I tend to think that the isolationist theory may explain similarities in some broad aspects of technology but not the multitude of point-by-point similarities found in pyramid construction and fitted megalithic masonry, necropolises, adobe-brick manufacture, mural painting and relief carving, calendar systems, trepanning, mummification, manufacture of bark cloth, the lost-wax process, ceramic stamps, weaving, reed boats, sun worship, marriage between sisters and brothers in royal families, specialized musical instruments, wheeled toys, parcheesi and other games, and many other particular technical and cultural characteristics.

The discovery in the Americas of tens of thousands of artifacts of definite Old World origin must also be taken into account. The great wealth of archaeological evidence that has been coming to light in recent years, no longer concealed as it was in the past, seems to tip the balance in favor of the diffusionist theory of contact between Old and New World civilizations.

However, the isolationists refuse to abandon their view. They concede that certain of the similarities between the higher cultures of Asia and the New World are a result of diffusion via the Bering Strait, but do not believe that massive dissemination of Neolithic or Bronze Age traits could have occurred by this route—and in fact very few of the traits shared by the higher cultures of the Old and New Worlds are found in the Arctic or Subarctic environmental regions through which such diffusion must have passed. The only other answer to the question posed by cultural similarities is communication across the open sea between continents.

Satisfied that he has proved that early man could have reached the New World in primitive vessels such as the balsa raft of the *Kon Tiki* voyage and the papyrus boats of the *Ra I* and *Ra II* expeditions, Heyerdahl has come full circle in his lifelong investigations. Since 1989 he has been in Peru working with a team of archaeologists who are conducting a series of excavations at Túcume on the northern coastal plains of Peru.

This Moche site, which dates from 100 B.C. to 600 A.D., has yielded a great number of artifacts unlike any others found in the New World. Heyerdahl believes that it was first constructed by foreign visitors to the area. On the coast just twelve miles from this site Heyerdahl has found a wooden steering oar that he is convinced came from an ancient Asiatic or Polynesian vessel. He would not be surprised to find fair-haired mummies, some of which have been found in other pre-Inca ruins. He also thinks the team may unearth wooden tablets such as those he found on Easter Island, which were inscribed with an undecipherable language found nowhere else in the world. He remains captivated by the pre-Inca legend of Kon Tiki Viracocha, the white-bearded sun king who came out of the sea to impart the secrets of an advanced culture to the coastal South Americans and later was driven off by rebelling vassals and set adrift on a raft in the Pacific Ocean.

Whether man crossed the seas between the Old World and the New before Columbus is a tantalizing question that has long excited the imagination of people everywhere. Chiefly because of the lack of original documentation, the subject has stirred heated controversy among scholars; but history must often be painstakingly reconstructed from oral tradition and archaeological evidence rather than from written sources alone.

In 1961 two respected archaeologists, Helge and Anne-Stine Ingstad, began an excavation at L'Anse-aux-Meadows on a coastal plain in Newfoundland. With an army of skeptics looking over their shoulders, the Ingstads were searching for "Vinland," the bountiful new land discovered by the Norwegian explorer Leif Ericsson, son of Eric the Red, who, according to Icelandic sagas written several centuries after the event took place, led a band of Norsemen across the sea to the west of Greenland. Other interpreters of the sagas believed that Vinland meant "land of grapes" and lay somewhere along the New England coast, where wild grapes flourish. Disagreeing with these earlier theories, the Ingstads closely followed the nautical descriptions of the sagas, which first led them to Labrador and finally to the northern coast of Newfoundland, where they discovered the indisputable Norse community at L'Anse-aux-Meadows. During eight summers of work they found the remains of eight timber-and-sod buildings, including a sauna and a smithy in which the Norsemen forged bog iron. Among their many discoveries was a distinctly identified Norse spindle whorl—a doughnut-shaped soapstone object used to spin wool into yarn—identical to the many found on archaeological sites in Scandinavia, Iceland, and Greenland.

No one can say for certain that L'Anse-aux-Meadows was Leif Ericsson's Vinland, but it is absolutely certain that Norsemen lived there around 1000 A.D. Prior to the Ingstads' discovery many scholars had discounted as pure fiction the Norse sagas' accounts of Norsemen voyaging to the North American continent. In 1976 the Norsemen finally won the honor long overdue them and were recognized as having preceded Columbus to the New World. President Ford proclaimed that each October 9 would be celebrated as Leif Ericsson Day to honor the Norseman who—in the words of the proclamation— "touched our shores centuries before the Italian explorer's *Niña, Pinta,* and *Santa María* sighted what is now the Dominican Republic." Some government bureaucrat must have forgotten that Columbus first landed at San Salvador in the Bahamas!

Like a debutante anxiously preparing for her ball, all of Spain has been making preparations during the past decade for 1992, the year that marks both the five hundredth anniversary of Columbus's discovery of America and the defeat of the Moors of Granada, the event that made Spain an independent European nation. Barcelona, which will host the Olympic games, and Seville, where Expo 92, the World's Fair, will be held, are undergoing urban face-lifts that will cost more than ten million dollars. Many economists warn that the country may bankrupt itself by spending so much, but for the proud Spaniards, this is a chance to show off Spain's illustrious past and to join the the world's leading modern nations.

Many Latin Americans, as well as members of Indian tribes in the United States and Canada, are not happy about the forthcoming celebrations. There is a furious criticism of the Catholic Church for considering the canonization of Queen Isabella, who arranged financing for Columbus's voyages. In 1990, Indian activists protested a Columbus exhibit at the Florida Museum of Natural History in Gainesville, claiming it was a racist propaganda show that downplayed the genocide and enslavement of the Indians by the Spaniards. Similar demonstrations have taken place all over the Americas, and several Latin American nations have refused to participate in the 1992 celebrations. In Mexico the government refused to accept the gift of a large bronze statue of Hernán Cortés from the Spanish government, because it would only serve as a reminder to the people of the destruction of ancient Mexican civilization and of the suffering of the indigenous population under Spanish rule.

In the Philippines, which was a Spanish colony for almost four hundred years, I witnessed this animosity firsthand in both ordinary citizens and top government officials. In 1985 I initiated a project to construct a replica of a Manila galleon. As part of the quincentennial celebrations in 1992 I would sail it between Manila and Acapulco following the route such galleons plied for three centuries. I spent two years batting my head against innumerable obstacles placed in my path to frustrate the project. I finally had an audience with President Aquino. She shattered my lifelong dream in short order. "Mr. Marx," she said, "for four centuries the Philippine people were enslaved by the Spaniards, and the last thing my people and I want is for you to glamorize and enhance the Spanish domination of the Philippines!"

Rather than enjoying fame as the "discoverer" of the New World, Columbus should be known as the man who renewed Europe's interest in the lands that lay on the far side of the Atlantic. During the so-called Dark Ages in Europe, geographical knowledge and maritime activity suffered a general decline. Men forgot that Strabo, Homer, Aristotle, Plato, Plutarch,

Seneca and many other ancient writers had referred to the existence of lands far out in the Atlantic Ocean. There seems little doubt that the geographical information recorded by such authors, much of which is understandably vague, was derived from accounts of early voyages far to the west, possibly even to the New World. The Renaissance, which flowered in the fifteenth century, marked a vigorous rebirth of hunger for knowledge and renewed activity. Columbus's "discoveries" spurred the curiosity and adventurous spirit characteristic of seafaring peoples.

In recent years a number of books and articles have appeared stating that Columbus did not set out blindly in search of unknown lands or a new route to Asia as he is popularly believed to have done, but was well aware of the existence of the New World. Columbus himself actually reported evidence of European contact.

During his second voyage he wrote of finding wreckage of a European ship on the island of Guadeloupe. Some months later, while cruising along the coast of Venezuela, his small fleet of vessels was approached by a large wooden canoe containing eighty men, whom he described as being of stout build with white skin and long blond hair and beards.

Although he and his crew attempted to communicate with these "strange men," they fled before their identity or origin could be established. Were they descendants of Norsemen who had reached North America five centuries earlier, or perhaps descendants of other Old World mariners who managed to set foot on those far shores? One thing is certain—they did not belong to any of the Indian cultures then extant in the New World.

There is a great deal of convincing evidence that there were also "great black gods" in the New World in pre-Columbian times. Shortly before Vasco Núñez de Balboa discovered the Pacific Ocean in 1513 while he was cruising along the Darién coast of Panama, he discovered a large colony of black-skinned people at a place named Quarequa. Balboa and several officers in his expedition reported that they were "Negroes from Africa and not Indians from the New World." Today the San Blas Indians live in this area, and although they are definitely not of Negroid stock, they have distinctive physical characteristics unlike those of any other natives of the New World. Their lore also asserts that their ancestors came from lands far away to the east, and their past has been associated with everyone from the wandering Lost Tribes of Israel to the Phoenicians.

Dr. Ivan Van Sertima, a respected anthropologist at Rutgers University, published the controversial book *They Came Before Columbus: The African Presence in Ancient America* in 1977. Van Sertima began his studies in 1970 when he came across extraordinary parallels between Africa and the Americas that indicated the presence of African influences on medieval Mexican and South American languages. Intrigued yet skeptical, he began researching those similarities and started to piece together a series of isolated archaeological discoveries. He became convinced that black African traders and explorers had reached the Americas, on both planned and accidental voyages. His critics in academia contended that if African Negroes came over they were most likely brought as slaves by the Phoenicians or other Mediterranean mariners. Van Sertima responded to these allegations by asking why, if that assumption was true, Negroid heads were objects of veneration among the Maya and the Aztec, and why the Olmec erected such huge monuments to them.

As a budding historian–archaeologist I had studied numerous books and archaeological reports about the presence of African Negro artifacts in the New World. Among the most convincing was the work of Professor Alexander von Wuthenau, an art historian who studied thousands of Negroid portraits in gold, copper, clay, and copal (a tropical resin) found in ancient Central and South America. I followed in his footsteps and made the same startling discoveries and assessments. These depictions of Negroes not only capture the dense close curl and kink of Negroid hair and the occasional goatee beard, which is unknown among the New World Indians, but also the broad noses, full-fleshed lips, projecting jaws, and coloration. They show African facial tattoos and scarification, ear pendants, and headdresses and coiffures.

Historian Frederick Peterson in his study of ancient Mexico emphasized "the strong Negroid substratum that intermingled with the Olmec." In September 1974 a Polish craniologist, Andrzej Wiercinski, presented a paper at the Congress of Americanists in which he reported that skulls from various Olmec archaeological sites "show a clear prevalence of the total Negroid pattern." A year later a Smithsonian Institution archaeological team reported finding two Negro male skeletons in a grave in the U.S. Virgin Islands that dated from 1250 A.D. The teeth of both skulls "showed a dental mutilation characteristic of early African cultures." The hand of one of the skeletons was clamped around an earthenware pot of pre-Columbian Indian manufacture. Anthropologist Ernest Hooten reports that some skulls found by archaeologists in pre-Columbian sites in the valley of the Pecos River in Texas and northern Mexico closely resemble crania of Negro groups coming from parts of Africa.

The most convincing proof that Negroid Africans arrived in the Americas during pre-Columbian times can be seen in the eleven colossal Negroid heads, sculpted from forty-ton blocks of basalt, that were found in the vicinity of Veracruz, Mexico, along with other artifacts with Negroid portraits on them. Nearby at Tres Zapotes the earliest-known wheeled toys were also discovered. The oldest evidence of mathematics and written dates was also found in this area—a cultural evolution that could only have occurred by introduction from another people. The Olmec, the New World's earliest "high culture," were the predecessors of the Maya and Aztec; they developed a very sophisticated civilization and established numerous ceremonial centers along the shores of the states of Tabasco and Veracruz facing the Gulf of Mexico.

In 1957 when I was living on Cozumel Island off the coast of Yucatán, I had the honor of meeting Dr. Alberto Ruiz, a noted Mexican archaeologist. Unlike many of the others I had met and would meet over the years, he believed that many mariners from the Old World had reached the shores of Mexico in pre-Columbian times. I assisted him in making an archaeological survey along the nearby coast of Quintana Roo, and we spent countless hours discussing this topic. At the end of the expedition I went with him to the other side of the Yucatán Peninsula to the Olmec site of La Venta, where four of the massive heads had recently been unearthed. These heads had military-type helmets and weighed between thirty and forty tons each. No one who has ever seen them would doubt they represent Negroes.

Samples of wood charcoal found in association with the heads gave a carbon-14 date of 814 B.C., plus or minus 134 years. Dr. Ruiz pointed out to me that the period covered by the extremes of the carbon dating was contemporary with the rise of the Nubian military as a decisive factor in the conquest and rule of Nubian pharaohs in Egypt's Twenty-fifth Dynasty. During that period these Negro Egyptian rulers were allied with the Phoenicians against the Assyrians. This is also the period when the Phoenicians, the greatest mariners in antiquity, began making sorties in the Atlantic Ocean.

However, there are a number of scholars, including Thor Heyerdahl, who believe that African Negroes most likely reached the Americas with the Egyptians. Heyerdahl's two expeditions in the *Ra I* and *Ra II,* which did not hew as close to historical re-creation as the epic *Kon Tiki* voyage, have been dismissed by some of his detractors as little more than publicity stunts. However, in trying to show how Egyptians and Negro Africans could have sailed to the New World in papyrus-reed vessels as early as 2000 B.C., Heyerdahl did prove two things: that it was possible for a papyrus boat to make an ocean crossing, and that since he and his crew were able to cross the Atlantic in a "laundry basket" or a "floating haystack," as some have quipped, then nearly anyone could have crossed it in ancient times in almost any kind of vessel.

Heyerdahl saw striking likenesses between reed boats depicted in frescoes in Egyptian tombs and others illustrated on ancient Peruvian ceramics, but what he failed to take into account was that there is no evidence that reed boats were used on the high seas by any group. Those built in Egypt and Mesopotamia, where there was no lumber at all, were used for short trips on rivers and lakes. The same type of watercraft are still in use today on Lake Victoria and elsewhere in Africa, as well as on Lake Titicaca in the Andes. Why then did he use a reed boat when the Egyptians in antiquity had much sturdier sailing ships at their disposal, unless he wished to make the voyage more uncertain and interesting, more like the *Kon Tiki* voyage? Neither Heyerdahl's focus on the Egyptians nor the type of vessel he selected was the most logical choice. The Egyptians were never noted for their seamanship and rarely sailed on protracted sea voyages. They depended on other maritime peoples, such as the Phoenicians, to attend to their maritime affairs.

A small number of Egyptian artifacts have been unearthed under less than clear circumstances in the New World. These include two Egyptian statuettes that purportedly were found under ten feet of sand on a beach at Acajutla in El Salvador, and several other Egyptian-looking statues and a copper disk bearing an engraving of three Egyptian-type pyramids and a sphinx that were found by grave robbers in Yucatán. In addition, shortly after Heyerdahl reached Barbados aboard the *Ra II,* a doctor on the island of Martinique reported finding an ancient coin, identified as dating from the Egyptian Second or Third Dynasty. However, since none of these items were seen *in situ* by archaeologists, there is some doubt of their authenticity.

The presence of tobacco, always thought to have been a plant originating in the Americas, was one of the startling discoveries made by French scientists who in 1977 treated the mummy of Pharaoh Ramses II, born in 1301 B.C. It was used to stuff the inside cavities of the body before burial. There is no evidence that the Egyptians ever smoked tobacco, but it has since been discovered in other Egyptian mummies. How did this American product reach Egypt? If the Egyptians did indeed reach the shores of the New World, with or without Negro Africans on board, it is likely that they did so aboard a Phoenician ship.

Rather than conclude that African Negroes reached the New World on Phoenician or other Old World vessels manned by "white men," we must recognize that they were no strangers to the sea. Negroid sea captains and mariners were known to serve in the Egyptian navy in the Nineteenth Dynasty and later on as well. There are also numerous records of African pirates making raids on pre-Christian Ireland. Coastal trade among the natives along the west coast of Africa dates back to the medieval period and most likely even earlier.

Although many of the New World Indian cultures trace their legendary origins to people who came from far away in ships, the first men actually arrived during the last Ice Age from Asia via the Bering Strait. Archaeologists debate when this took place. Most agree that this migration took place sometime between 25,000 and 12,000 years ago, when North America was covered by great masses of ice. Sea levels were down more than three hundred feet, exposing the seafloor between Alaska and Siberia and creating a dry land bridge between the two continents. Not all scholars agree with these dates. Dr. Louis S. B. Leakey, who is highly respected for his work in Africa, claims that man has been in the New World for more than a million years. Stone tools have been found in the Mojave Desert of California that Leakey and others have dated as between 50,000 and 80,000 years old, which would mean that America was inhabited at the time of the Neanderthals, and stone tools found elsewhere in North America push this date back a million years. But other archaeologists argue that the stones may have been shaped naturally and are skeptical of Leakey's dates. Whatever dates are correct, there is no disputing the fact that early man reached the New World long before anyone was making transoceanic voyages.

Dr. Georg Debetz of the Institute of Ethnography in Moscow believes that all pre-Columbian Americans may be descended from a band of about fifty people who crossed the Bering Strait around 23,000 B.C. Debetz bases his belief on the fact that the original Americans had limited blood types and an ethnic uniformity characterized by dark hair and eyes, tan skin, largely hairless bodies, and somewhat Mongoloid features, which are all characteristics of early Asian peoples. He may be right about the fact they were all Asians, but few scholars believe that only a handful crossed the Bering Straits.

Whether or not the first migrants were coastal people or possessed any maritime skills is not known, but they could have been daring seamen if other evidence is considered. There is unequivocal proof that Asians populated Australia via the sea nearly 40,000 years ago, but traveling by boat in tropical waters is not as difficult as it would have been in the northern latitudes. It is believed that at least as early as 8,000 years ago early man was fishing and hunting whales by boat off the coasts of Alaska and western Canada. However, archaeologists—trained by the nature of their work which is primarily on land—look to a land bridge as the most likely way the Asians reached the Americas.

Archaeologists have the reputation of being among the most skeptical of scientists. After a lifetime working in the field I have found that it generally takes a major earthquake to change their opinions. In 1974 I became embroiled in a controversial event that serves as a good example. Until 1974 it was accepted fact that early man did not reach Florida until 3,500 years ago. Now we know that Stone Age men were living in caves in Florida as early as 12,000 years ago. This startling fact would have been discovered twenty years earlier if archaeologists had given consideration to evidence from a Florida sinkhole found by an amateur about fifty miles south of Tampa, near Sarasota.

This evidence came to light in 1958 through the determination and devotion of Bill Royal, a retired Air Force colonel living in Venice on the Gulf Coast of Florida. Royal, an avid sport diver, spent a great deal of time diving in the myriad limestone sinkholes that dot the state. Near his home in Warm Mineral Springs, which has long been a flourishing sulfur-water health spa, Royal was astonished to find large stalactites hanging from the roof of many submerged caves, an indication that at one time they were above water. Digging in the sediment of a cave forty-three feet below the surface, he discovered several Paleo-Indian skeletons and a lot of bones from animals that have been extinct since the last Ice Age. Royal was very excited by his find and contacted a geologist, who studied the caves and determined that the stalactites had formed between 1,000 and 20,000 years ago. He then turned over the bones to an anthropologist, but both bones and the scientist disappeared and Royal had to start all over again.

Over a period of months, Royal dug into the sediment of several caves and found a number of stone spear heads, two bone needles, various animal bones that had been worked into tools, and the remains of five more skeletons. After his repeated pleas to the University of Florida, an archaeologist visited the site. After a cursory visual inspection of the site he pronounced the artifacts and bones to be no more than five hundred years old.

Ten years later, after I met Royal and became interested in what he had discovered, I took these same artifacts to ten archaeologists, all of whom dated them between 10,000 and 15,000 years old. The catch was not telling them where the objects had been found before they analyzed them. If they had known, I doubt they would have trusted their observations and made an objective assessment.

During the summer of 1959, Chet Huntley sent an NBC television crew down to film Royal at work in the sinkhole. Dr. Eugenie Clark, a well-known marine biologist who specializes in shark studies, was diving with him, and while filming was in progress they discovered another human skeleton. This skeleton had a complete skull containing the brain, which was in a remarkable state of preservation. The high hydrogen sulfide content of the 87-degree-Fahrenheit water in Warm Mineral Springs had created an anaerobic environment that protected the brain and other organic material that came to light.

Carbon-14 dating revealed that the skull and brain were about 10,000 years old. The oldest extant brain previous to this find was less than 2,000 years old, so this discovery created a great deal of excitement in the scientific community. However, instead of receiving a note of gratitude from the academic establishment, Royal and Clark were accused of perpetrating a hoax. One expert stated that Royal had found the skull in Europe, planted it in the sinkhole, then faked its discovery for the sake of the television program being filmed. Here was sound evidence that man was in Florida about 8000 B.C., but no one—at least not the experts whose opinion counted—would believe it. Bill Royal, a modest, quiet man, was stunned.

Anyone else would have thrown in the sponge at that point, but not Royal, although he would have to wait many more years before the experts admitted his evidence was sound and revised the history of early man in America. Royal spent more than five thousand hours exploring the spring on his own, from its upper levels down to the bottom at 230 feet. Instead of bringing bones and artifacts to the surface, he left them *in situ,* hoping eventually to persuade an archaeologist to examine them.

I first met Bill Royal in 1968, and after several dives and hours of examining his previous finds, I was convinced that he had made a fantastic discovery and decided to assist him. I tried in vain on both sides of the Atlantic to get archaeologists to join us. I was repeatedly told that I was assisting Royal in his hoax. I brought the matter to the ear of several Florida politicians, and finally in March 1971 the Florida state underwater archaeologist, Carl Clausen, was ordered to conduct a survey of the spring. He was skeptical from the outset and told Royal so. Clausen spent a week excavating an undisturbed section of the floor of one of the caves, and beneath seven feet of sediment he discovered several human bones that dated as 10,300 years old. This should have brought vindication for Royal. Here was a qualified archaeologist finding the oldest human bones in North America under unexceptionable conditions. However, Clausen insisted on secrecy, requesting Royal to keep the find quiet until he could undertake further excavation on a larger scale.

Several months later, Clausen did indeed return with a large team and plenty of equipment, but to Royal's great surprise, he announced that he would work in Little Salt Springs, a sinkhole three miles from Warm Mineral Springs. Royal had already explored this sinkhole and recovered artifacts and human and animal bones, none of which were more than 5,000 years old. Royal had been able to prevent Warm Mineral Springs from being plundered, but scores of sport divers had explored Little Salt Springs and removed untold numbers of artifacts, so it was far from being an undisturbed site. After two months of work and a considerable expenditure of public funds, Clausen discovered that Royal had been correct: nothing they found was more than 5,000 years old.

A year and a half later, Clausen was replaced as state underwater archaeologist by Wilburn Cockrell, and Royal had to start all over again with another skeptical archaeologist. Unlike Clausen, whose specialty was shipwrecks, Cockrell was interested mainly in early man in North America, but he was very hesitant about working in Warm Mineral Springs, since many scientists still considered Royal a crackpot. Cockrell approached the project professionally. Rather than recovering bones and artifacts on his first dives, he carefully gathered sediment and pollen samples surrounding these objects. Most of the samples dated between 10,000 and 12,000 years old. Cockrell realized that it was conceivable that the bones and artifacts could have been planted, but certainly not under hundreds of tons of sediment and deep layers of extinct vegetation. Cockrell knew then that he had the opportunity of a lifetime.

Over a period of months he excavated a number of undisturbed buried sites in various caves in Warm Mineral Springs, and every artifact proved to be around 12,000 years old. Objects removed from the hundred-foot-high mound of debris on the bottom of the sinkhole are in a remarkable state of preservation, because the underground springs that feed Warm Mineral Springs have been sealed off from the air for thousands of years and there is no oxygen dissolved in the water to foster deterioration. Cockrell brought in other experts to assist him. Unfortunately a lack of state funding eventually brought the project to a halt for almost a year, although he continued the work in his spare time. In October of 1973 he invited me to spend some time working at the site with him. I was astonished to find that Royal was no longer a participant in the project. He had been discarded, as happens all too frequently when scientists take over a project from an amateur.

On one of our dives, while collecting pollen samples in a burial area, Cockrell found an atlatl—a spear-throwing hook, a simple but effective implement that enabled a man to hurl his spear from a relatively safe distance, yet with enough force to pierce the tough hide of his quarry. Such tools were known to be used in Asia as long ago as 8000 B.C. But until the atlatl was found in Warm Mineral Springs, no one had had any idea they were used at such an early date in this hemisphere. Bill Royal's discovery of early man in Warm Mineral Springs has rewritten the prehistory books.

Cockrell, who is now a Florida State University professor, has continued his research at Warm Mineral Springs. The site is now recognized as having the continent's oldest ceremonially buried Indian skeleton and has furnished conclusive proof that humans hunted Ice Age saber-toothed cats and giant ground sloths more than 10,000 years ago. Plant fossils and pollen are also being collected from the sinkhole, and Cockrell has said, "Ultimately we hope to be able to reconstruct the climate and have an image of the environment and its people."

The Spanish might well have failed in their New World conquests if the Indians had not initially believed them to be the returning "bearded white gods" who had visited their lands in the heroic past and promised to return again. Many of the conquistadores who followed in Columbus's wake reached areas of the New World presumably never before visited by Europeans and they reported scores of cultural similarities to Old World peoples. When these observations reached a startled Europe, many theories evolved, attributing the amazingly developed native American cultures to influences as widely varying as Egypt, the Hittites, Babylonia, Phoenicia, and even the Lost Tribes of Israel and the "lost continents" of Atlantis and Mu.

Since that time, hundreds of authors have presented theories about which peoples were the first to reach the New World, but until recently none was able to dethrone Columbus. At one time during the sixteenth century so many theories circulated that a judge of the Holy Inquisition found it necessary to declare it heresy to believe that the New World could have been discovered by anyone other than a Spanish Catholic. The fact is that Columbus was an Italian Jew from Genoa.

Periodically a new candidate for discoverer of America is reported in the press or announced in a scientific journal. These events are commonly met with skepticism or hostility by those still loyal to Columbus; for some of them, Columbus's discovery is an article of faith, and they fail to appreciate that the fact that others reached the shores of the New World before him in no way detracts from his achievement. During the past few decades alone, claims have been made for many different peoples: Africans, Arabs, Basques, Carthaginians, Chinese, Egyptians, Etruscans, Greeks, Hindus, Irish, Japanese, Jews, Norsemen, Phoenicians, Polynesians, Portuguese, Romans, Russians, Tibetans, Turks, and Welshmen. Many of these claims are backed by nothing more than nationalistic pride, but other are supported by some evidence. Modern technology has given scientists exciting new tools with which to explore and measure the past. In light of recent archaeological work and historical research, some scholars have jeopardized their academic reputations by publicly declaring their conviction that Columbus was preceded by various Old World mariners.

One such controversial scholar is Dr. Barry Fell, a Harvard

University professor of linguistics. Several years ago the publication of his book *America B.C.* created a storm of controversy. After painstaking research, Fell concluded that Celtic mariners crossed the Atlantic from either Spain or Portugal about 3,000 years ago and settled first in the New England area before migrating as far west as Oklahoma. He believes that some of their settlements lasted until around the time of Christ, after which they intermarried with American Indians, and their descendants still live among us today. Stone structures in New England that were once dismissed as of no historical importance have been identified by Fell as temples to Celtic gods. Some he thinks were observatories for regulating the calendar of Celtic festivities and possibly for predicting eclipses.

One of the oldest Celtic settlements Fell cites was in southern New Hampshire near North Salem, along a branch of the Merrimack River. There is considerable evidence that an ancient Celtic people erected numerous temples and circles of standing stones used in their religious festivals. On many of the stones they cut inscriptions using the ancient Celtic alphabet called Ogam, which Fell believes was invented by the Phoenicians and used by the Celts on both sides of the Atlantic. One of these is known as the Bourne Stone, which was discovered around 1680 in Bourne, Massachusetts. No one was ever able to make any sense of the writing on it until Fell saw it.

According to him, the letters on the Bourne Stone are a mixture of Ogam and Iberic and record the annexation of a large part of present-day Massachusetts by Hanno, a prince of Carthage. On Monhegan Island off the coast of Maine another stone inscription was brought to Fell's attention. Written in Celtic Ogam, it read: "Cargo platforms for ships from Phoenicia." In 1780 a strange stone building was discovered near Mount Hope Bay, Rhode Island. Fell translated an inscription on one of the building's lintels to read: "Voyagers from Tarshish this stone proclaims." The Biblical seaport of Tarshish was somewhere on the coast of Spain, most likely at present-day Cádiz, and was famous for its intrepid sailors and the size of the ships they sailed throughout the known world. Around 533 B.C., Tarshish was destroyed by the Carthaginians, who took over its trade. Fell contends that it was at this time that Iberian Celts and the Carthaginians became partners, making profitable voyages between North America and the Mediterranean. The chief products from North America were probably hides, copper, and furs.

Fell has investigated and deciphered more than five hundred ancient rock inscriptions, scattered throughout the world, that were written in various European and Mediterranean languages in alphabets that date back more than 3,500 years. In many cases these messages form America's oldest archives and bear witness to ocean crossings by many different ancient mariners.

In 1979 a team of archaeologists from the University of Massachusetts at Amherst conducted a survey of several stone structures that Fell had identified as cells for Irish monks who followed in the wake of St. Brendan. Locally they had been called "monk's caves" for as long as anyone could remember. Although the archaeologists were unable to determine when the structures had been built, they announced that they were most likely constructed in the nineteenth century. They based their findings on the discovery of nineteenth-century pottery, ceramics, a gun flint, and other artifacts. This is the predictable evaluation one can expect from a team of scientists who deliberately set out to debunk a colleague, which was evidently the case in this survey. Finding a penny dated 1944 doesn't prove that a Civil War fort was built at that date, only that someone lost a coin there in 1944 or later. Old structures could have been used for centuries, and the debris left by the latest inhabitants doesn't date the construction of the structure.

Another scholar who has frequently been criticized by the academic world is Dr. Cyrus Gordon, who recently retired as chairman of the Department of Mediterranean Studies at Brandeis University. Dr. Gordon is both an archaeologist and linguist and began his studies relating to pre-Columbian contact

between the Old and New World back in 1930. One of his
main themes is that Semitic tribes of the eastern Mediterranean
did indeed visit North America thousands of years ago—an
opinion that has created a great deal of argument.

In 1872, a large stone bearing a strange inscription was
discovered near Paraíba on the bulge of Brazil. For many years
it was thought to be a forgery. Dr. Gordon studied it for years
and in 1968 announced that the inscription was genuine Phoenician. He believes that the vocabulary and grammatical usage,
which led earlier experts to doubt its authenticity, are in fact
good idiomatic Phoenician that compares with other Phoenician script that has been found in the Mediterranean since the
Brazilian stone was found over a century ago. Dr. Gordon has
translated the inscription to read:

> We are Sons of Canaan from Sidon, the city of the King.
> Commerce has cast us on this distant shore, a land of moun-
> tains. We set [sacrificed] a youth for the exalted gods and
> goddesses in the nineteenth year of Hiram, our mighty king.
> We embarked from Ezion-Geber into the Red Sea and voy-
> aged with ten ships. We were at sea together for two years
> around the land belonging to Ham [Africa] but were separated
> by a storm and we were no longer with our companions. So
> we came here, twelve men and three women, on a new shore,
> which I, the Admiral, control. But auspiciously may the ex-
> alted gods and goddesses favor us.

During the past few years, Gordon has been involved in
several other controversies concerning stones allegedly bearing
inscriptions made by Mediterranean peoples in ancient times.
In 1968, Manfred Metcalf, a civilian employee at Fort Benning,
Georgia, found a flat piece of sandstone, approximately nine
inches square, that was covered with strange symbols. He was
intrigued and brought the stone to the attention of Dr. Joseph
B. Mahan of Georgia's Columbus Museum of Arts and Crafts.
Dr. Mahan, a specialist in American Indian archaeology, has

long believed that some of the tribes in the United States trace their roots back to ancient Mediterranean cultures. For example, the Yuchi, an old Georgia tribe now resettled in Oklahoma, were racially and linguistically distinct from other American Indians. According to their own legends the Yuchi's ancestors came from a land "far to the east across the ocean." Mahan sought assistance from Dr. Gordon, who has not been able to decipher the inscription but feels the script shows strong similarities to Minoan writing dating back to about 1000 B.C. during the Bronze Age. Another expert in ancient Semitic languages, Dr. Stanislav Segert of the University of Prague, agrees with Gordon that the text is Minoan but thinks it dates back to around 2000 B.C.

Encouraged by these findings, Mahan then sent Dr. Gordon a photograph of still another inscribed stone, which was gathering dust in the Smithsonian Institution in Washington, D.C. This stone had been discovered in 1885 by Smithsonian archaeologists under one of nine skeletons in a burial mound near Bat Creek, Tennessee. The archaeologists had erroneously concluded that the inscription was in Cherokee. When the results of the excavation were published in 1894, a photograph of the stone was inadvertently printed upside down and its significance went unnoticed. After studying it, Dr. Gordon agreed with Mahan that it had been misidentified. Gordon reported that the writing style was that of Canaan, the "promised land" of the Israelites. He translated the inscription to read "for the land of Judah." The circumstances of the stone's discovery rule out any chance of fraud or forgery, and Gordon claims that "the inscription attests to a migration of Jews, probably to escape the persecution of the Romans after the disastrous defeats in 70 and 133 A.D."

In a book entitled *Natural and Aboriginal History of Tennessee,* published in the early 1800s, John Haywood, chief justice of the supreme court of Tennessee, wrote that many Roman coins were found in Tennessee and adjacent states. More recently, Canaanite coins of the Bar Kokhba Rebellion (132–35

A.D.) have been found by farmers in Kentucky around Louisville, Hopkinsville, and Clay City. Living today in eastern Tennessee there is a small group of dark-skinned people known as the Melungeons. They are neither Indian nor Negro but Caucasian. According to their legends, they are descended from Mediterranean people who came to the New World some 2,000 years before Columbus.

Dr. Robert L. Stieglitz, a professor of history at Rutgers University, has taken up the banner where Dr. Gordon's work stopped. Dubious at first, he started by examining the work done by both Dr. Gordon and Dr. Fell. Once he was confident their conclusions were scientifically sound, he explored new areas of research on the fascinating but controversial subject of pre-Columbian contacts with the New World. He thinks that after the Jewish revolts against the Romans, various bands of Jews fled. They went first to the western Mediterranean, most likely to Spain or Portugal, and then later, either through accident or by connection with Mediterranean sailors who were acquainted with deep-sea navigation, they reached the New World.

It is encouraging that there are distinguished institutions of learning as well as scholars that are open to reassessment of the pre-Columbian history of the Americas in the light of a growing body of evidence. In 1966 the Smithsonian Institution published a 447-page book entitled *The Early Formative Period of Coastal Ecuador,* written by Drs. Betty J. Meggers and Clifford Evans, a husband-and-wife team of distinguished archaeologists. Not all pre-Columbian contact with the New World came from Europe or Africa. This monumental book has 196 illustrations of artifacts they uncovered during a five-year excavation of a coastal site near Valdavia, Ecuador, and identical artifacts found in Japan from a Japanese culture that flourished about 3000 B.C. When the book was first released it made headlines around the globe, since these scholars produced indisputable proof that the Japanese had reached the New World 5,000 years ago.

This is the oldest datable evidence proving contact between the Old and New World. The majority of artifacts from the site were pottery, the oldest ever found in the Americas. This pottery was identified as Jomon ware from the island of Kyushu in Japan. Because the Ecuadorian cultures of that era had no pottery-making techniques, either it was made in Japan and brought over by Japanese fishermen or mariners who accidentally landed on the northwestern shores of South America, most likely after an eight-thousand-mile sea voyage, or these same strange visitors taught the local inhabitants how to make the pottery. The archaeologists also found in association with the pottery a collection of skulls that are definitely not characteristic of early physical types of American Indians, but rather closely resemble the medieval Japanese.

At another site in Ecuador these archaeologists found evidence of still another Japanese occupation, this one dating from around 500 B.C. At this second site, in addition to a vast amount of ceramics they discovered remains of buildings, net sinkers, coolie yokes, and other artifacts—all of unmistakable Japanese origin. Fortunately, these two extraordinary and significant discoveries were made by respected archaeologists, and academia was silent for a change. If a nonacademic had made the discoveries the scholars would have been screaming "hoax" as they did in the case of Bill Royal. Under ideal conditions, archaeologists would always be the ones to unearth clues to the past. But this is not an ideal world, and amateurs who are prepared and sensitive to the material can play an important role in helping fill in the picture of the past.

There is also mounting evidence that the Chinese visited the shores of America in the distant past. At another site in Ecuador, archaeologists uncovered substantial evidence of Chinese occupation dating from the early Han Dynasty, about 200 B.C. From historical documents we know that about this time, a period during which the Chinese were obsessed with discovering medicinal drugs, a Chinese named Hsü Fu received permission and an enormous subsidy from the emperor of China to search for drugs in the eastern ocean. In 219 B.C. a fleet of vessels was assembled to carry some three thousand young men and women across the Pacific. The fleet sailed east and never returned. The proximity in time of this documented one-way voyage and the early Han Dynasty artifacts excavated in Ecuador may well be more than a coincidence.

There is historical evidence of another Chinese voyage to the New World in 499 A.D., an expedition from which the mariners returned to China. The voyage was led by a Buddhist priest named Hwui Shan. Manuscripts recount that after many months of hardship at sea the voyagers reached a land they named Fusang. In his written report to the emperor, Hwui Shan described the inhabitants of Fusang and their customs as well as the character of the land, which corresponds with the northwest Pacific coast in the vicinity of Oregon and Washington. It is known that during that period the Chinese utilized very large oceangoing sailing vessels, some with as many as four decks and possibly weighing over one thousand tons. The Chinese knew the directional properties of the lodestone as early as 2600 B.C. and were using the magnetic needle, a primitive form of compass, at least as early as the fourth century B.C. They developed geographical knowledge very early, and the spherical-earth theory dates back in China to at least the time of Christ.

Apparently the Chinese were still making crossings to the New World as late as the sixteenth century. Spaniards on an exploratory voyage to the Gulf of California in 1544 reported finding several large Chinese junks at anchor there. Chinese aboard the vessels managed to tell them that they had been coming to those regions for trade with various Indian tribes for many centuries.

But there is evidence the Chinese had much earlier contact with the New World. Peanuts have been found in Pre-Columbian sites in Chekiang province in China dating from between 2100 and 1811 B.C. In addition, a large cache of Chinese bronze coins and a bronze mirror dating from 1200 B.C. have been found at Victoria in British Columbia, and many other hoards of Chinese coins and artifacts have been unearthed along the shores of the northwest coast of America. During the nineteenth century when the first white settlers reached the areas along the Columbia River they discovered that the Wishram Indians possessed thousands of old Chinese coins, which they said had been obtained from sea traders from China.

Early settlers in the Northwest also discovered the remains of many ancient Oriental sailing vessels along the beaches. Artifacts found in association with some of the shipwrecks confirmed they had come across the Pacific from the Orient many centuries before. In 1925 an ancient Chinese junk was unearthed during construction of an oil storage tank in Los Angeles Harbor. Fifty years later, two sport divers, Bob Meistrell and Wayne Baldwin, accidentally discovered two stone anchors weighing 450 pounds each, as well as numerous ballast stones, off Palos Verdes, California. Archaeologists determined that these were the type of anchors used by the Chinese, and geologists confirmed the finding by proving that the stones originated in China. Of course, the skeptics responded that the stones could have been brought over as ballast on a modern ship. However, about the same time as this discovery, a similar find that left the skeptics baffled was made by a noted scientist. During a deep-water survey off San Francisco, Dr. Ching Chang Woo, a marine geologist working for the U.S. Geological Survey, recovered still another Chinese anchor from over a depth of one thousand feet while dredging for bottle samples. The thickness of the manganese crust on this anchor proved beyond any doubt that it was of pre-Columbian origin.

Not long ago a New York art collector bought a fifth-century-B.C. Chinese manuscript on silk found by two tomb robbers. This remarkable manuscript may shed light on links between early China and the New World. The collector turned it over to scholars at Columbia University, who deciphered the archaic calligraphy. Twelve creatures figure in the manuscript's border. Among them are antlered deities with long protruding tongues. They bear a marked resemblance to the supernatural creatures found in New World art of roughly the same period. Several months ago a Mexican archaeologist published a report describing the similarities between the pottery of the late Chou decorative styles of China (700–200 B.C.) and those of the Tajín culture of Veracruz in Mexico.

In 1971 a team of Russian scholars made international news announcing they had evidence that Asians had reached the New World at least 1,000 years before Christ. Among the evidence they offered were that the purely American word "tobacco" had penetrated a number of Oriental languages and dialects in hoary antiquity and that certain ancient Tibetan documents and maps make reference to "a green land lying far across the Eastern Ocean" (the Pacific).

Deep in the tropical forests of western Honduras at the ruins of Copán, another ruined Mayan city, there is a remarkable stone sculpture, believed by some to be a representation of Indra, the chief deity of early Hindu religion, riding an elephant. The profiles of two elephants appear on another stela at the same site, which dates from about the eighth century. How did sculptures of elephants, unknown in the New World at that time, come to be made? At Copán there are no fewer than three images resembling Hanuman, the monkey-faced god celebrated in the *Ramayana,* one of India's great epics.

Some of the largest temples in Mexico are believed to have representations of other Hindu gods, such as Siva, Ganesha, and Surya. Comparison between Hinduism and early Mexican religions reveals some striking resemblances. Even more intriguing is the similarity between the architectural styles of the Maya and Aztec and those of India and Hindu-influenced Southeast Asia. In both areas the major structures were pyramidal, often with serpent balustrades and surmounted by temples employing the offset arch, with sanctuaries, symbolic altars, and sculptures and inscriptions.

For more than a century, as ruins have emerged from the concealment of jungle growth, a number of scholars have expressed amazement at some striking similarities between ancient cultures in Asia and the New World. Several years ago Dr. Victor Segovia, a Mexican archaeologist, discovered two stone friezes on a ruin near Campeche in Yucatán that are almost identical to friezes on ruins in Cambodia. Many scholars feel there are more Asian-American similarities than Mediterranean-American similarities, despite the Mediterranean's closer proximity to the Americas.

Some researchers contend that the peoples of the Far East developed nautical sciences at an earlier period than did early inhabitants of the Mediterranean world. From earliest times they utilized more advanced sailing vessels and techniques than their contemporaries in the west, which enabled them to sail close to the wind, a feat that was not perfected in the Western world until the beginning of the Renaissance. Although some ancient peoples who sailed in the Pacific, including the Chinese, Japanese, and Indonesians, had large wooden sailing ships, it is believed that the first transpacific contact between Asia and the New World was effected with dagger-board sailing rafts. Historians had generally considered lashed-log sailing rafts to be unseaworthy for long voyages. But Thor Heyerdhal's epic *Kon Tiki* crossing and several similar voyages subsequently made by others prompted a reevaluation. A number of experts now think such sailing craft were probably both safer and faster for crossing the Pacific than even the large, unwieldy Spanish ships that plied the Manila galleon route from the sixteenth to the nineteenth century.

Given the growing body of evidence, there seems little doubt that long before Columbus not only did "bearded white gods" reach the New World, but black and yellow "gods" as well.

2

Great White Gods from the East

There is an assumption that early-fifteenth-century European ships that made the arduous transatlantic crossing during the dawn of the age of exploration must have been far superior to those in use one or two millennia earlier. It is also generally believed that a vessel in the pre-Columbian era could only have traversed the ocean by accident, aided by great good fortune. We know, however, that this is not the case. As early as 3000 B.C. the Babylonians had established maritime commerce with India, and by 1200 B.C. the Phoenicians were making frequent voyages to the Azores, a group of islands in the North Atlantic west of Portugal, to which they belong today. The Azores lie far out to sea, a third of the distance between Europe and continental North America.

Another common misconception is that ancient Old World vessels were too small for transoceanic voyages. By 2500 B.C., Egyptian shipwrights were constructing wooden merchant vessels well over a hundred feet in length and powered by a large square sail. These ships traveled as far as the Syrian coast for lumber and down the Red Sea for incense, ivory, and gold. During the tenth to fifth centuries B.C., the smallest craft the ancients considered practical for Mediterranean trading voyages were from seventy to eighty tons burden. From the fifth century B.C., merchant vessels of from 150 to 500 tons were common. Some were able to carry as many as six hundred passengers on extended voyages. By the middle of the third century B.C., the Greeks were building grain freighters of nineteen hundred tons burden—ships that were ten times the size of Columbus's *Santa María* and at least twice the size of the largest galleon used on Spanish voyages to and from the New World.

The fact is that the size of a vessel has little relationship to its seaworthiness. Over the past century there have been more than 120 intentional solo or two-man extended ocean voyages in small sailing craft less than twenty feet long. In the late 1980s a Frenchman actually crossed the Atlantic on a Windsurfer. Among the most notable were an English adventurer's eighty-four-day solo voyage from the Moroccan seaport of Casablanca to Florida in a six-foot boat, the recent voyage of William Verity from Florida to Ireland in a home-built twelve-foot sloop, a Japanese Boy Scout's ninety-three-day crossing from Japan to San Francisco in a nineteen-foot sloop, and a thirty-day Atlantic crossing in a twenty-four-foot craft manned by an intrepid toeless, fingerless sailor.

The initial voyages of discovery were probably accidental —vessels were carried across the oceans by storms or contrary winds or currents. Since the advent of recorded history there have been many accounts of East Asian vessels driven onto American shores as far south as Acapulco. In the Atlantic this was an even more frequent event. A good example is the Portuguese explorer Pedro Alvares Cabral's unanticipated discovery of Brazil while attempting to round the continent of Africa early in the sixteenth century. Even as late as the nineteenth century there were hundreds of accounts of sailing ships blown across the Atlantic by stress of wind and weather.

Strabo, the first-century-B.C. Greek geographer, wrote of

a Phoenician fleet returning from an exploratory expedition along the west coast of Africa sometime around 1200 B.C. that was blown off course and fortuitously found shelter at Madeira. The ships might easily have missed the Madeira archipelago, which lies off the Atlantic coast of Morocco, and been blown across the Atlantic to the New World by the same westerly wind that was pushing it off course. Because of the prevailing northeasterly winds and westward-flowing currents, a voyage from the Straits of Gibraltar down the African coast or to any of the off-lying Atlantic islands, such as the Canaries, was an easy feat. However, trying to get back was another matter. With only a square sail, which was what propelled the vessels used for exploration and trading, it was impossible to beat against the prevailing trade winds and contrary currents. The only alternative for ancient mariners was to head well out into the Atlantic and work their way north until they could pick up the westerly winds that would enable them to reach the Mediterranean again.

Some scholars contend that primitive mariners could not have survived accidental transoceanic drift voyages because their provisions would have been inadequate for unexpected voyages of long duration. This may have been true of small fishing boats but certainly not for exploratory or trading vessels. In any event, it has been proved that if adequate water is available, a man can survive for fifty days or longer without food. Furthermore, contrary to popular belief, seawater and fish juices can provide a supplementary water source. In 1954 a French physician named Alain Bombard made a successful solo crossing from the Canary Islands to Barbados. Bombard spent sixty-five days in a fifteen-foot rubber raft that carried neither food nor water. In the nineteenth century there were known accidental drifts in the Pacific. Nine Japanese made an unplanned drift of eleven months before finally reaching Hawaii. There were two others between Japan and North American waters of seventeen and eighteen months duration. In both cases a number of the crew survived the ordeal.

Since a number of ancient authors wrote of the existence of lands on the other side of the Atlantic, we can surmise that some of those ancients who reached the New World must have returned to tell of their discoveries. How did the early navigator with only primitive methods at his disposal set and keep a course for his destination when he was such a long distance from home? Several historians have suggested that mariners may have followed along the coastline of North America and then made relatively short open-ocean crossings between Newfoundland, Greenland, Iceland, and the British Isles before working down the coast of Europe and eventually reaching the Mediterranean and home port. This hypothesis, however, is not one acceptable to a sailor. The persistent belief that early mariners navigated primarily by hugging the shore has been disproved. Nothing is more fraught with peril and therefore more assiduously avoided by sailors on an unknown coast than hugging the shore.

Also, the shore-hugging theory was based on the assumption that mariners had neither the means nor the ability to find their way on the high seas out of sight of land. It is true, perhaps, that the earliest seafarers had no instruments, but the theory does not take into account the extraordinary ability that mariners in some areas of the world, notably the South Pacific, have even today of reckoning position with remarkable accuracy. How could the Phoenicians have navigated across more than eight hundred miles of open ocean to the little Azores again and again? From time immemorial even such relatively undeveloped people as the Hawaiians were able to sail to Tahiti and other South Pacific regions thousands of miles across open water and then return home, accomplishing this when their culture still belonged to the Neolithic Age. It is thus hard to believe that such skilled and scientifically oriented peoples as the Phoenicians, Romans, and others in the Old World couldn't navigate with some order and precision on the high seas.

Many theories and inventions we think of as modern were discovered and in use thousands of years ago, albeit in modified form. We know that as early as 4000 B.C. the Babylonians maintained a constant vigil of the movement of heavenly bodies and were well versed in astrology, as were the Egyptians, Greeks, Chinese, Hindus, Maya, and Aztec. It is on the foundation of these ancient discoveries that modern science has risen and blossomed. In the second century B.C., the Greek astronomer Hipparchus calculated the solar year at 365¼ days minus four minutes—an error of only six minutes. He calculated the lunar month at twenty-nine days, twelve hours, forty-four minutes, and three and a third seconds, which according to modern calculations is only one second off. About the same time, Eratosthenes, a Greek geographer, astronomer, and mathematician, fixed the value of a degree and measured the circumference of the earth. His instruments were primitive, yet he made no more than a 10 percent error. The achievements of these early scientists are astounding.

Although only a very few examples of early land maps have survived, we know that they were widely used by the Egyptians and Babylonians, who employed land-surveying instruments as early as 3000 B.C. The Phoenicians, whose culture was greatly influenced by the Egyptians and Babylonians, probably were using sea charts by 1500 B.C. The Greeks certainly had charts; there are references to them in a number of ancient sources, and by the time of Christ a number of cartographic and geographic theories had been advanced.

The most notable ancient cartographer and geographer was the Greek Alexandrian Claudius Ptolemaeus, better known as Ptolemy. Around the middle of the second century A.D. he produced the *Geographia,* a monumental contribution to scientific thought. The *Geographia* was a comprehensive geography of the known world. Using an astrolabe—the forerunner of the modern sextant—to establish latitude and dead reckoning to determine longitude, he fixed the positions of more than eight thousand places with only minor inaccuracies. Ptolemy's great achievement, like so many intellectual fruits of the classical world, was lost following the decline of the Roman Empire and not rediscovered until the middle of the fifteenth century, when it was brought back into use. The maps and charts used during the Middle Ages were little more than stylized sketches and were quite primitive compared to those of the Hellenistic cartographers.

Considering the sophistication of calendric computations and astronomy used in both Old and New World cultures, it would seem reasonable to conjecture that techniques of celestial navigation were in use soon after men took to the seas, sailing beyond familiar shores in search of expanded opportunities for food or commerce. During the almost 1,500 years the Phoenicians reigned as undisputed masters of the seas, they must have had some methods of orienting their vessels when out of sight of land. What a shame that the Phoenician seafarers and merchants were not keepers of historical records; at any event, there are none extant to tell us details of their accomplishments. As early as 1500 B.C. they were making frequent trading voyages to the British Isles, to the Azores, and to other off-lying Atlantic islands—voyages that require a certain level of nautical science.

In the first century B.C., Strabo wrote that the Phoenicians went to extremes to keep their navigational methods and sea routes secret. Unfortunately their knowledge was lost when their sea power waned and they were eclipsed by the Roman Empire. Strabo reports that once when a Phoenician vessel was heading for Cornwall on the coast of Great Britain to pick up a cargo of tin, the captain found his vessel shadowed by a Roman ship that had been sent to discover the source of the tin, a necessary ingredient in the manufacture of bronze. When both vessels were in the vicinity of the treacherous rock-strewn water off the fog-shrouded island of Ushant at the entrance of the English Channel, the Phoenician captain deliberately changed course, heading into shoal water, where both ships were wrecked. Strabo says the Romans perished, victims of their curiosity, but the Phoenicians escaped on pieces of wreckage, and the captain was later recompensed by the state for the loss of his vessel and the sacrifice he had made to protect the Phoenician tin monopoly.

Strabo also writes that the Phoenicians used the stars to navigate by. Homer mentions this method of navigation in his *Odyssey*. Saint Paul, describing his shipwreck at Malta in the Acts of the Apostles, states: "When for many days neither sun nor stars had been visible from the driving ship, the crew abandoned all hope, for the sun by day and the stars by night serve the helmsman as a guide." It is known that the extensive geographical knowledge and navigational skills of the Polynesians and Micronesians were based on celestial techniques, probably derived from contact with more advanced Asian civilizations such as the Japanese and Chinese.

In the Western world the first historical reference to the magnetic needle, or "sailor's needle," occurred in 1180 A.D., but it is thought that it was in use as early as the fourth century. The Norsemen and others who navigated the unpropitious seas of northwestern Europe and the northern Atlantic, where even at midsummer overcast skies are common, had fewer opportunities to utilize the methods of celestial navigation and probably relied on some primitive form of compass.

To establish latitude, ancient mariners most likely used the astrolabe, developed by the Babylonians around 3000 B.C. It still served as the principal instrument for Columbus and his contemporaries 4,500 years later. It is doubtful if the ancients had any accurate means of determining longitude, other than dead reckoning.

Global climatic changes should also be considered in trying to understand the navigational feats of mariners in antiquity. These climatic deviations are known from historical records and also from geological and paleontological studies. During the heyday of the Norsemen, between 800 and 1200, good weather prevailed in Europe, making their voyages easier than they would be today. Greenland was aptly named at the time, because great sections of this large island were actually green with dense vegetation. Then a few centuries of colder climate followed. During the winter of 1322–23 the entire Baltic froze solid, and there are reports that six years later the mouth of the Nile River was impassable because of floating ice packs. During the first half of the seventeenth century, Iceland was blocked by ice for six months each year; it is blocked for only a few weeks today.

But let us return to the Phoenicians, the greatest mariners of antiquity, for the story of far-reaching seafaring and trade in the Mediterranean starts with them and they were most likely the first Europeans to cross the Atlantic and reach the New World. They sailed greater distances than anyone had before, and for well over two millennia after them no one ventured as far. Shipbuilders, manufacturers, miners, and metalworkers, the Phoenicians and their descendants, the Carthaginians, were the first to sail out of the Mediterranean through the Straits of Gibraltar into the "Great Lake."

The Bronze Age origins of the Phoenicians are hazy. By the second millennium B.C., a Semitic-speaking people calling themselves Canaanites or "merchants" had evolved from a mixture of indigenous tribes and Semitic immigrants who filtered to the coast of present-day Lebanon from the hinterland. Later, this ethnic heterogeneity was leavened by the addition of sea-wise Aegeans who fled the barbaric invasions. Gradually these people became the Phoenicians Homer referred to as a "race of mariners."

From the outset the Phoenicians were a pragmatic people, looking for profit rather than conquest and less interested in cultural refinements than commerce. They were hemmed in on the east by high, heavily forested mountains that rose close to the rocky coast, and were unable to develop large-scale overland trade to the southeast because of the Arab monopoly of the caravan routes. So the Phoenicians turned to the sea. They learned astronomy from the Babylonians and plied the trackless oceans setting a course by the stars. Confident and brave, the men of Tyre, Byblos, Sidon, and the lesser cities ventured where no one else dared. Beyond the familiar waters of the eastern Mediterranean, where ships were seldom out of sight of land, they sailed past Sicily, the Balearic Islands, and Iberia. Their first encounters with the forbidding Atlantic, with its strange winds, currents, and creatures of the deep, were probably on their voyages to Cornwall, England, where they obtained valuable metals. The Phoenician entrepreneurs ranged far afield establishing commercial outposts wherever they could drive an advantageous bargain, exchanging trinkets, which they mass-produced, for much more valuable goods.

Phoenicia was made up of a collection of city-states that shared a common culture. For centuries, led by Tyre and Sidon, it was the commercial center of the ancient world, exploring, colonizing, and trading. By the time the Phoenicians reached their apogee in the twelfth century B.C., they had been trading for a millennium. Egyptian tomb reliefs of the mid-third millennium depict a stubby merchant ship from Byblos on the Nile. Byblos's early trade fattened on the Egyptian and Mesopotamian markets for the pine and cedarwood of Lebanon. The Canaanites of Byblos also dealt in the resins and perfumes of Arabia, which were in great demand. But as the empires of the Nile and the Tigris and Euphrates burgeoned, there was an intensified need for metals. Thus Byblos, and soon after the other Phoenician cities, became a vital link in the lucrative metal trade.

The Phoenicians' galleys exported eclectic ideas and technology along with trade goods. The Phoenicians were not artistically creative or innovative, preferring to copy the designs of others, but their craftsmen and metallurgists were adept at working gold and ivory, carving wood, and smelting iron. They knew how to produce transparent glass and exported a great deal of linen, wool, and silk cloth. Some of it was embroidered and dyed with Tyrian purple, the most highly prized dye of antiquity, which was extracted from the murex snail. They built and furnished ships, temples and even cities for other states.

The Phoenicians frequently presented rich gifts to foreign

rulers to entice them into future trade, and they used such offerings to assuage potential invaders, who could easily crush their small cities. The kings of eight of the sea cities made common cause in 877 B.C. and presented an offering to the Assyrian king as he stood poised with his armies on the northern frontier of Lebanon. A court scribe recorded what they bought: "gold, silver, tin, copper, copper vessels, linen robes with many colored borders, big and little apes, ebony boxwood, ivory and walrus tusks." The tusks are surprising and may have been obtained through trade, or possibly the Phoenicians had penetrated north of the British Isles into the Arctic regions.

The Egyptians had been sailing to Punt, probably on the Red Sea near present-day Somalia but perhaps farther down on the southeast coast of Africa, since at least 2600 B.C. for myrrh, electrum, and other precious goods. About 2300 B.C. a wealthy helmsman named Knemhotep died at a town near the Nile's first cataract. Hieroglyphics found in his tomb explain that with a captain, Khui, he made eleven profitable trading voyages to Punt, bringing back incense, gold, ivory, exotic animals, and woods such as ebony, highly prized in treeless Egypt. In 1493 B.C., Queen Hatshepsut sent to Punt an expedition of five great galleys, which returned two years later with a rich cargo including gold and thirty-one potted myrrh tree saplings, which particularly delighted the queen.

Throughout history, gold has been the basis for many an unlikely partnership. Five hundred years after the Egyptian queen sponsored the expedition to Punt, Solomon, king of the Israelites, and Hiram, king of Phoenician Tyre, organized a joint fleet to seek the fabled bounty of Ophir, an area that may have been the Punt of the Egyptians. This was the beginning of a mutually profitable trading alliance. Solomon had married a pharaoh's daughter, and it is possible that he learned through the Egyptians where Punt/Ophir was. He had two assets to bring into the partnership—his knowledge of Punt/Ophir, and a Red Sea port that was a perfect staging point for a naval expedition into the Red Sea or the Indian Ocean. Israel was still without the materials to build ships and had no shipwrights or mariners. The Tyrians could supply these better than anyone else. Ezion-geber, near modern Eilat, was selected as the site for construction of the fleet. Hiram sent timbers and sails, men to build the vessels, and experienced seamen and officers to sail them, "and these, in company with Solomon's servants, went to Ophir and brought back 420 talents of gold to King Solomon," of which Hiram received his share.

The secretive Phoenicians made every effort to discourage commercial competition by concealing raw-material resources and trading routes. They formed a partnership with the Hebrews only because they needed access to a Red Sea port and because initially they did not know how to reach Ophir. Business was business with the Phoenician merchants, and it is to be presumed that once they had been shown the way, they no longer needed a partner. The Hebrews never made the voyage again. In fact, a century later the Israelites, under Jehoshaphat, tried to reach Ophir; but the ships they built without Phoenician aid sank as soon as they were launched.

The Phoenicians were so secretive that they may never have committed any of their vast knowledge of geography and navigation to writing. They did offer spine-chilling tales of ghastly demons, treacherous tides, and entangling seaweeds that lay in wait for anyone who ventured out into the Mare Altum, the high sea. More than once a Greek or Roman ship shadowing a Tyrian or Sidonian galley must have been lured onto the rocks, as in Strabo's account, or led on a wild goose chase. Heedless of danger, the Phoenicians sailed north, past Brittany to England, in quest of tin and other products. Phoenician coins and other artifacts have been found in the Azores, which are almost one thousand miles from the Straits of Gibraltar; no one knows when the Phoenicians first reached those isles. They also frequented the Canary Islands, from which they collected a valuable vegetable dye, superior to the murex purple.

One of the greatest sources of mineral wealth in the ancient world was the Iberian Peninsula, and sometime before 1100 B.C., the Phoenicians sailed westward 2,300 miles to found a colony in the mysterious land of Tartessus, in southern Spain. For many centuries Tartessus was the distributing center for prodigious amounts of Iberian gold, silver, copper, iron, lead, and mercury. Tartessus, the Tarshish of the Bible, was an obscure city of veiled origins somewhere near the mouth of the Guadalquivir River, but its remains have never been found. Its highly cultivated people were very active in the early bronze trade. Tartessus became an ally of Carthage after 800 B.C. and was destroyed around 533 B.C., perhaps by the Carthaginians. At some time in its history, perhaps, voyagers from the city left in present-day Rhode Island the inscribed stone lintel mentioned in chapter 1.

Carthage was founded on the fertile North African coast near modern Tunis in the ninth century B.C. by a band of Tyrians who had fled an Assyrian siege of their city. Greek legend held that Carthage was founded in 814 B.C. as the result of contention over the throne of Tyre by rival factions. The colony grew into a powerful and wealthy city in its own right, though tainted with a gruesome tradition of infant sacrifice, which persisted there long after it had ceased elsewhere. Soon after, the settlers of Carthage took over many of the western Phoenician colonies and founded new ones at various strategic locations. The Tyrian settlements at Gades (Cádiz), which had access to the gold mines of southern Spain, came under Carthaginian occupation around 600 B.C. Most amazing of all, the Carthaginians were able to bar Greek exit from the Mediterranean, which came to be called the Internal Sea; and they carved out for themselves an African empire second in size only to Egypt's.

Many of the voyages of the Phoenicians and Carthaginians were long ones, and a number of them were launched under the auspices of the Egyptians. Around 600 B.C. the Egyptian pharaoh Necho sponsored a Phoenician fleet that sailed from

Ezion-geber on the Red Sea in an attempt to circumnavigate Africa. The expedition was successful and returned to Egypt via the Straits of Gibraltar during its third year. The trip lasted so long because the explorers spent extended periods ashore in search of valuable products and planting crops to provision their ships.

In 1658, early New England settlers found a stone, measuring forty-five inches long, fifteen inches wide, and five inches thick, with a two-line inscription on it. For generations it was used as a doorstep for an Indian mission, and eventually it ended up, forgotten, in the basement of a museum. A number of historians believed the inscription was Norse until Dr. Barry Fell examined it and translated it to read: "Proclamation of annexation. Do not deface. Hanno of this place takes possession."

Although Hanno was a common Carthaginian name, one Hanno was a prince of Carthage and in the service of Hiram III, king of Tyre, Phoenicia's premier city. It is quite likely that he is the Hanno referred to in the inscription. He was an able seafarer who explored and colonized the west coast of Africa early in the fifth century B.C. On his first voyage of exploration outside the Pillars of Hercules, he founded seven cities and a trading post along the African coast and probably reached as far south as the coast of present-day Gambia or Sierra Leone. An account of this voyage survives in a Greek manuscript dating back to the tenth century, which was no doubt copied from a much older document. The Greek document also refers to a second voyage made by Hanno "in which he did circumnavigate the northern ocean." Sometime between his first and second voyages he became the king of southern Spain, and his principal port was Gades.

According to Aristotle, the Carthaginians were known to have discovered an island in the Atlantic "large in extent, fertile in soil and full of navigational rivers, but uninhabited . . . the first discoverer fixed there; but the Carthaginians ordered that none of their subjects should settle there." This description could not refer to Atlantic islands such as the Azores or Canaries because they have no navigable rivers. Other ancient sources also mention this discovery and remark that other settlers were not permitted because Carthage feared losing too many of her citizens and wished to reserve this island as a sanctuary to which they might retreat when necessity arose. According to the Portuguese chronicler Antonio Galvão, writing early in the sixteenth century, "in 590 B.C. a fleet of Carthaginian merchants sailed from Gades westward through the great sea trying to find land; they discovered what we call now the Antilles and Mexico."

While doing research in the Royal Academy of History archives in Madrid, I came upon a fascinating document written by a bishop who visited Yucatán around 1550. He reported that while visiting the village of Mani, near Mérida, he saw a number of strange buildings, unlike any others he had seen in his travels throughout the peninsula, but resembling ruins he had seen in the Holy Land. The stone roofs of the buildings were held in place by iron rods. Iron was unknown in the New World until after the arrival of the Spaniards, or so we have been led to believe. From the village elders the bishop learned that legend attributed these buildings, which were centuries old, to a band of white men who had come from a place called Carthage. Possibly some of the survivors of that once preeminent seaport, rather than become vassals of the Romans, had sailed to the New World and established a colony in Yucatán.

The Phoenicians and Carthaginians have not come down through history as sympathetic characters. Apart from their genius for trade, their undisputed mastery of the seas, and their bold explorations, they are remembered as their adversaries represented them, a brutal and venal people. Unfortunately, they cannot speak for themselves, as they left no literature or artistic testament to their daily lives. All of their records went up in flames during the siege of Tyre by Alexander the Great. In 346 B.C. a similar fate befell Sidon during that city's destruction by Persian troops. Every man, woman, child, and beast was exterminated; all the manuscripts, archives, and works of art in the city were destroyed. Carthaginian archives and libraries were also obliterated when the Romans razed Carthage in 146 B.C.

The Phoenicians and Carthaginians were great mariners, but were by no means the only ones who could have visited the New World. Etruscans, Greeks, and Romans may have done so. The Etruscans were a highly cultivated people who flourished in west-central Italy until they were absorbed by the upstart Romans. Their origins are somewhat of a mystery, although it is thought their ancestors came from Lydia in Asia Minor. A few eminent scholars, primarily Italians, contend that the Etruscans were the first to discover the New World. They base their conviction on similarities in pottery, jewelry, and tomb designs found in the New World with those of the Etruscans. There is also a close resemblance between Etruscan polygonal walls and ruins of polygonal walls found in Peru. The Etruscans took to the sea around 1700 B.C. However, they were never known to be far-ranging mariners like the Phoenicians and Carthaginians, and there is no evidence that they ventured far from their own coastline.

The Greeks have occasionally been proposed as discovers of the New World, but there is scant evidence to support this theory. The Greek biographer Plutarch did write that "there were Greek communities beyond the Atlantic that were unable to perpetuate the Greek tongue and they thinned out because of admixture with other inhabitants."

The Romans have been often portrayed as relatively timid sailors who neglected maritime trade. However, the reality is that they followed in the wake of the Phoenicians and Carthaginians, albeit less singlemindedly, and their ships are thought to have ventured as far as Southeast Asia and China. After conquering much of the British Isles, fleets of Roman ships plied between Italy and England in much the same way the Spanish fleet shuttled back and forth between Spain and its New World colonies more than 1,500 years later.

No less an authority than Plato, who lived from about 427 to 347 B.C., wrote that "far to the west of the British Isles were other islands beyond which, at the edge of the sea, stretched a great continent." In 150 B.C. the Roman historian Pausanias wrote about a group of islands west of the Atlantic whose inhabitants were red-skinned and whose hair was "like the mane of a horse." The Roman consul Metellus Celer has left us an even fuller account. In 62 B.C. he was officiating in Gaul when the king of a neighboring province brought him several exotic-looking men with red skins and black hair. The consul was told the men had been blown across the Atlantic in a large wooden canoe and cast up on the coast. There appears to be little doubt that the Romans were aware of land on the other side of the ocean.

At the Roman ruins of Pompeii a pineapple is depicted in a mural. The pineapple is a native New World plant. Even critics of the theory of early voyages, such as the plant taxonomist Elmer Drew Merrill, have accepted the Pompeii pineapple as proof of contact between the continents.

A Greco-Roman torso of Venus was discovered in the Gulf of Mexico near Veracruz in the 1880s. It would be tempting to use the marble statue as proof of contact in antiquity, but it could have been brought to Mexico at any time before or after Columbus. However, in recent years ancient Roman artifacts have been excavated from pre-Columbian archeological sites in Central and South America. Dozens of classical Greco-Roman terra-cotta oil lamps were recently uncovered in northern Peru in pre-Inca tombs. A third-century Roman terra-cotta head was discovered in apparently unequivocal association with a twelfth-century tomb in the state of Mexico.

The most compelling indication of Roman contact with the New World was found in 1961 when Dr. García Payón of the University of Jalapa discovered a hoard of Roman jewelry in six graves near Mexico City. Dr. Robert Heine Gelhern of the University of Vienna and Professor Hans Boehringer of the German Institute of Archaeology have identified them as of second-century-B.C. Roman origin. Scientific dating of the bones and other material found in association with the jewelry indicates that the burials took place no later than 100 B.C. It is possible they could have been brought over on a ship other than Roman, but it is certain they were brought over during the pre-Columbian era.

Roman coins have been unearthed in many areas of the Western Hemisphere, usually under circumstances that rule them out as evidence of pre-Columbian Roman presence, but two of the finds are worth mentioning. Near York, Maine, there is a rock on the beach bearing an inscription in Latin that has been an object of curiosity since the time of the first settlers. Nearby a Roman coin bearing a date of 237 A.D. was found. In the 1880s a ceramic jar filled with several hundred Roman coins, dating from the reign of Augustus down to 350 A.D., was found on a beach in Venezuela. The hoard is now in possession of Mendel L. Peterson, formerly with the Smithsonian. Close study of the worn, small-denomination coins indicates they are not a numismatist's misplaced collection but were probably a Roman sailor's ready cash, either buried up on the beach for concealment or washed ashore from a shipwreck.

In 1978 a farmer in Missouri unearthed Roman-style metal items and a bronze drinking cup that is identical to several found at Pompeii. Tests of the metals indicate they were manufactured by methods in use in Roman times.

According to legend, Saint Brendan, the patron saint of County Kerry, voyaged across the northern Atlantic to the New World with Irish monks to preach the word of Christ several times during the sixth century, preceding the Norsemen by three or four hundred years. On one of his missions he allegedly reached as far south as Florida and the Bahamas, encountering in both places other Irish monks who had arrived before him. According to Professor Carl O. Sauer of the University of California, when Norse explorers set out about 600 A.D. to colonize Iceland and Greenland, they found in each place traces of earlier Irish religious settlements. It was, he believes, the arrival of Norsemen that drove the Irish farther west

until they reached the shores of America and settled at Belle
Isle, between Labrador and Newfoundland along the St. Lawrence River, eventually merging into the culture of the Algon-
quin Indians.

"Christian Ireland from its beginnings lived in a special
awareness of the sea," Professor Sauer writes, "not a sea to be
feared or to try the limits of man's courage, but [one that]
stirred the imagination and drew men to seek what lay beyond
the far horizon." Such beliefs must have fostered the development of considerable navigational and shipbuilding skills. Saint
Brendan sailed in a curragh, a cowhide vessel built on oak
frames with tarred joints. Roman geographers describe seagoing curraghs as the principal ocean craft of the British Isles;
some were large enough to mount a square sail and carry over
twenty men. These craft were unsinkable and could have
crossed the ocean even in stormy weather.

In 1474 the Florentine scholar Paolo Toscanelli wrote: "In
the year 734 of Christ, when the whole of Spain had been won
by the heathen Moors of Africa, the island in the Atlantic
named Antillia was inhabited by an archbishop from Oporto
[in Portugal] with six other bishops and Christians, men and
women, who had fled from Spain by ship, together with cattle,
belongings, and goods." Several sixteenth-century historians
recorded that in 1477 inclement weather forced a Portuguese
ship far across the Atlantic and after a long period of hardship
it reached a place called Antillia, where the crew found seven
towns whose inhabitants spoke Portuguese. The people there
said that their ancestors had fled from Spain and Portugal at the
time of the Moorish conquest when King Don Rodrigo had
been killed. The place where they settled, according to the
sixteenth-century chronicles, was New Spain or Mexico.

Other contemporary historical accounts state that after
these Portuguese mariners managed to return to their home-
land, the Portuguese kings sent out a number of expeditions to
find Antillia, but because they were too fainthearted to sail far
enough west they all failed.

The Vikings were sailing and wreaking havoc along the

shores of Europe by the middle of the seventh century. On most of the forays they sailed from headland to headland, more or less following the coastline. Their epic sea travels began when the Norwegian and Danish Vikings started crossing the North Sea and making piratical raids in the British Isles, culminating with the big westward thrusts to Iceland and Greenland. We know they went as far west as L'Anse-aux-Meadows on the north coast of Newfoundland, and there is also a possibility that they voyaged to Mexico and Central America.

There is little evidence of contact between the Old and New World during the Dark Ages. The Portuguese were the next on the scene, centuries after the Norsemen. There are over one hundred charts predating 1492 that depict large landmasses and islands in the Atlantic. The most famous, the so-called Chart of 1424, shows many of the islands of the Caribbean, calling them Antillia. It was probably drawn by a Venetian, since Venetians were the best chart makers of the period. There are a number of documentary accounts of a Portuguese ship that in 1430 was driven by a tempest across the Atlantic and eventually reached a large landmass where there were settlements of people who spoke Portuguese and other European languages. A similar accidental crossing by a Portuguese ship returning to Lisbon from the Canary Islands is known to have occurred in 1447. The Portuguese even knew of the Sargasso Sea, located in the vicinity of Bermuda; it was described in an atlas of 1436. In May 1989 a large rock was discovered in the Bahamas with the date 1450 and two sailing ships inscribed on it; the ships are similar in appearance to the caravels used at the time.

There are still many obscure points in the history of these early Portuguese navigations that cannot be explained adequately in spite of the efforts of researchers who have pored over documents in archives and libraries in search of clues. Perhaps further information will turn up—perhaps from a private archive, of which there are still quite a few in Europe. Data about Portuguese history are scarce, because Portugal's archives and libraries have suffered a great deal over the centuries. During Spanish rule (1580 to 1640) all accounts of early Portuguese discoveries were destroyed. The fires that followed the great Lisbon earthquake of 1755 totally obliterated the India House and other depositories where records were kept. Much of what archival material remained in the country was subsequently looted or destroyed by invading French forces.

According to Fernando Columbus, his father knew of these early Portuguese voyages and they influenced him considerably, "particularly about the island called Antillia or Antilla that lies some two hundred leagues westward of the Canaries and Azores." There were many stories in circulation about lands to the west, and Toscanelli wrote of a westward route to the Indies that would be shorter than the one sought by the Portuguese. Columbus is said to have received into his house a man known as the Anonymous Pilot who, before he died, told him of a route to the west. Much speculation surrounds this shadowy figure; it is possible that he may have given Columbus definite details, even a chart to follow, which would account for the absolute certainty shown by Columbus when he discussed the project with others. During a trip that Columbus made to Iceland he met a party returning from Vinland, so there can be no doubt that Columbus knew of the existence of the New World before he set sail in 1492.

In light of the overwhelming amount of evidence already available and more that will doubtless be uncovered in years to come, the focus will inevitably shift from which was the first Old World people to reach the shores of the New World to which ancient group made the greatest cultural contributions to the Indians of the New World.

3

The Making of an Adventurer

For me, adventure is a way of life, and it's a life I wouldn't change for anything in this world. Risk and chance excite and challenge me. For as long as I remember I have been fascinated by the idea of actively seeking the past. My curiosity has taken me to over a hundred countries in the past forty years, and I have actually worked in more than half of them. I have explored under the sea and on land, and have lost track of time researching ancient manuscripts in musty archives and museums. For years I've said that I will retire and try living a normal life, but no sooner have I completed an expedition than several more opportunities are presented to whet my appetite for further adventures.

My lifetime yen for adventure no doubt grew out of the circumstances of my childhood. My birth, in a little house in the shadow of a Pittsburgh steel mill on December 8, 1936, was unusual in one respect—my head was encased in the caul, or fetal membrane. My Yugoslav mother and grandmother were thrilled, because a child born with a caul is considered to have a rosy future. Since antiquity many cultures have believed a caul is a charm against drowning. Since I have survived so many accidents at sea that I can't even remember them all, I have to believe being born with a caul *has* brought me luck.

Like many Europeans, my father, who was an Austrian immigrant, was fascinated by stories of lost treasures. As far back as I can remember, he used to spin fanciful tales about vast hoards of gold and fabulous treasures that were hidden all over the world. These tales sank deep into my young mind, and I was certain that one day I would search for and find numerous treasures. I learned to swim at an early age and used to dive with homemade goggles in the murky lakes and rivers near my home. Probing through the mud and twisted branches of long dead trees that lay strewn along the bottom, I found it easy to imagine the faint outlines of the twisted hulk of a wreck. I imagined what it would be like to probe deeper, deeper, deeper, into the strongroom of a treasure galleon. From the age of six I was oblivious to almost everything else and read everything concerning sunken and buried treasure that I could get my hands on.

To learn more about Spanish galleons I soon advanced to reading about Spanish history, which led me into the exploits of Columbus and other early explorers. Vikings and Norsemen soon captured my interest as much as tales of lost treasure. Fortunately there were a number of people of Scandinavian descent in my neighborhood. A couple of Swedes were happy to have such a rapt audience and soon had me convinced that the Norsemen were the first to reach the New World. One of them gave me a Viking ship model that was my most prized possession for many years.

One day in the third grade when we were studying about Columbus, I made a serious academic blunder—I insisted that the nun was mistaken in telling us that Columbus was the first to discover America. My repeated protestations led to a paddling by the principal, but not even a sore bottom made me change my mind. From that time on the kids in school called me Eric the Red. They meant it derisively, but I was quite proud of this distinction. I didn't let the matter die. At the Carnegie Museum I sought out the curator of the department that handled the fascinating display of Viking artifacts. Here I was, an eight-year-old kid confronting a grown man with a Ph.D. and expecting his support and affirmation. To my great dismay he informed me in no uncertain terms that Columbus had absolutely been the first European to reach the New World. Over the years I would meet countless others like him who would tell me I should concentrate on sports like other kids my age and leave historical inquiry to those more qualified. That night I cried in the dark. But I also vowed that one day I would prove him wrong. It was that night that I first conceived the idea of someday sailing a Viking ship replica across the Atlantic.

My parents were divorced about this same time. Home wasn't a good place to be, and I began to explore the world beyond Pittsburgh. I would disappear from home for days, sometimes for weeks, wandering alone and penniless to points seven or eight hundred miles away. My first long bike trip was to Mingo Junction, Ohio. The next year, when I was nine, I rode my bicycle from Pittsburgh to Chicago, stealing milk and butter from stoops and picking fruit from orchards. A year later when my bicycle had been taken away from me, I hitchhiked all the way to Minnesota to see the Kensington Stone, which had an inscription describing how the Norsemen had visited those regions long before Columbus arrived. Years later I was dismayed when the stone was proved to be a fake. When I returned from these unauthorized expeditions, I was a hero among the neighborhood kids. My mother, relieved to see me again, would briefly smother me with affection. Then, in a few weeks, I would be off again. So extreme was my wanderlust that legions of teachers, child psychologists, and priests were called in to curb it, but to no avail. Pittsburgh was the end of the world as far as I was concerned, especially since it was so far from the sea, where I was certain my destiny lay.

Finally, at the age of thirteen, I left home for good. I hitchhiked until I reached Atlantic City, New Jersey, where I made friends with a deep-sea helmet diver named Joe Novak. Joe and his kindly wife had no children, and they took me in when I convinced them I was an orphan. I started my career as a boat hand on Novak's salvage vessel. As I watched him go down and come up in his hard-hat rig, working on pier pilings and other mundane underwater projects, I was thrilled beyond words—and I vividly recalled my father's tales of sunken treasure. After much begging on my part, Novak reluctantly taught me how to dive. Soon I was doing most of the diving on each job, since Novak preferred staying on the surface, nursing a bottle of brandy. It was an experience so absorbing that I was more certain than ever that my future was inextricably intertwined with the sea and the unknown treasures and adventures it held.

One day after a fierce winter storm I read in the newspaper that the heavy seas had uncovered what several experts claimed was a Viking ship. I rushed up to the site in great expectation and fought my way through a horde of curious spectators to see the wreck. What little I knew at this time was enough to convince me that this was no Viking ship. The fastenings and long iron nails were machine-made, and the planks had been cut by a modern saw. Photographs I sent to the Smithsonian Institution in Washington proved me right. The wreck was determined to be an early-twentieth-century fishing vessel. Novak commented that I should become an archaeologist, and at the time I thought that it was a good idea.

The Juvenile Court authorities were hot on my trail, and Novak, to whom I had now told the story of my family, sent me up to Bridgeport, Connecticut, to work with another Polish hard-hat diver who had a small salvage firm. On my very first job I had the horrifying experience of having to pull out the bodies of two men who had crashed in a small plane into Long Island Sound. They were the first of more than three hundred bodies I have recovered from underwater sites around the world, from modern disasters and ancient shipwrecks and sunken cities. Soon after this experience I was to find my first treasure under a pier piling—a gold pocket watch.

After reading an article about people out in southern California who were practicing a new sport called skin diving, I knew that was the place for me. I headed west to Los Angeles to live with a great-aunt and returned to school again, although it was not school but the sea that held me in its grip. I spent every possible moment on or in it.

Within a few days of reaching California I made contact with some divers in the Los Angeles area and sampled the sport of skin diving. What a thrill! With fins I could reach the bottom twice as fast as before and with half the effort. Face masks in those days were primitive things made of hard rubber that had to be sandpapered down to fit the contours of one's face, and snorkels were usually nothing more than a length of garden hose. But primitive or not, both these pieces of equipment made a tremendous difference. I could dive deeper, see better, and never really have to surface completely. Soon I was initiated into the use of the recently developed Cousteau-Gagnon "Aqua-Lung," or scuba gear, which made the cumbersome, complicated helmet rig Joe Novak had taught me to use seem prehistoric. A whole new world beckoned me.

I feel almost antiquated when I think how far skin diving has come since those days. The skin-diving club I joined, the Los Angeles Neptunes, was one of the few in the world and the second one established in the United States. Most of the members were men in their forties who had pioneered the sport in the late 1930s and 1940s, inventing or developing much of the equipment in use today. Skin divers were such a rare breed when I started diving that people would gather on the shore as we came out of the water in our weird equipment, half expecting one of us to say, "Take me to your leader."

Most of my early dives were devoted to exploring and spearfishing, but I soon discovered that diving was a good means of supporting myself as well. On weekends I could average between fifty and a hundred dollars a day recovering lost outboards, anchors, fishing tackle, and even golf balls. This led to bigger and better jobs, such as collecting marine specimens for universities and government agencies, and also underwater photography, which was a new and highly profitable field.

It was on one of my first underwater photography assignments that I had my first brush with death. I was diving from a rocky stretch of coast near the Palos Verdes cliffs, taking still photographs of some small fish, when I spotted a group of sea lions playing around some nearby rocks. As I approached, they suddenly started to screech and swim around frantically, some trying to scramble onto the offshore rocks and others trying to reach shore. At first I thought they were afraid of me, but then I saw the real cause of their panic. It was a sight I'll never forget: four killer whales, each about twenty feet long. The killer whale is among the most voracious creatures in the sea, as vicious and powerful as the great white shark, but much more intelligent, since it is a mammal. Despite the playful antics of Shamu and his semidomesticated cousins who entertain at Sea World, killer whales in the wild have been known to ram boats at high speeds and devour the occupants.

I was, if possible, more panic-stricken than the sea lions. I didn't even try to swim for safety—not that I could have outdistanced those monsters anyway. I just froze, sinking like a stone to the sea floor about thirty feet down. This was probably my salvation (luckily I had plenty of air left in my tank), for, as I looked up, the killer whales closed in, expertly cutting off their victims' line of retreat to the shore. Seconds later the surface was a churning caldron of blood. Smaller sea lions were cut in half with one crunch from those massive jaws, while the larger ones, some weighing up to five hundred pounds, were finished off in three or four bites. In two minutes there was nothing left of the twenty-odd sea lions but gory bits and pieces that filtered down on top of me in the now murky water. Fearing that the killer whales might notice the tidbits they had missed—and me in the bargain—I quickly set out for shore, hugging the bottom like a snake. I was so rattled by the horrifying scene I had just witnessed that I abandoned my underwater camera with its case, which had taken me a month to build, on the bottom and was never able to locate it again.

Most of the members of the Los Angeles Neptunes were content with spearfishing and grabbing lobsters and abalone, so I had difficulty convincing a few that we should start searching for old shipwrecks. Then I showed up at one of our meetings with a handful of gold coins. The *Winfield Scott* was one of the numerous California gold rush ships that wrecked along the coast in the 1850s. She lay in shallow water near Anacapa Island off the coast of Santa Barbara. She soon became known as "Marx's gold mine," because I managed to recover several hundred gold coins and numerous pieces of gold jewelry from under her steel sides. If six guys went diving with me I always found more than they combined. It was just lucky! After the coins petered out on this wreck we began exploring others and then got into diving for placer gold nuggets and gold dust in the rivers of northern California.

I knew that good research was the key to success in finding sunken treasures, so I devoured every book, magazine article, and old newspaper account on the subject, taking notes assiduously, until my records filled a dozen footlockers. I never seemed to tire of collecting these records or probing deeper and deeper for facts. Of course, the trick was sifting the truth out of all the fanciful fiction masquerading as fact that had been published about sunken treasure. I became quite an expert and before long had people contacting me from all over the United States about shipwreck data.

After graduating from high school I enrolled in day courses at Los Angeles City College and night courses at UCLA, majoring in the earth sciences, with my interest focused on history and archaeology. As a result of researching shipwrecks I came across a substantial amount of information about several pre-Columbian Asiatic ships that had been discovered along the West Coast over the years, as well as Oriental artifacts that had been discovered on land.

The idea that Asians might have beaten my Norsemen to the New World piqued my curiosity. I decided to find out more. One of my college professors told me that a quantity of Ming dynasty porcelain had been discovered at two different sites along beaches in northern California and Oregon, and this got me started on my quest for the "great white gods"—or in this case, great yellow gods.

The first site I went to was at Drake's Bay, so named because Sir Francis Drake is believed to have careened his ships there during his circumnavigation of the globe (1577–80). Drake's Bay is a stunningly beautiful place about twenty-five miles northwest of San Francisco. In 1950 only a handful of people lived there, raising cattle and fishing. Just about everyone I met had a small collection of Chinese porcelain sherds that they had found along the beach after storms. They were certain an old Chinese junk lay just offshore, but pointed out that the bay was a spawning ground for the great white shark and only an idiot would dive there. But neither the menace of sharks nor the frigid temperature of the murky water could keep me from diving. I spent several days exploring and recovered several dozen porcelain sherds, six iron cannonballs, and some lead musket shot without seeing any sharks. The cannonballs and shot disturbed me, since I knew they wouldn't normally be found on an Asiatic vessel.

I took the artifacts to several museums, and an expert at the University of California in Berkeley cleared up the mystery of why Chinese porcelain was mixed in with cannonballs and shot. He explained that the *San Agustín,* a Spanish galleon of the type known as a Manila galleon, such as plied the seas between Manila and Acapulco during the colonial period, had wrecked in this area in 1595. He said what I had found most likely came from this shipwreck. So I had finally found my first Spanish treasure galleon, but most of the wreck lay buried under tons of sediment. For many years I planned to return to this site one day and find the rest of the wreck. After years of bureaucratic obstacles, I was able to obtain a permit from the State of California, and in June 1989 I relocated the wreck site.

I am currently waiting for an excavation permit to continue work on this site.

The second suspected Asiatic shipwreck was located near the mouth of the Nehalem River in Oregon. There too I talked to quite a few local people who had found Chinese porcelain sherds along the beach. They too told tales of these objects coming ashore from a Chinese junk lying offshore. At least there, although the water was cold, I didn't have to keep looking over my shoulder for sharks. I spent two weeks combing the seafloor, but found only modern wreckage. Some time later I learned that a large block of beeswax with the date 1679 inscribed on it had washed ashore. This made me think that another Manila galleon might be the source of the porcelain sherds that washed up on the beach from time to time, since the galleons typically carried tons of export porcelain destined for European markets. My hunch proved correct years later when I found documentation in the Spanish archives indicating that the galleon *San Francisco,* carrying a large amount of Chinese porcelain, had been lost in this area in 1707. So perhaps, I thought, the Norsemen were the first to reach America after all.

One evening as I was leaving an anthropology class the professor asked me to stay behind for a chat. He asked me if I was interested in going to Guatemala for a week with him, and even before I knew all of the details I jumped at the opportunity. Two close friends of his, a married couple, had gone to visit the ancient Mayan ruins of Tikal in northern Guatemala and had disappeared after leaving their chartered plane at a nearby dirt airstrip. I had just been learning about these very ruins in another of my classes, and here I had a golden opportunity to visit them. With several Mayan guides and a police officer we spent the week trekking through the dense jungles in a futile search for the couple, who were never found.

Archaeology came alive for me during this expedition as my college professor crammed his lifetime of knowledge about Meso-American civilzations and other facts into me. At night he recounted legend after legend of the great white gods as we lay in our hammocks unable to sleep because of the squadrons of relentless mosquitoes. I was hooked—determined to devote a good part of my life to investigating the legends of the great white gods.

During the Korean War, I joined the U.S. Marine Corps, and after boot camp I was assigned to the Marine Corps base at Camp Lejeune in North Carolina, where I was in charge of salvage operations. This improbable place turned out to be a treasure hunter's paradise. Only a stone's throw away was treacherous Cape Hatteras, known to generations of seamen as the "graveyard of the Atlantic." No one can say with certainty how many shipwrecks lie scattered in this area—the estimates range from six hundred to three thousand.

The notes in my footlockers, which I had had shipped from California, indicated the wrecks included Spanish galleons, German submarines, copper-laden Victory ships, and sailing vessels with rich cargoes of gold dust inbound from California via Panama. During my year at Camp Lejeune, I probably spent more time chasing after old shipwrecks than actually working for the Marine Corps. I was then transferred to Vieques Island, between Puerto Rico and the Virgin Islands, to run the Marine diving school. Between classes, I usually had several weeks of spare time. I made good use of them by visiting many of the other Caribbean islands in search of sunken and buried treasures.

My three-year stint in the Marines temporarily satisfied my wanderlust. I managed to see a great deal of the world: Hawaii, Wake, Guam, Okinawa, Japan, Korea, Greenland, Iceland, most of the countries touching on the Mediterranean, and the greater part of the Caribbean.

I spent my spare time chasing after shipwrecks everywhere I was stationed. In those days very few people were diving, and my activities on shipwrecks made me quite well known to the press and public. I was frequently contacted for various unusual diving jobs, and my superiors let me run off on any adventure that arose, because they were pleased with the publicity that my capers brought to the Marines. I continued my research on pre-Columbian contacts with the New World, and soon I realized that I had been mistaken about the Vikings being the first to reach the New World. In Europe I met museum curators and university faculty who shared my beliefs in these facts, but in the United States most scholars were reluctant to risk their reputations by stating that Columbus was a johnny-come-lately.

In 1955 the press announced that fishermen off Boston had made a sensational find, the remains of a Roman shipwreck, and had brought up seven amphorae from the site. The National Geographic Society asked me to investigate the wreck site. I took six Navy UDT divers along to assist me. We never got into the water. One look at the so-called Roman amphorae convinced me that they were Spanish olive jars, similar in appearance to the amphorae used in the classical world, but used as storage jars throughout the Spanish colonial period. Since then more of these olive jars have occasionally been recovered from that site and from other sites in the United States. Each discovery prompts erroneous headlines about Romans or other ancient mariners reaching America. The latest find occurred about ten years ago when the national press carried stories that a Greek shipwreck had been discovered near Roatán Island off the coast of Honduras. This time when I was contacted by NBC-TV to investigate the site I was smart enough to request photographs of the "Greek amphorae." Once again they turned out to be Spanish olive jars from the mid-eighteenth century.

Several months after the disappointing sortie up to Boston, I was asked to investigate another suspected Old World shipwreck off Sable Island, Nova Scotia. A figurehead identified by several experts as of Viking origin had washed ashore, and people were convinced a Viking ship lay nearby. I was thrilled at the prospect of fulfilling my dream of proving the Norsemen had reached America. I wasted little time getting up there. I was greeted by hordes of media people who thought they would get the story of a lifetime and various museum experts from both the United States and Scandinavia. To everyone's chagrin, especially mine, the shipwreck turned out to be a Canadian fishing boat from around the turn of the century. It had most likely been skippered or owned by someone of Scandinavian descent, since I found other Viking carvings on the superstructure and the name *Vinland* on the stern nameplate.

To compensate for this embarrassment I did have an exciting find some months later in the Caribbean. I was sent with several Marine officers to scout for likely liberty ports for an armada of naval vessels carrying Marines on maneuvers in the Caribbean. In Martinique I visited the local museum and learned that woodcutters had recently discovered a cave with a number of skeletons and artifacts in it. A museum staff member took me to the cave. We found that the site had been plundered. Holes had been dug everywhere, and the bones were strewn about. I asked permission to dig myself and was both amazed and thrilled to unearth a small ceramic head with definite Semitic features and a long beard. Later I showed it to a number of experts. Before I told them where it had been found, I asked their opinions. Without exception each authority said it was most likely Phoenician and definitely of pre-Columbian origin. So once again I was on the trail of the great white gods.

A six-month cruise in the Mediterranean with the Sixth Fleet provided the opportunity for my most memorable experiences while I was in the Marines. I was attached to the fleet as a diver. My duties were few. Mainly, I had to make inspections of the bottoms of the fleet's vessels. I also searched for the occasional lost article, which in several instances was sadly the body of a drunken sailor or Marine who drowned while returning to his ship. When we were in port I spent every available hour exploring the ruins of the classical world, visiting museums and talking with historians and other experts. While my Marine companions were ashore chasing women and trying to drink the place dry, I was amassing vast amounts of knowledge that I was able to utilize to great advantage later in life. Not that I didn't like women and wine, but I was mesmerized by history! The highlight of the tour was diving on classical wrecks. I had opportunities to dive on several Roman shipwrecks off Naples and a Greek galley off Crete that carried a cargo of marble columns and other building materials.

I remember the three days I spent in Cádiz Bay in 1954 as if they were just last week. I knew that the Spanish city of Cádiz was founded by the Phoenicians and has probably been used as a seaport for the past 4,000 years. Consequently I knew there had to be countless shipwrecks there. It was sheer luck that I selected a cove that was the best spot to explore in the whole enormous bay. La Caleta, as the cove is named, is surrounded by land on three sides, with two large Spanish forts on both sides of its mouth. I had no idea when I started diving that these forts were then being used by the Franco government for housing political prisoners; however, I knew something was up, because each time I surfaced I saw policemen and soldiers waving machine guns at me. I just ignored them and continued my explorations.

Later I was to learn that La Caleta was the main Phoenician anchorage and was also used for centuries by other cultures. I had never seen anything like it, and I had never been so excited. I was in an underwater museum. The entire seafloor was paved with debris from dozens, perhaps hundreds, of shipwrecks spanning thousands of years! It was surreal. Disney couldn't have done a better job of designing a set with more interesting objects from antiquity. There were thousands of classical-period amphorae all over the bottom and enough ceramic objects to fill several museums. My most interesting discoveries were eleven bronze and six marble life-size statues of Phoenician, Greek, and Roman manufacture. I raised three of them many years later, and they are on display in the Cádiz Archaeological Museum. Iron and bronze cannon, as well as countless anchors, lay askew like so many fallen logs. Using a small rubber raft and diving with scuba tanks I spent about eight hours each day just swimming about and marveling at what I was seeing. Little did I realize at the time that six years later, when I got back to this place again, most of what I had seen would have disappeared, plundered.

All good things have to come to an end, and this expedition had a decidedly dramatic finish. I was on the bottom totally wrapped up in what I was seeing when I heard one huge engine after another turning on. I realized with a start that the fleet was raising anchor and getting ready to sail. I frantically tried to get back to my ship, or for that matter to any of them, but before I was even halfway I realized I'd never make it and I would have to go ashore. Here I was in a black rubber suit with no identification or money, and I knew if I went ashore I would receive a far from pleasant welcome from the Spanish military and police, who had been trying to chase me away for days. But I had no choice, so I rowed back to the beach inside La Caleta and was met with swarms of angry Spaniards wielding guns—an event that, over the years, would be repeated numerous times in other countries.

I couldn't speak a word of Spanish at the time, and no one seemed to understand English. All I could do was stand there dripping wet, point at the departing fleet, and hope for the best. Luckily for me, it was a religious holiday in Cádiz and a big fiesta was going on when I landed. While the military and the police were arguing over who had the authority to arrest me, two distinguished gentlemen galloped up on fine Andalusian horses and in perfect English asked me if there was a problem. I told them my story, and they said they would be happy to help me. My rescuers told the soldiers and police that they would get me to the American consulate and back to my ship, and I was released into their custody. They produced some clothes for me and accompanied me to the fiesta, where I got a taste of marvelous Spanish hospitality.

What wonderful luck I had once again. I couldn't have been rescued by two more fantastic men. It was almost uncanny. Both men were historians who specialized in the classical period. Don Manuel Jiménez Fernández was a professor at the University of Seville, and Don Manuel González Byass owned the largest wine and brandy bodega in Spain and was the author of several history books.

The following day we learned that the Sixth Fleet would be in Barcelona in three days' time and I could join my ship there. My hosts would lend me the train fare to Barcelona. The two days I spent with these men were as exciting as the time I had spent on the bottom of La Caleta, and it was a turning point in my life. While they regaled me with historical facts about Cádiz Bay and other places in Spain, I kept them spellbound by describing what I had seen on the bottom of the bay. Even more fantastic was the fact that both were adherents of the theory that the Phoenicians and others had most likely reached the New World before Columbus. I remember the university professor saying that if word ever leaked out that he said that Columbus was not the first to reach America, he would surely lose his job and probably be exiled to some faraway Spanish colony. Before departing for Barcelona I promised my new friends that I would return one day to work on the shipwrecks in Cádiz Bay.

I kept my word, returning six years later in 1960. When I came back to Spain it was primarily to begin researching primary documents in the Spanish archives. I had no idea what a kettle of worms I was getting into and how many years of frustration were to follow—frustration that continues today. I loved working in the archives, ferreting out the past from fragile ancient documents written in spidery cursive. My historical research turned up mention of a staggering number of shipwrecks in Cádiz Bay. There were over 2,500 recorded ancient shipwrecks—and many others for which no records exist—as well as five Phoenician and Roman settlements. Whenever I had time away from the archives over the next two and a half years I would be on the bottom of Cádiz Bay exploring. Under the auspices of the Cádiz Archaeological Museum I was given permission to search these waters and just within a two-mile radius of the inner port.

I located fifty-four classical-period shipwrecks and ninety-seven of later dates without using any of the sophisticated equipment available today, such as sonar, magnetometers, and metal detectors. Most of my finds from the colonial period were the result of clues I found in documents. Most of the classical shipwrecks I found by relocating spots where fishermen told me they had snagged things in their nets. Neither the Spanish government nor I could find funding for undertaking any extensive salvage efforts at the time, but I did recover millions of dollars' worth of treasure and artifacts during this period, which I turned over to the Cádiz Archaeological Museum.

No place on earth is more fascinating to me than Cadiz Bay, and every year since 1970 I have approached the Spanish government for a permit to salvage shipwrecks there, but I have been continuously stymied by unrelenting bureaucracy. For the past twenty years the government has been preparing a law to cover shipwreck exploration. Until the law is passed, no one can work on shipwrecks. Meanwhile, however, one of the world's most precious archaeological resources has been almost totally destroyed. Cádiz Bay was of little importance when I started my explorations, but it has become the largest and most important port on the Iberian Peninsula. The greater part of the bay area has been subjected to monumental filling and dredging, obliterating any hope of excavating the historic relics in this unique underwater museum.

In 1978 I went through another round of sheer frustration with the Spanish bureaucrats. During the years I had spent researching and diving in Spain prior to the *Niña II* voyage and also afterward, I had taken hundreds of slides of the artifacts and objects of treasure I had recovered and turned over to the museum, and I used these slides in lectures on underwater archaeology that I gave around the world. With time some of the slides faded, so I wanted to photograph the objects again.

In November 1978, when Jenifer and I went to the museum to photograph the artifacts, we discovered that most of them had disappeared. The current director of the museum had no idea what had happened to any of them. He questioned the employees, but no one seemed to know anything. Naturally, I was very upset, since I had spent hundreds of hours, not to mention lots of money, recovering them. I threatened to hold a press conference. The museum director, fearing a scandal, was at wits' end. We conferred for several days and finally worked out a deal. In return for promising not to hold a press conference and to keep the loss of these treasures a secret, he would issue me an excavation permit for La Caleta and I would receive 50 percent of all duplicate finds. The director assured us that he had the necessary authority for issuing this permit and wrote me a letter of intent. I was thrilled that at long last I would be able to gather data for the Phoenician ship replica I had dreamed of for so many years.

Several months earlier, two Canadian businessmen, Donald C. Webster and Michael Needham, had approached me about forming a shipwreck salvage company with them. Now I had a project—and what a project! When I told them about the forthcoming permit for La Caleta, they were as ecstatic about the project as we were. Within a month they raised almost a million dollars, and we formed a company named Phoenician Explorations Ltd. I assembled a first-class team of divers and archaeologists, who were ready to start as soon as we had the permit. I went to Spain to expedite matters, stopping first at Madrid, where I had a four-hour audience with King Juan Carlos, who is an avid sport diver. He said he looked forward to diving at La Caleta once we got started and offered me the loan of one of his own boats, the *Pato Loco*—"Crazy Duck." With the king of Spain's backing I thought nothing could stop the project. I was sure the years of anguish and frustration dealing with Spanish bureaucrats were over. I was wrong.

I rented a big house near Cádiz for our team and got together a considerable amount of equipment. We were poised to begin as soon as the museum director issued the excavation permit. The days passed, and still there was no permit. One

day he informed me that I would have to go before a committee in Madrid, consisting of archaeologists and museum directors from all over Spain. He assured me this was just a formality—something that had to be done before the permit could be issued. While waiting for this meeting, I flew to Palma de Mallorca, where I spent several days diving with the king and his cousin, Prince Michel de Bourbon, who had become one of the investors in Phoenician Explorations. We had a great time, recovering numerous artifacts from several Roman shipwrecks. Several newspapers carried articles about our diving activities. There was still a moratorium in Spain restricting any activities on shipwrecks, but since we were diving with the king I never gave it a second thought.

It was the period following Franco, who died in late 1975, and various political parties that had long been outlawed were vying for power. Several of the Madrid papers were run by socialists with political ambitions, and they made the most of embarrassing the king. The day before I was to meet with the committee in Madrid, several articles appeared in the newspapers about the king's shipwreck diving in Palma, and a minor "Watergate" ensued. The paper learned about my impending permit and had a field day. Because Bourbon was both a cousin of the king and an investor with my company, the king was accused of nepotism, as well as breaking the law by recovering artifacts from a shipwreck.

Although I had requested a permit only for La Caleta, the museum director extended the permit to cover about two hundred miles of the coast of Andalucía once he knew I had the backing of the king—which was rather a strange thing to do in a country that had never issued a single permit for excavation of shipwrecks. I tried to dissuade him from including such a large area, but he insisted, saying that he wanted us to investigate wrecks that fishermen had located all along this coast. Once this fact became known, even the newspapers that were usually favorable to the royal family came out with articles and editorials lambasting the king.

Things were going sour on all sides. The meeting that was

supposed to be a minor formality turned out to be a major catastrophe. When I met with the commission in Madrid I was informed that not only did the director of the Cádiz Archaeological Museum have no authority to issue a permit, but neither they nor anyone else in Spain could authorize my project until the government passed shipwreck legislation. I could hardly believe it. It was politics again, the same problem I had faced for years. Cádiz is located in the province of Andalucía which had been granted a certain degree of autonomy, including rights to all archaeological sites. The museum director in Cádiz had assumed that he could grant me an archaeological excavation permit, based on Andalucía's right to such sites. However, the commission was entirely made up of federal bureaucrats, who decided that the rights to all archaeological sites did not include those under the sea. I was devastated and headed for Brazil to investigate the reported discovery of a Greek shipwreck site.

In 1985, King Juan Carlos invited me to inspect what was happening to the shipwrecks I had found in Cádiz Bay so many years before. I spent a month combing the seafloor, growing more depressed each day. More than two-thirds of the shipwrecks, and certainly countless others that I had not located, had been annihilated by the dredging and landfill activities. Since that time even more have disappeared forever. Since 1985 I have fought to stop this wanton destruction, but to little avail. UNESCO, which has a mandate to protect cultural sites worldwide, chose not to get involved, and the Spanish press, agreeing with the government and the private sector, maintains that the economic development of the Cádiz region is of more importance than old shipwrecks. I understand this, but my fight will continue in the hope that at least a handful of the shipwrecks that remain hidden under the bottom sediment can be saved.

While I was in the Marines, I completed a number of correspondence courses from the universities of Maryland and Illinois. Combined with the college credits I already had from

UCLA and Los Angeles City College, those credits brought me within one semester of a bachelor's degree. So I resumed my studies at UCLA, but found it very hard going after my experiences. Sometimes I had the feeling that I knew more about the subject than the professor and that the best way to learn was out in the field, supplemented with research in libraries, and not in a stuffy classroom. I never finished the semester. I was keenly interested in the ancient Mayan civilization of Yucatán and Central America, and when I learned that a small movie production unit was going to Mexico's Yucatán Peninsula to film the ancient, majestic pyramids and temples of the Maya, I couldn't resist joining them, offering to work in exchange for my transportation, lodging, and food.

I went for a couple of months and stayed for three fascinating years, exploring the undeveloped Yucatán. When the movie was completed, the production team returned to the States, but I stayed on to explore the ruins that dotted the land. The whole time was an extended adventure, sometimes rough but never boring. I trekked into the dense jungles, staying a couple of weeks at a time. I descended into the *cenotes,* or sacrificial wells, to recover samples of Mayan artifacts for museums, and I hunted jaguar and wild boar in the dense jungles of Quintana Roo.

In time I settled on the island of Cozumel, which in 1956 was an out-of-the-way paradise. I helped a local entrepreneur start the island's first tourist hotel and operated a fishing business. The islanders, most of whom were Maya, were *muy simpatico,* the island was beautiful, the water was clear as gin, and the gorgeous fish on the coral reefs were large and plentiful. Most of my daylight hours were spent underwater on the magnificent multicolored reefs surrounding the island. At night I talked to the local fishermen, who often knew the locations of wrecks. This research led me to a half-dozen ancient relics that lay on the nearby reefs. The wreck that fascinated me most was a large vessel with some twenty iron cannons that lay on a dangerous reef off the Yucatán mainland opposite Cozumel.

Local legend had the wreck filled with an immense treasure in gold and jewels. With several American friends, I mounted three well-planned expeditions to the wreck, and we brought up thousands of artifacts, but very little treasure—only a gold pocket watch, several pieces of jewelry, and a few coins.

For over three years I worked hard to determine the origin of the mysterious ship. I had many clues, but none of them was definite. The identification of this wreck became an obsession. I gave up my life and work on the island and moved to Washington, D.C., to be close to the libraries there as well as the National Archives, where I labored feverishly for three months until the final crucial piece fell into place to complete the puzzle. I was able to identify the ship as a Spanish merchantman, the *Matanzero,* which sank in 1741 while sailing from Spain to Veracruz, Mexico. I had enjoyed the research almost as much as the diving, and I felt great satisfaction at having solved the mystery.

During the time I lived on Cozumel Island I spent as much time in the jungles of Quintana Roo in search of clues of the great white gods as I did chasing after shipwrecks. This was the real reason that I had come to the Yucatán Peninsula, and I was to experience a dream come true.

4

El Gringo Loco

On sixteenth-century Spanish charts, the eastern half of the Yucatán Peninsula appears as a huge empty territory, with a few names of bays and capes inked next to the shoreline. In 1956, when I arrived on the scene, the map of Yucatán still looked much the same, except that the territory had a name, Quintana Roo, in honor of a minor hero of Mexican independence. For over three hundred miles of coastline, from Cape Catoche in the north down to Chetumal, the capital of the territory, on the Belize border (then called British Honduras), there were fewer than ten villages, none of which had more than twenty families. But the coast was densely populated in comparison to the area inland, where there wasn't another settlement for fifty or sometimes a hundred miles from the coast.

In the 1950s, Quintana Roo was still pretty well isolated from the outside world. With a total population of a thousand (except for Chetumal) scattered over an area of twenty thousand square miles, there was little demand for an airstrip, and the three dirt roads that led into the territory from the states of Campeche and Yucatán were passable only in the dry season. Sea communications were little better. Cozumel is separated from the Quintana Roo coast by a channel only twelve miles wide, but few of the islanders would venture across in the small local boats for fear of being swept away by the strong northerly current that runs through the channel on its way to join the Gulf Stream. There were a few turtle fishermen who worked over on the mainland at times, and several smuggling boats that occasionally went down to British Honduras for contraband, but it was not until I had three little schooners with auxiliary engines built, the *Aguilucho,* the *Clipper,* and the *Bluebird,* that anything like steady communications started between Cozumel and the nearby mainland coast.

Today this same area that was so primitive during my exciting sojourn is one of the most important tourist developments in Mexico and nothing like the area I knew and loved. Cancún Island in those days had only one small fishing village with a half-dozen thatch huts and was covered with overgrown Mayan ruins. Now the island resembles Miami Beach and only a fraction of the ruins remain, the others having been destroyed by the indiscriminate bulldozing that initiated the government's massive resort project. When I returned to Cozumel about fifteen years ago for a week's vacation, the changes were so drastic that I broke into tears and fled after two days. I like to remember the place the way it was in the old days.

The only reassuring thing had been to find a number of old friends. Almost as soon as Jenifer and I stepped off the plane I was greeted by a short, bronze-skinned Maya, Taolé, who had worked on one of my boats as a barefoot lad and was now a prosperous middle-aged man. The word spread that *el gringo loco,* the crazy *gringo* who spent all his time in the jungle or under the water, was back, and I had the pleasure of introducing Jenifer to people I'd talked about and had missed.

When I first arrived on Cozumel the village jail also served as a makeshift museum; various carved stones and other objects found in the Mayan ruins were strewn around, though no one had any idea where most of the items had been discovered. Two large stone heads of bearded men over three feet high naturally stirred my interest and reassured me that I was in the right area in my pursuit of the great white gods. One of the store owners in town also had a collection of several hundred clay figurines from both Cozumel and the mainland. Among them were two dozen or so statuettes depicting bearded men with definite non-Indian features. From photographs of these finds, various experts in Europe and the States identified most of them as appearing to have come from the eastern Mediterranean.

Several months after my arrival I met Pablo Bush Romero, a Mexican millionaire who was an amateur archaeologist. Don Pablo, as he was called, told me that near Mérida, the capital of Yucatán, he had bought a number of clay figurines of Oriental-featured men from a peasant. The National Museum in Mexico City identified them as Japanese from around 500 A.D. In a cave on Cozumel a hunter had recently discovered a bronze disk with three pyramids and a sphinx engraved on it. I later tracked down the missionary to whom he sold it. He provided me with a photograph, copies of which I sent to six museums around the world. The consensus of opinion was that the disk appeared to be Egyptian and over 3,000 years old.

I knew from research that the Spaniards who first arrived in Cozumel in the early sixteenth century had been amazed by various things they encountered. They found large stone crosses erected all over the island, and the Indians told them legends of white men coming to the island many times over the centuries in large ships. It took little more to convince me that this area was one of the best places to start my quest.

Quintana Roo was not only one of the least accessible regions in the Western Hemisphere but one of the most hostile. However, I was totally ignorant of this when I decided to take the *Aguilucho* over to the mainland for a short reconnaissance several months after settling on Cozumel. All that the islanders could tell me was that no one lived over there but a few Indians and one or two families with copra plantations. I suppose I expected just a bigger version of Cozumel, but I was in for a shock, and so were the four attractive young schoolteachers staying at my hotel who persuaded me to take them along.

Even before we anchored the *Aguilucho* offshore I could see that there was a big difference. Cozumel was green and lush, but this was a real jungle, which started right at the thin strip of beach and became higher and denser the farther inland it went. We rowed to shore and were immediately greeted by swarms of sand flies and mosquitoes, which had obviously not had a square meal in a year. We had, of course, come without any insect repellent, but were determined not to let a few thousand insects faze us. We set about building a thatched lean-to for our campsite. The two boatmen were smarter. They slept on board the *Aguilucho,* ostensibly in case the anchor dragged in the night, but also to keep out of range of the pestilential insects.

After we had eaten supper I set off for a stroll down the beach with one of the teachers. Not far from the campsite, we spotted a huge loggerhead turtle—it must have weighed four hundred pounds—scooping a hole in the sand. We sat down to watch her lay her eggs. My companion kept saying, "I feel someone is watching us watch the turtle." She was so insistent that I finally climbed a high sand dune behind us to have a look. I saw nothing but the long strip of beach reflecting the bright moonlight, with the impenetrable dark bush behind, and was starting back when someone charged out of the bush right past me, heading for the beach. It was a large jaguar, its mottled gold-and-black coat unmistakable even though I had never seen a live one before. Within seconds it had pounced on the loggerhead's neck, sending up a jet of blood that spurted on the petrified woman sitting only twenty-five feet away.

I was totally unarmed; in fact, the only weapons I had brought along on this lark were spear guns for underwater fishing, and they were back at the campsite. Picking up a piece of driftwood—not that it would have been of much more use than a matchstick—I ran past the jaguar, grabbed the school-teacher around the waist, and sprinted down the beach without stopping until we reached the campsite. She was in hysterics by then, and the other three joined in as soon as they caught sight of her, spattered with blood from the decapitated turtle.

I don't know which was worse, the jaguar or four scream-ing women, but for a few minutes I felt like going back to join the jaguar. I yelled for my two boatmen to come and help, but even with three of us we could hardly hold down the hysterical woman, who was screaming and thrashing around in a frenzy. The other three calmed down as soon as I could explain that their friend wasn't wounded, only frightened, but they started up again as soon as they heard the word "jaguar," convinced it would come down the beach to attack our camp. I was sure the loggerhead was a big enough meal to satisfy a couple of jaguars, but I had the boatmen build four bonfires around the lean-to, and the three of us sat up on guard duty all night, armed with spear guns. No one would have been able to sleep anyway, since a steady parade of land crabs, lizards, frogs, and snakes crawled all over us and even inside the sleeping bags.

With the first light of dawn the expedition, which had been planned to last a week, was over by silent consent. Exhausted, swollen with insect bites, and thoroughly shaken, we broke camp and headed for Cozumel.

My next trip to the mainland was in the way of a badly needed apprenticeship with one of the best hunters in Quintana Roo, Miguel López, who runs a chicle enterprise in the north-ern part of the territory. I had taught Miguel how to dive on Cozumel and had decided to take him up on his invitation to go hunting with him. It was obvious from that fiasco of a first expedition, in which we hadn't even left the beach, that I had a lot to learn before I could go exploring the Quintana Roo back-lands.

I could have been in New York in a tenth the time it took me to reach Miguel's main chicle depot at Leona Vicario, about twenty-five miles from the coast on one of Quintana Roo's "highways." First I had to go to Isla Mujeres, north of Cozumel. It was called the Island of Women because of the thousands of Mayan statues, all of women, that the Spanish conquistadores found there in the early sixteenth century. The weekly boat, the *Cisne*—I can't think of a less appropriate name for that tub than *Swan*—managed to make Isla Mujeres without breaking down more than twice, which I was told was a record, and then continued across to the small fishing village of Puerto Juárez on the coast, where Miguel was waiting to meet me.

As we jolted along the road to Leona Vicario, Miguel told me I had come at a good time, since he had been planning to take supplies to one of his camps in the jungle and bring out the chicle the men had collected for him. Chicle until recently was the base of chewing gum; it is made from the sap of a tree that grows wild all over the rain forests of Central America. Expecting that we would have to walk, I was surprised the next morning to see that we were going to travel first-class—by narrow-gauge railroad.

We rode an open flatcar pulled by two mules and loaded with supplies, which included two large sea turtles Miguel had bought in Puerto Juárez, flipped over so that they wouldn't suffocate from their own weight. Several Indians walked along the track in front, cutting away just enough of the undergrowth to let the mules and flatcar pass. The jungle was so thick on each side and overhead that we seemed to be going through a never-ending green tunnel.

Twice the mules acted uneasy, and I thought there might be a jaguar lurking nearby, but both times Miguel grabbed his rifle, bounded off into the bush, and returned with a type of wild boar called *jabalí*. We talked a lot about hunting in general and jaguars in particular, and Miguel told me that jaguars often kill turtles when they come up to the beach to lay their eggs, but that they rarely attack humans unless cornered. If I was so interested in jaguars, he would make sure I got a crack at one before I went back to Cozumel.

By evening we had reached an Indian settlement of several huts, where we were to spend the night. It looked as if the life of these people had changed little since the time when their Maya ancestors were building temples at Dzibilchaltún and Chichén Itzá. They still made their *milpas,* or corn patches, by burning a clearing in the jungle, and they still planted the corn by digging a little hole with a fire-hardened stick. Their huts were no more than thatched roofs on poles, although one of them, which must have been the headman's, had sides on it as well. Aside from the few cows and the dozens of semidomesticated, scrawny dogs slinking around—animals brought originally from Europe—there was little to indicate that the Spaniards had arrived at all.

Miguel, who is half Maya himself and understands the language, learned that a big jaguar had been bothering the village. It had killed several cows and attacked a man, who was badly mauled but survived. Miguel decided to lay a trap for the jaguar that night. He tied a dog to a stake in the corner of a low-fenced corral, with a piece of raw meat just out of reach so that it howled and barked incessantly. Then he placed us, nine men in all, around the corral. I thought this was a bit dangerous, since someone might shoot the person opposite, but then Miguel was the hunter. He gave me his own good rifle and used one of the primitive shotguns the Indians make themselves (another European innovation). Their ammunition is also homemade, and they use the cartridges over and over, simply refilling them with scraps of metal and glass mixed with powder. Oddly enough, they work.

It was agonizing to stand absolutely still for hours, not even able to swat at the millions of mosquitoes gorging themselves on us. I was beginning to regret ever mentioning my desire to shoot a jaguar to Miguel when the dog suddenly stopped yapping—our long-awaited visitor had arrived. A tense minute or so passed, during which it dawned on me that the jaguar would have to get past us to reach the dog. I was wondering if it would find one of the sentries more interesting than the bait when the animal made a tremendous leap from the bush right over the corral between Miguel and one of the villagers. Eight cannon seemed to explode, drowning out my rifle crack, while the jaguar was still in flight, and it fell dead right on top of the startled dog. Its body was riddled, and I looked carefully for signs of my rifle bullet, finally finding it in the left hind paw—a great shot. "Never mind," Miguel said. *"Tigres* move fast. You'll know to compensate next time." I hoped so, for the next time I might not have eight homemade bazookas to help out.

We started out on the jungle express the next morning and late in the afternoon reached the chicle camp, a clearing dotted with about twenty huts and a high windmill for drawing fresh water up from a *cenote.* I noticed that all the supplies we were unloading, except for the turtles and a few sacks of rice and beans, were cases of tequila. Miguel explained that the *chicleros* were good hunters, and tequila was what they wanted from the outside, not food.

By nightfall most of the fifty or so *chicleros* had returned from their rounds. They were a tough, taciturn bunch, uncommunicative even after downing astonishing quantities of tequila. Arguments were settled quickly, and privately, with long-bladed hunting knives. The only men I can think of comparable to the *chicleros* are the sixteenth-century *boucaniers*—not their successors the buccaneers, but the half-wild hunters who roamed the deserted north coast of Hispaniola selling *boucan,* or smoked meat, to passing ships. Like them, the *chicleros* are a mixture of escaped convicts and men who are not lawbreakers but simply prefer complete freedom, even with incredible hardships, to the restrictions of society. Out there in the jungle nobody bothered them. In fact, except for Miguel and his two Indian helpers, I was the only outsider who had ever visited the camp.

For the next two weeks Miguel and I hunted nearly twelve hours every day. It was an invaluable education for me. Miguel was as much at home in the jungle as I was underwater. He seemed to glide through invisible openings in the bush, while I, only two steps behind, would become enmeshed in a tangle of vines. To me, the noise in the jungle was at first just noise— birds screeching and monkeys chattering and howling just for the hell of it. But Miguel showed me how the sounds change and can mean, for one thing, the presence of a jaguar or ocelot, the same way that underwater the reactions of the smaller fish often signal the approach of a shark. But Miguel tracks game mainly by smell. I eventually got so that I could smell out a jaguar also; there's no mistaking that pungent, musky odor, and if you ever skin a dead jaguar it almost knocks you out. However, on this trip we never got closer than the smell, although we feasted royally on the small, succulent Yucatán deer, pheasant, and *jabalí,* a leaner, more tasty version of domestic pork.

One day we were tracking a jaguar that Miguel had "smelled out" when we heard a shot nearby. We rushed in the direction of the shot, cursing our luck that someone else had gotten the jaguar first, and then stopped dead at the scene before us. One of the *chicleros* was lying with a bullet in his head and both hands neatly severed at the wrist, and another *chiclero* was calmly nailing the dead man's hands to a tree. The dead man, the *chiclero* explained, had been stealing chicle from his area for months, and he had finally caught him in the act; the thief's hands were nailed up as a warning to other would-be thieves. Miguel did not look at all shocked. "The *chicleros* have their own jungle justice," he said, "brutal, but effective. Just forget the whole thing. The police don't dare show their faces around here anyway." No one in the camp ever mentioned the dead man's absence, and that was the end of it.

At the end of two weeks I had to get back to Cozumel, jaguar pelt or no jaguar pelt, and asked Miguel if I could borrow a mule to ride back to Leona Vicario. But he said that we could both take the "train" the next day, since he was out of supplies and had to return also.

Sometime in the middle of the night we were awakened

by heavy pounding on the door of the thatched hut that nearly shook us out of our hammocks. Miguel went to the door and found several very drunk *chicleros* who had run out of tequila and wanted more. He told them he was completely out of supplies, and when they kept insisting, he slammed the door shut. As he turned away, a machete blade sliced through the door, missing him by inches. More *chicleros* congregated outside, shouting demands for tequila and accusing Miguel of holding out on them. After a while, someone said, "Let's burn Miguel's house down. We'll teach him not to play games with us." At this Miguel threw me his pistol, grabbed his rifle and machete, and quietly cut an opening in the rear wall, through which we crawled.

In seconds the flimsy hut was ablaze; in minutes there was nothing left but a small pile of smoldering ashes. We spent the rest of the night hiding far back in the jungle, and the next morning, after the *chicleros* had gone out on their rounds, we grabbed two mules and rode back to civilization, if you could call Leona Vicario civilization. Miguel not only didn't report the incident to the police (nor would he report the murder), but also planned to go right back to the camp with another load of supplies, assuring me that he would be in no danger as long as he was careful not to run out of tequila again.

From then on I spent more time on the mainland than I did on Cozumel. The *Aguilucho* could make the trip straight across in two hours; I would cruise down the coast looking for a likely spot, hop ashore, and tell my boatmen to come back for me in a week. At first I concentrated on hunting, but now that I was armed with both a pistol and a good all-purpose .30-06, the jaguars were making a point of avoiding me. I ran into everything else: deer, packs of *jabalí,* a few anteaters, which look dangerous with their long clawlike nails but are completely harmless, and monkeys by the thousands. I found that the general rule about jaguars not attacking unless cornered doesn't apply to their smaller cousins, the ocelots. They try to compensate for lack of size by being extra vicious and have a nasty habit of leaping down from overhanging branches. My guess is that an ocelot could not kill a man unless it fastened on his throat, but they can certainly leave some healthy scratches before you shake them off your back.

When I finally tracked down my first jaguar, it was almost too easy. He was polishing off the last of a *jabalí*—I had heard the rest of the pack squealing as they crashed through the bush —and I was able to get close enough for a good head shot. He was a young male, only about six feet from nose to tail, but with a fine pelt. Two men from the small Indian village on the coast showed me how to skin him properly and cure the hide, which they do by stretching it on a frame, scraping the inside, and rubbing it with salt. Hunting lost excitement for me after that. I began to take over small groups of tourists, four to five men to a party (no women, after that first fiasco), but when I was alone, as long as the animals didn't bother me, I didn't bother them, except for the occasional deer or *jabalí* for food. I was much more interested in another quarry—Mayan ruins.

One of the most thrilling moments of my life was when, on one of my first expeditions, I came across the ancient walled city of Tulum, perched on a cliff overlooking the sea across from the southern tip of Cozumel. It was so beautiful, so elegant, and so fascinating. A team from the Carnegie Institution had partially restored the ruins in 1922, but before long they had become almost completely concealed by jungle growth again. Nothing was easily visible but the bleached limestone walls on the seaward side. Tulum had been the capital of almost all the eastern coast of Yucatán at the time the Spaniards arrived, before the long wars of conquest eventually left the region almost depopulated.

There were several smaller ruins scattered along the coast. I had already found one small temple not far inland, literally stumbling upon it in a tangle of undergrowth. I was sure that the dense jungle farther inland concealed other remains of the Maya civilization, unknown to anyone, since the Spaniards had not settled in that part of Yucatán and few of the Indians survived.

The first three hunting parties I took to the mainland

stayed fairly close to the coast, but my fourth party was an adventurous group of men who were game to go anywhere with me. We decided to travel as far inland as we could go in four days and then work our way back to the coast at a more leisurely pace, hunting along the way. On the morning of the fourth day, when I figured that we were about twenty miles inland and should head back soon, we came upon a slightly clearer patch in the jungle, which was probably the remains of an old Maya corn patch. The thin soil had become so exhausted from years of burning off and intensive cultivation that even centuries later the vegetation there was not as dense and high as the surrounding jungle. In the center the undergrowth rose in a slightly elevated mound that I knew from experience must conceal some ruin. Hit by one of the sudden cloudbursts that are so frequent in Quintana Roo (except when one is lost, out of water, and dying of thirst), we made a dive for the mound, hacked away the tangle of vines covering the entrance, and crawled inside a small, dark room.

After a while our eyes had become accustomed to the dimness, and one of the men exclaimed, "It's a damned shame I didn't bring my camera and flash attachments. It would be great to photograph these colored drawings." I looked up at the wall he was pointing to and could scarcely believe my eyes. There were frescoes depicting three vessels that looked like Greek or Roman galleys, each of them with dozens of men standing with shields, spears, and long-handled swords in their hands. I knew that the Maya were supposed to have made very large dugouts, in which they traveled as far as the Greater Antilles and Nicaragua, but these were not dugouts by any stretch of the imagination. After brushing away some of the cobwebs and mold covering the paintings, I could see that the men in the vessels had light reddish hair and beards and certainly did not look like Maya or any other indigenous American race.

Only a few months before I had been at Chichén Itzá as the guest of Don Fernando Barbachano, who managed both that site and another famous Mayan city, Uxmal, and probably

Bearded clay head with eastern Mediterranean features found by Marx on Cancún Island. (This and all other artifacts are of pre-Columbian origin, unless otherwise stated.)

A mosaic in Lebanon depicting a man carrying an amphora aboard a Roman galley.

Marx and Wilburn ("Sonny") Cockrell discussing a human skull, more than 9,000 years old, found in Warm Mineral Springs, Florida.

Bronze axhead of pre-Columbian eastern Mediterranean origin, found among some ruins on Cozumel Island.

Marx, in bright shirt, with friends studying the Sacred Cenote at Chichén Itzá in Yucatán in 1956.

Bill Royal surfacing with two 9,000-year-old human skulls in Warm Mineral Springs, Florida.

Jade Aztec artifacts recovered by Marx in the Lake of the Moon on top of the Toluca volcano, Mexico.

Ceramic objects, including one with a face of a man, and a fragment of ornate alabaster recovered by Marx from one of the mysterious sunken buildings off the northern end of Andros Island, Bahamas.

Carving of a bull on the wall of a ruin at Tulum, Quintana Roo, Mexico, dating from before the tenth century. The conventional view is that bulls were first brought over by the Spaniards in the sixteenth century.

Marx examining the bull carving at Tulum.

Mayan clay figurines found in
a sinkhole (cenote) by Marx.

Marx, in center, with part of his
crew of the Viking ship replica
Alfie, in Limerick, Ireland.

Mysterious glazed platter,
believed to be of Phoenician
origin, found off Salvador,
Brazil.

Life-size marble figurine of a woman, painted white by the Maya. It is believed to be of pre-Columbian Old World origin.

Two of the second-century
Roman amphorae found on a
Roman shipwreck in the
Bay of Guanabara, Brazil.

Marx with the Guanabara
amphorae.

Marx meeting with village chief in Yucatán who claimed to possess ancient writings about Old World contact with the Americas.

Marx presenting gift of candles to village chief in Yucatán.

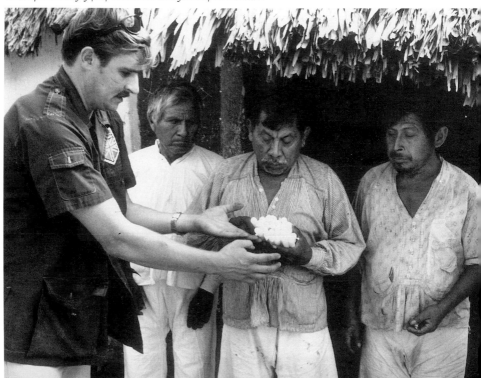

Marx on the bottom of the Lake of the Moon, in the Toluca volcano, Mexico, holding a large piece of incense and a clay mask of a man.

Some of the many clay figurines of the goddess Tanit, Phoenician and dating from the sixth century B.C., found by Marx on a wreck off Tyre, Lebanon.

Two Hindu figurines, sixth or seventh century A.D., found in Guatemala.

One of the many massive basalt Negroid heads discovered in Oaxaca, Mexico.

An article that appeared in the
Brazilian magazine
Manchette in 1976,
concerning the discovery of
Roman amphorae by the diver
Roberto Teixeira. The article
states that the amphorae
are Greek.

Strange ceramic head of a
bearded man found by Marx in
a cenote near Tulum, Yucatán.

Phoenician bronze coin, from
about the fifth century B.C.,
found in the Bahamas.

Stone carving of a man with Semitic features and a beard, found in a Mayan ruin in Chiapas, Mexico.

Marx holding figurines of the Phoenician goddess Tanit.

Barnacle-covered grinding stone found by Marx on the Roman shipwreck in the Bay of Guanabara, Brazil.

Mysterious clay figurine of a bearded man, believed to be Phoenician in origin, discovered by archaeologists near Veracruz, Mexico.

Figurine of a bearded Oriental man found by archaeologists near Veracruz, Mexico.

Bronze bell, believed to be of
Roman origin, found near
Mérida, Yucatán.

Clay head of a man with Old
World features and a beard,
found by Marx on Cozumel.

A clay head of a bearded man
discovered by archaeologists
under a ninth-century Aztec
ruin in Mexico City. It has
definite Semitic features.

Bronze sword blade dating from the Bronze Age, of European origin, discovered among some Mayan ruins near Mérida, Yucatán.

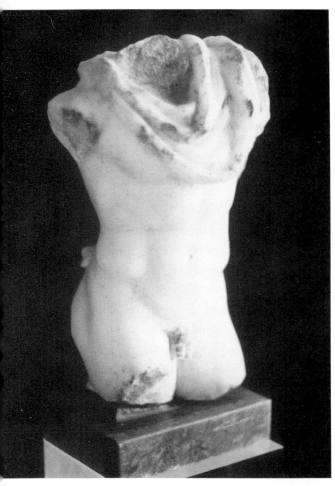

Roman torso of Venus, made of marble, discovered in the Gulf of Mexico in a fisherman's nets during the past century.

knows more about the ancient Maya than anyone else in Mexico. We were wandering around the ruins one morning, discussing my plans for diving in the sacred *cenote* if I could get the government's permission, when Don Fernando stopped at a stone column and pointed to the carvings, which depicted a series of bearded men with straight noses and deep-set eyes— very un-Maya-like. I remember Fernando saying: "Roberto, these men here are not Indians. Look at the features and the beards. You know that neither the Maya nor any other pure-blooded Indian in Mexico has facial hair, or at least not enough for a beard."

"Then who do you think they are?" I asked.

"For years I have been thinking about this," he answered, "and I am convinced that there was some sort of contact between the Old World and America, or at least Mexico, before the Spaniards arrived. But when I bring this up with the different archaeologists who come here, they just say I'm crazy."

"Then we're both crazy," I exclaimed, "because I think you're right!" For a long time I had been skeptical of Columbus's so-called discovery of America. His voyage was highly publicized and came at a time when Europe was ready to expand on a large scale, but that did not mean it was the first. This is not to belittle his feat; it was extraordinary in many ways. But if the printing press hadn't been developed, and if the Europeans had not settled permanently in America but had disappeared the way the Vikings did at Newfoundland, we might know even less about Columbus than we do about Leif Ericsson.

For days afterward Fernando and I talked excitedly about our theory of pre-Columbian voyages to the New World. I had read a lot about ocean currents, early methods of navigation, and what little is known of the ships and voyages made by the Phoenicians, Carthaginians, and other ancient Mediterranean peoples and thought that such voyages were more than possible. But the discussion always ended with Fernando's insisting that no one would ever take us seriously. "People are conservative," he would say. "Look how long it took them to accept Copernicus, or Darwin. But maybe someone will find some irrefutable proof. Maybe you, Roberto, with all your diving in these waters, will find the remains of a Phoenician or Greek ship. That certainly would be proof enough."

I never imagined I would strike pay dirt so soon after Fernando had inspired me to search for clues. I was now straining my eyes at what looked like three ancient Mediterranean ships (whether Phoenician, Cretan, Greek, Roman, or what, I couldn't tell), all bearing bearded men. Without any means to photograph the scene, I knew that I would have to make sure I could find the site again. I estimated we were about twenty miles inland, but it is so difficult to judge distances traveled in the jungle, since one never walks a straight line, that it could just as easily have been ten or forty miles. I climbed the highest tree in the area, hoping to spot some distinguishing feature, or perhaps the coast, but I could see nothing but the perpetual haze that hangs over the Quintana Roo jungle, and beneath it a solid carpet of green.

I had a hard time convincing my trigger-happy team of the importance of the find, but they finally agreed to forgo hunting for the next few days and help me clear the area around the ruin. Late the next afternoon I was hacking away at some stubborn undergrowth about thirty yards from what we thought was the only ruin when one of the men yelled to me from the other side: "Hey, white hunter, I found some horses we can use to ride out of this damned jungle."

From the beginning this man had been particularly skeptical of "all this fuss over some old paintings," as he put it, and at first I thought that this was his idea of a joke. But as I approached he started to crawl into a small hole in the bushes that turned out to be the entrance to another temple he had discovered only thirty-five feet from the first one. It was no more than six feet square and four and a half feet high, and so well concealed that the rest of us had overlooked it completely.

I rushed over and squeezed my way inside the tiny room,

already crowded with three other men. The ceiling and two of the walls were covered with a thick calcareous deposit, but visible on the other two walls was another series of frescoes, this time with horses—dozens of them, grazing, frolicking, and running, and some with riders. Again I was pop-eyed in amazement. According to historians and paleontologists, there had been no horses in America (except the small prehistoric ancestor of the horse, which became extinct before man appeared) until the Spaniards brought them over in the sixteenth century. Yet from what I knew of Mayan architecture and history, this building, which was little more than a Mayan hut reproduced in limestone, had been built and probably abandoned long before the Spaniards ever arrived.

One of the men, seeing how turned-on I was over this second find, joked: "Boy, you're going to commit suicide when we get back and find out that some jerk came over here and painted these things a few years ago." I didn't think it very likely that some unsung Michelangelo had been wandering around the Quintana Roo jungle recently with his little paint box. No, those frescoes were old; the only question was how old. Either they had been painted soon after the Spaniards arrived—although none of the riders wore armor, which is how horsemen always appear in the few post-conquest codices that survive—or, as I believed, dated from a considerably earlier period. What I had to do was get some photographs of the buildings and the paintings, so that experts on the Mayan civilization could tell me.

By this time we were getting low on food and water, and since I was not exactly sure of our location, I decided it was prudent to head back the next morning. We had already cleared an area of about 100 by 150 feet with the larger of the two ruins in the middle, but the bush grows back almost overnight in Quintana Roo. To be on the safe side I took my yellow rain poncho, which would be easy to spot from the air, and stretched it across the flat roof of the larger ruin, weighting down the corners with boulders. Then I climbed four high trees on each side of the rectangular clearing and hung strips from the red canvas door flap of a pup tent and other brightly colored pieces of cloth.

The next morning, after a quick breakfast of dehydrated foods, we broke camp and set off on a compass course that I estimated to be the most direct route to where the *Clipper* was waiting for us offshore. Three days later we stumbled out on the beach, completely exhausted, even though I calculated, by carefully counting my paces on the return trek, that the site was only ten, rather than twenty, miles inland. After so long in the almost sunless jungle, the bright reflection off the white sand blinded us at first, and we did not realize that we were only half a mile from where the *Clipper* lay at anchor. As soon as we reached the boat we celebrated by drinking gallons of water and then threw all our stinking clothes overboard and dove in ourselves to wash off some of the nine days' accumulation of filth. The saltwater bath didn't loosen the hold of the scores of ticks embedded in our skin, though, and we entertained ourselves during the trip across the channel by extracting them with lighted cigarettes.

I knew I had to act fast or the path we had chopped through the jungle on our way out would be completely overgrown, making it more difficult to find the site again. I couldn't entice any of the men from the hunting party to go back—I couldn't really blame them, since they had come for a vacation, not an ordeal. Not surprisingly, after the harrowing stories they told around the hotel bar, none of the other tourists was interested in helping me relocate the "fresco site." And since none of the islanders was willing to go either, no matter what salary I offered, I decided to go alone.

After a few days of resting and writing to various archaeologists who I knew would be interested in the find, I set off again with my best camera equipment. During the crossing to the mainland, I managed to persuade one of my crewmen to accompany me inland. He wasn't at all enthusiastic but consented when I offered him a daily wage equivalent to a week's.

The boat dropped us off at the same spot where we had come out of the jungle before. I told the remaining crewmen to take the boat back to Cozumel, since the hotel was full and all three boats would be needed for fishing parties, and then return to pick us up in seven days. Actually I expected we would be back in about four days at the most, since on the way out I had marked our trail by chopping every third or fourth tree trunk, and the two of us alone could travel much faster than the hunting party.

At first it was easy going. The jungle is not as thick close to the sea as inland, and the path, in addition to being marked already, was still fairly clear from our machete work on the way out. A few hours from the coast a heavy cloudburst hit us, and we headed for the shelter of a large tree to be sure that the camera gear stayed dry. These cloudbursts stop as suddenly as they start, and soon thin rays of sunlight began filtering through the thick foliage overhead. The only trouble was that we couldn't find the narrow trail again. This probably would not have happened to someone more experienced in jungle travel, but after searching for several hours I had to admit that we were lost.

Taolé, my companion, suggested that we backtrack all the way to the coast and go along the beach until we found the beginning of the trail again. This was certainly the only sensible suggestion, but I don't make any claims to being sensible, and I hated the thought of losing a whole day to get more or less right back where we were then. I was sure I could find the ruins by following the compass heading and blazing a new trail, and even if we were off by a mile on either side, I could always spot those brightly colored markers I had left by climbing any high tree.

As soon as darkness approached, we found a small clearing and pitched camp for the night. We were both exhausted, and after a quick meal of canned beans we dropped off to a sound sleep. Awaking the next morning to the playful chattering of the monkeys, my first movement after unwrapping myself from a cocoon of mosquito netting was to reach under the folded blanket beneath my head for my pistol. It was gone. Then I noticed that my rifle, which had been lying on the floor of the tent between Taolé and me, was gone too. I shook Taolé awake, and we made a rapid inventory of our gear and supplies. The two sacks full of canned rations, which Taolé had been carrying, were missing, as well as a five-gallon plastic water container. My pack, which contained more food, was still there, but only because Taolé had been using it as a pillow; my camera bag was there, since it had no value to the thief or thieves, but it was open, and cameras, lenses, batteries, everything had been drenched in dew. The only water we had left was the four canteens on my web belt, which I had hung on a branch. Our nocturnal visitors had missed that and our two machetes, also, stuck in the same tree.

Taolé and I rushed over, grabbed the machetes, and started to charge into the bush after the thieves, but then we came to our senses, realizing that they could have covered a mile just while we were checking our losses. We returned to the campsite and sat dejectedly, not saying anything to one another, but mumbling curses at the robbers, ourselves, and everything in general.

Anyone in his right mind would have said, "That's the breaks. You've had bad luck, so give up for now." But, unfortunately for Taolé and me, my mind never works that way, especially when I'm obsessed with a goal, like photographing those frescoes. We broke camp, and I led the way, blazing a trail that pointed inland instead of seaward. I was working up nerve to tell my plan to Taolé, who had been muttering to himself since we started that we were headed the wrong way, or so it seemed to him, when the truth dawned on him.

"Eh, *Capitán,*" he said, "are you crazy? The sea is in the opposite direction."

"*Hombre,* are we going to let a little thing like the loss of our guns and part of our supplies force us to give up?"

"You *gringo loco!*" yelled Taolé. "Everyone on Cozumel

says you are crazy, and they are right. How do we fight the *tigres* if they attack us? What do we do when we have no more food and water?"

I showed him that my pack was full of dehydrated food, enough to last, if we ate only two small meals a day, for four or five days. The water was a more serious problem, but I was sure we could catch a supply of rainwater with my poncho when we reached the site. I also offered to double his already astronomical salary, but the clincher was my agreeing to give him one of my best suits, with all the accessories. Taolé's eyes shone as he imagined himself the best-dressed sea dog on Cozumel, although I was at least eight inches taller than he.

The next morning I was sure we would find the ruins before the day was over. I planned to spend a few hours photographing the frescoes and then head back on the trail the hunting party had helped me clear. I figured we would reach the coast in less than three days. Just to be on the safe side I climbed a high tree to see if I could spot my markers, but there was nothing except the usual unending carpet of green under the same bluish haze.

During the next two days, as we climbed dozens of other trees, this view was to be repeated over and over again, always looking exactly the same as our last sighting. We spent the next two days crisscrossing the area, hoping to find either the site or the marked trail, and then on the third day, I told Taolé that we had better start back to the coast immediately, since we had barely a day's supply of food left and absolutely no water. Taolé said that would be foolish. It would take us several days at the minimum, and it would be better to keep heading inland, since we were already near the road that ran down the peninsula from Mérida to Chetumal. My maps had been in one of the stolen sacks, and I couldn't check on the road, but I knew there was one, and Taolé's suggestions had certainly seemed more sensible than mine from the start. So we headed inland.

Each day, convinced, or at least hoping, that we would reach the road before nightfall, we stumbled on, catching

iguanas to roast—until the matches ran out and we had to eat
them raw—and drinking what little water we could find in
rock crevices. By our seventh day in the jungle, we were both
so weak we had to rest an hour for every half hour we spent
hacking the bush, and our palms were so blistered we had to
use both hands to swing a machete. By this time the insects
were having a hard time finding any place on our bodies that
hadn't already been pierced, but that didn't seem to daunt
them. I don't know how many times a day one or both of us
struggled up a tree, feeling certain we would sight the road.
There was nothing, nothing, nothing. I do know I vowed on
the average of once every five minutes never to set foot in the
jungle again or even look at a photograph of it.

That evening, as we kept up a steady conversation to forget our empty stomachs, I casually asked Taolé how he knew
about that road. He said he had once taken a bus trip on it from
Mérida to Chetumal that had an overnight stop at Peto.

"Peto!" I screamed. "Peto is the very center of the peninsula, at least a hundred miles from where we started on the
coast!" I was not sure how far we had traveled, but even if we
had been moving in a straight line we couldn't be much more
than thirty miles inland, and that left seventy more miles to go.

My mind had not been working very well for the last few
days, imagining all sorts of wild fantasies as we stumbled
along. In fact, I couldn't remember exactly what I was supposed to be doing on this expedition. But this sudden revelation
must have shocked me back to my senses, such as they were,
and I realized that our only chance was to head due east until
we reached the sea, or until we dropped. Taolé was already
asleep, and I joined him, stretched out on the bare ground, since
we had already discarded our heavy bedrolls and tent, and my
camera bag, somewhere along the way.

When I tried to rouse Taolé the next morning, he refused
to budge, protesting that he just wanted to lie there and die,
but after I smacked him across the face a few times he seemed
to come out of his trance and got up. Then I discovered that I
did not have my compass, nor could either of us remember

when I had last used it. Guiding ourselves by the sun, which we had constantly to climb trees to sight, we set out on what I believed to be an easterly course but later calculated must have been more like a southeasterly one.

For the next three days we kept on as steadily as our weakened condition would allow, our only nourishment being the liquid we wrung out of different vines Miguel had told me were not poisonous (and some I wasn't sure about). Then during the afternoon of the third day we stumbled upon a *sacbe,* one of the elevated causeways the ancient Maya built to connect their cities and ceremonial centers. According to everything I had read about the Maya, no *sacbe* was known to exist in this unexplored section of the peninsula, but I wasn't exactly elated over our discovery—my only thoughts were on food and water. The *sacbe* ran in the same direction we were headed (which I thought was due east), and we decided to use it, since the vegetation covering it was not as thick as the rest of the jungle.

Archaeology and history were the farthest things from my mind when, two or three hours after starting out along the *sacbe,* we almost tripped over what turned out to be one of four large stone wheels that lay strewn over the *sacbe.* They were all perfectly round, about three feet in diameter, and made of some kind of hard rock that was not limestone, the one rock normally found in that area. I knew this was another important find, since it was a commonly accepted fact that none of the pre-Columbian civilizations in America either knew of or used the wheel. This had been another topic in my long talks with Fernando Barbachano. He disagreed with this theory, since wheel-like objects were depicted in several Mayan frescoes and carvings, and several pre-Columbian toys that had functioning wheels had recently been excavated. Again there was no proof that these four stone wheels had not been made after the Spanish conquest, although this part of the peninsula had not been populated since around the thirteenth century. But we could not afford to stop, wheels or no wheels, and continued down the *sacbe* after a few minutes.

The following morning, the eleventh since the boat had

dropped us off, we were trudging along the *sacbe* when it abruptly ended at the edge of a large lake, one of the few on the entire peninsula. The water was cloudy and tasted stale, but we didn't care about taste and foolishly drank so much and so quickly that in moments we were both rolling on the ground with severe cramps and vomiting. Then we started all over again, taking small sips. We were relieved to find that our swollen tongues returned to almost their normal size, but were furious with ourselves for having discarded all our empty canteens, which meant that we could not carry any of the water with us.

We started to walk around the lake, which was several miles in circumference, and soon sighted an Indian hut on the other side. Even though we ran the whole way, the short twilight had turned to pitch black by the time we neared the hut. I had learned a few words in Mayan from my Catholic missionary friends in Cozumel. Taolé was a full-blooded Maya, but he had lived on Cozumel all his life and knew even less than I did. I shouted out greeting, but the Indians must have thought we were evil spirits, since they all took off screaming into the jungle. We were too hungry to worry about them and gorged ourselves on green bananas growing around the hut and a clay jar full of tortillas.

Afraid the Indians might decide we were thieves instead of spirits, we thought it best to get plenty of distance between us and the hut. We took all the tortillas, several dozen bananas, a few ears of corn, and two gourds filled with water, leaving behind in payment our only possessions: my good wristwatch and Taolé's gold chain, minus the holy medal, which had broken off and been lost sometime during our trek.

With our bellies full for the first time in days, we kept going all that night and the following day, stopping only to climb trees for a sun sighting. By the evening of the thirteenth day, we were out of water again and had not a drop of saliva to help chew and swallow the remaining raw corn and dried tortillas (my idea of what a wooden shingle would taste like, only worse). But that night, as we lay down to sleep, I was sure I smelled the sea, and I assured Taolé we would reach it the next day. Early the next morning we both climbed a tree for a sun sighting, and when we saw a flock of pelicans fly overhead, even the skeptical Taolé had to agree that the sea was very near.

Before starting out we had to tear up the rag hanging on my back, which had once been a shirt, to tie around Taolé's feet. He had started out on this venture wearing sandals, which had fallen apart after a few days, and the clumsy moccasins he had made from a piece of deerskin we found in the hut did the same. I could hardly look at his feet without getting sick. We had tried taking turns with my boots, but he couldn't keep them on, since my feet were twice the size of his.

Around noon on the fourteenth day we detected the unmistakable sound of voices through the usual jungle din. People, and that meant food and water! Whooping with joy, Taolé and I dashed in the direction of the voices and burst into a large clearing containing a number of huts, obviously a *chiclero* camp. But one of the *chicleros,* who was standing about ten yards from the edge of the clearing, suddenly pulled out a pistol. We stopped dead and dove for the ground as six shots zoomed overhead. Perhaps the *chiclero* thought we were bandits, I reasoned, and as soon as the firing stopped, I cautiously raised my hands to show we were unarmed—we had even thrown away our machetes as we dashed to the clearing. Taolé would not even move, but lay flat on the ground with his eyes squeezed shut, praying very rapidly out loud.

We were soon surrounded by about twenty ruffians who looked like characters from a Pancho Villa movie. Every one of them was carrying some sort of weapon, ranging from semiautomatic rifles to antique blunderbusses that should have been in a museum. They fell back at the approach of a burly shirtless man with a man of black hair, who resembled a gorilla more than anything human. He walked over to me—Taolé was still prone, praying more fervently than ever—grabbed me by the hair with one hand, and proceeded to smash me across the face with the other. He stopped as suddenly as he had started and walked away. Meanwhile several men had grabbed Taolé and given him a few knocks. They dragged us both to what appeared to be a large cage; I later learned it had held a pet jaguar belonging to the gorilla, who went by the name Barbanegra, or Blackbeard. He had shot the beast recently when it scratched his face, adding a few more scars to the collection that gave his face such a menacing aspect.

Even in my half-dazed state I was beginning to suspect that this was no *chiclero* camp. We had, as it turned out, stumbled upon the base of a well-known group of *bandidos,* who were about the only authority in that part of Quintana Roo. But this I did not learn until later. At that point my main concern was over what these characters, whoever they were, intended to do with us. We were given no food or water, and since the cage was unprotected by any trees, we roasted in the sun for the rest of the day and then shivered that night after being soaked by a heavy rain shower.

The *bandidos* apparently made their own booze, which I think was fermented heart of coconut palm, and drank steadily all day. I don't know if they were celebrating our capture or if this was routine, but by nightfall many of them had fallen into a drunken stupor, including Barbanegra, obviously the gang's leader. At first Taolé and I were too frightened to sleep, but we must have dozed off. We awoke some time later to find our cage moving: four drunks were carrying it toward a fire blazing in the middle of the clearing and yelling for everyone to come and watch the show. Inserting a long pole through the cage, they started to swing us over the fire—not very close at first; they obviously enjoyed our screams as the heat blistered our bare feet (Barbanegra had appropriated my boots) and wanted to prolong the fun.

But their fun was cut short by several shots. The four drunks almost dropped the cage but fortunately set it down away from the fire, as Barbanegra lurched toward us, waving a smoking pistol. He smashed one of our tormentors across the face with his pistol and another with the flat of his long hunting knife, but the other two took off for the jungle before Barbanegra could reach them. He dispersed the onlookers, threatening to skin alive the next man who acted without his orders (the unauthorized entertainment was, apparently, the reason for his rage, since I'm sure he had nothing against a little torture in itself), and had our cage moved next to his hut for safekeeping.

The camp was soon quiet, except for great snuffling snores from Barbanegra's hut. Neither Taolé nor I could sleep with our feet so badly blistered. I heard something move outside the cage and poked Taolé, sure that our tormentors had returned, but instead the face of a young girl appeared out of the dark. At first I thought I was dreaming, since we had seen no sign of any women in the camp that day, nor did she look like any of the local Indians. Motioning to us to be quiet, she handed in a gourd filled with coconut water and two pieces of salted venison, which we quickly devoured.

Speaking in a low whisper, since Barbanegra's hammock was only fifteen feet away, she told us that her father was the headman of a small village about fifteen miles inland from the coastal ruins of Tulum. That explained her appearance. I knew the village, which was inhabited by descendants of Chinese laborers who were brought over to British Honduras in the nineteenth century after the Negro slaves were emancipated and had escaped to settle in Quintana Roo. This same gang of *bandidos,* the girl explained, had raided her village two years before and, after killing several of the men and raping most of the women, had stripped the village bare and carried her off as a hostage for tribute payments. She lived as Barbanegra's concubine and was going to have a child soon. She broke her story off, as Barbanegra snorted and stopped snoring altogether, and after grabbing the now empty gourd, she quickly disappeared into the hut again.

Taolé and I felt almost as sorry for the girl as we did for ourselves. She had told us that her father could not help her because Barbanegra had threatened to kill her if the police were told of the raid or her capture. But even if he decided to take the chance, I knew that the nearest police force, except for the two-man contingent on Cozumel, was at Chetumal, more than 150 miles away, and besides, probably no one knew exactly where the bandits had their camp.

The next morning it almost seemed as if we were waking from a bad dream. We were let out of our cage and given a big breakfast of tortillas, black beans, and cocoa to drink. When we finished, Barbanegra appeared, sat down with us, and began firing questions at us in such rapid Spanish that I could barely understand him, since I was used to the slow, singsong accents of the people on Cozumel and the rest of Yucatán. After a while I learned that he thought we were spies sent by the police to locate his camp. My accent convinced him finally that I was a *gringo* tourist, but he would not believe the story about looking for ruins, or that Taolé was a boatman. He kept pulling on Taolé's nose, saying the only noses he'd ever seen like that were on policemen. The questioning ended abruptly when Barbanegra stood up and said it didn't matter who we were, because we knew the location of his camp, and he would have to kill us.

For the rest of the day Taolé and I were completely ignored and even left to wander around the camp, well aware that we would be shot at the first move we made for the clearing. We mostly sat around nursing our blistered feet and trying to stay inconspicuous. There was no reason to think that Barbanegra had not been serious about having to kill us. Our only consolation was that he didn't seem to be in any particular hurry.

We were given a fish head each and some more beans and tortillas for supper and then tied to a large tree for the night, a decided improvement over the cage, which had been too small for us either to lie down or stand up in. By sundown the men were all drunk again. Most of them had passed out, while a few played dominoes or practiced knife-throwing, something they were experts at even when dead drunk.

For hours Taolé and I twisted and rubbed the half-inch

hemp rope holding our arms and legs to the tree, but it would not loosen. We had not seen the Chinese girl all day and feared that she might have been observed talking to us the night before, but sometime around the middle of the night, she appeared again, moving silently out of the bushes behind the tree. She quickly cut the ropes and handed us a gourd of water and a rag bundle containing venison and tortillas, then slipped off into the darkness. I knew she hoped we would be able to help her return to her village somehow, and I promised myself we would not let her down.

The ropes had been so tight around our legs that we had to crawl into the bush. Then I remembered the rope, which the *bandidos* would be able to tell had been cut by a knife, so I crawled back, retrieved the pieces, and rejoined Taolé. About fifty yards from the camp, we broke into a stumbling run and crashed through the bush until we fell panting to the ground. While we lay there trying to catch our breath, I reflected that we were both weak, almost naked, had blistered, bleeding feet and only a small amount of food and water. In our condition we couldn't last more than a few days in the jungle, even if the bandits didn't immediately track us down, as I feared they would.

I was sure we were near the sea. The saltwater fish heads we had been given for supper seemed to confirm that, and I decided our best chance lay in heading for the coast. Taolé disagreed, saying that was exactly what the bandits would expect us to do, but not wanting to waste time arguing, I got up and started to backtrack in order to work my way around the camp, heading in the direction I thought was east. Looking back, I saw Taolé following. We passed within a hundred yards of the camp and froze in our tracks when the camp's pack of mangy dogs broke out in a chorus of barking, but one of the *bandidos* yelled to quiet them down and we continued on, soon running into a narrow path that led in the direction we were headed. The going was easier, and we were able to keep up a fairly steady trot for several hours. Fortunately my sense of direction had not been off. We were very weak, and the next two miles seemed like twenty. But the intensifying scent of the sea spurred us on, and suddenly there we were on the coast. We emerged from the jungle on the shore of a deeply indented bay called Bahía del Espíritu Santo.

We turned north along the shore, but after a few minutes spotted a thatched hut up the beach. If we turned back, the closest settlement would be more than a hundred miles to the south, so we would have to sneak around the hut. When we crept closer, we saw with relief that it was only a roof thatch covering four dugout canoes. Checking that no one was about, we rushed out of the bush and started to launch one of the dugouts. It occurred to me that it would be insane to leave the other three behind for our pursuers. We spent precious minutes searching for vines strong enough to tow them with—bashing in the bottoms with rocks was ruled out because of the noise. We tied the three dugouts in a line behind ours and started paddling furiously down the middle of the bay for the open sea.

In less than a quarter of an hour the sun rose in a blazing ball of fire in front of us, and I knew that the bandits would notice our disappearance then, if they had not already done so. The other dugouts slowed us down considerably. Aside from the weight, they swayed continually from side to side, creating extra drag. But the tide was coming in and they would have drifted ashore in no time if we had cast them loose. There was, of course, the chance that we had failed to see other dugouts on the beach, but there was little we could do about that.

By the time the sun was overhead I estimated we had covered almost half the twenty miles to the mouth of the bay. We cast off the other dugouts, which increased our speed three-fold, even though we had to rest more than we paddled. By about four that afternoon we were only a short distance from the bay's entrance, but the closer we got, the stronger the force of the northerly current, which runs along the Quintana Roo coast. I was afraid we could not clear the bay before we were pushed onto its northern shore, since we were drifting sideways faster than we could paddle forward.

Taolé and I must have dropped off to sleep from sheer exhaustion soon afterward. Suddenly we were both in the water; something, probably one of the many alligators that live in the bay, must have come up under the dugout and flipped it over. Whatever it was, it did us a big favor, for I heard rifle shots and noticed that we had drifted north to within half a mile of the shore. The bandits had followed us, heading around the bay by land, and were firing at us from the beach. We grabbed for the two paddles floating nearby and, holding on to the dugout's carved keel with the other hand, kicked frantically away from the shore.

Either we made poor targets in the water or the bandits were bad shots, because fortunately the bullets splashed pretty wide. About an hour later it began to get dark, and we figured it was safe to turn the dugout over. We didn't stop paddling until we were a mile out from the bay, where the two-knot current began to carry us north without any further effort on our part. We had another stroke of luck besides that timely heave from the alligator. This canoe would undoubtedly have foundered in any seas more than a foot high, but there was a flat calm, and we drifted along scarcely aware we were moving.

Taolé and I had both dropped off to sleep again as soon as we realized we were safely out to sea and did not wake until sunrise. We were about a mile from shore and had already drifted to within several miles south of Tulum. The sea was still calm, and Taolé suggested that we try to take the dugout all the way to Cozumel, the southern tip of which is almost directly across the channel from Tulum. I vetoed this plan when dark storm clouds started to line the horizon, signaling the approach of a squall. Tulum was uninhabited, but there was a large copra plantation, named Tancah, located only five miles north, and Taolé said he knew the owners, the González brothers.

While the current carried us north we also paddled toward

shore, but the squall hit us before we could reach the opening in the reef in front of Tancah. Swamped by the heavy seas, we clung to the overturned dugout and were soon thrown over the reef by a large comber, which left us unhurt in the calm, waist-deep waters of the lagoon. Several Indians came out in another dugout and helped us ashore, where we were met by the González brothers. They were astonished to see us alive: my boat had been cruising up and down the coast for the last ten days after we failed to appear at the rendezvous point, and only the day before it had left Tancah for Cozumel, the crew having given us up for dead.

The two brothers were hospitable in the best Mexican tradition. Not only did they clothe us, but seeing what a sorry state we were in, they had their wives and maids give us the best nursing care they could. We could not keep down solid food and were fed broth every hour or so while the women tried to clean and medicate the hundred and one cuts, scratches, and burns covering us.

I felt more exhausted than I had ever thought possible, but neither Taolé nor I could sleep soundly that first day. Tancah was only thirty miles as the crow flies from the spot where the *bandidos* had been firing at us the evening before, and we were sure they would follow us. Late that afternoon we sat on the wide verandah with the two brothers and over a few tequilas told them what we could remember of our experiences at the time. They did not show the least surprise at our story about the *bandido* camp, and seeing that we were really serious in our fears that we would be followed to Tancah, they admitted that they paid a large monthly tribute in money, bullets, and cigarettes to Barbanegra in return for his keeping his hands off the plantation—the classic protection racket, Yucatán-style. That was little comfort to us, since I could hardly expect Barbanegra to honor the agreement in our case, especially after we were told that no one else knew the location of their camp.

Everything else about Barbanegra was well known in the district. The brothers told us that he had been a famous guerrilla leader in the mountains around Veracruz during the Mexican Revolution, which started in 1910 and lasted in some areas through the 1930s. Even after the revolution triumphed, he continued the fighting, having fallen out with the new leaders of the republic. After his followers had either deserted or been killed, he made a long trek overland to Quintana Roo, where he was joined by malcontents and criminals from all over southern Mexico, and he virtually ruled the district.

When I told them about the Chinese girl who had helped us escape, they verified her story. Her name was Lola Lung, they said, and she had actually been betrothed to one of their nephews when she was taken hostage. I could hardly believe that all these things were such common knowledge, yet no one had done anything about them.

"There is nothing anyone can do," one of the brothers commented bitterly. The government knew about the bandits and their activities, he explained, but was unable to control them. Ten years before a twenty-four-man force of policemen had been sent to round them up. Ten of the twenty-four had been found by their companions in the jungle, beheaded, and the rest of the force never succeeded in finding even a trace of the bandits. Since then no further efforts had been made.

Exhaustion won out over curiosity, and Taolé and I fell asleep before we could learn any more about Barbanegra and his crew. The next morning one of the brothers announced that a plane would be coming to pick us up. I thought it was a joke, but he said that they had a rough airstrip located halfway between their house and the ruins of Tulum. They had radioed to Mérida for the plane the evening before, and it would be arriving soon. After a fast breakfast, several Indians half carried us to a jeep, and we were driven at lunatic speed through the coconut grove along the beach to a clearing that they called an airstrip but that bore a closer resemblance to a rock quarry.

We sat there nervously scanning the sky for signs of the plane, half expecting the bandits to burst out of the jungle that surrounded the strip. Before long, a twin-engined Beechcraft made a pass over us, banked, and then made one of the bumpiest landings I have ever seen. We thanked the González brothers as they hoisted us aboard, and moments later we were on our way to Mérida. Below us for the first hour was a solid floor of dark green without a road or hut, exactly as it had looked from the countless treetops Taolé and I had climbed in the last two weeks.

On landing in Mérida, we were met by police officers, to whom we gave a brief account of our experience in the bandit camp with as precise a location as possible. Then the American consul appeared and rushed Taolé and me to a hospital, where we were to stay for more than a month. We had been thin to start with, and during the seventeen-day ordeal I had lost more than forty pounds and Taolé only slightly less. We were both suffering badly from dysentery, which in my case was compounded by malaria, although I had probably contracted it on a previous expedition.

About two weeks after we had reached Mérida, several hundred soldiers were landed on the shore of the Bahía del Espíritu Santo, but when they reached the camp they found it deserted, except for a few barking dogs that had chosen to remain behind. The force spent several weeks combing the area without finding a trace of the bandits.

After only a few days in the Mérida hospital, my recent experiences began to seem less like an ordeal and more like just another interesting adventure. I forgot about the vows I had made never to set foot in the jungle again and was already thinking of those frescoes and the four stone wheels we had found on the *sacbe*. Brief mention of my finds appeared in the international press. Most comments were skeptical—understandably so, I suppose, in view of the absence of any proof. This only made me more determined to return and make photographs. Friends and scholars I kept in correspondence with all reminded me that "a photograph is worth a thousand words."

The most encouragement came from John Goggin, professor of anthropology at the University of Florida. Goggin was a kindly man and had taken me under his wing when I met him in Mérida during one of his digs on a Spanish colonial site. As soon as I returned from my first expedition I had written to him about the frescoes and even sent him several potsherds, as well as slivers of the wooden lintels from the entrances to the two ruins, so that he could date the site. Goggin offered me his full support, promising to come down and make a thorough study of the ruins as soon as I had a foolproof way of locating the site.

Nearly two months passed before I could search for the "fresco ruins." I knew that finding the wheels would be easy. It was simply a question of starting out from the lake along the *sacbe*. But the frescoes were another matter. Dreading the thought of spending weeks, or even months, wandering all over the jungle again, I decided to search by air, which is what I should have done the moment I returned to Cozumel after first discovering the ruins. Once sighted from a plane and marked on a map, they would be much easier to locate from the ground.

I knew the pilots in the Mexican air force wing stationed at Cozumel, and I often hitched rides on the four or five pre–World War II T-6 training planes the United States had generously donated to Mexico after our Air Force had declared them unfit for service. I contacted my friend Chucho, whom I considered the best of the pilots, and he agreed to fly me over the mainland the next day.

Rushing out to the airfield shortly after sunrise—the best time for searching over the jungle, before the haze gets thick—I found that Chucho had not yet recovered from a heavy bout with tequila the night before. I chewed him out for letting me down. "Roberto, my friend," he slurred, leaning heavily on my shoulder, "you know I wouldn't let you down. I have arranged for the best pilot in the whole Mexican air force to fly you. Paco," he yelled, "take the *señor* and fly him wherever he wants to go."

Paco's appearance was not exactly reassuring. He was a kid dressed in greasy overalls who looked scared to death. I was to find out that he had good reason to be. He was the plane's mechanic with only a few hours' flying time under his belt, none of them solo. I should have suspected something was wrong when Paco kept crossing himself and murmuring Hail Marys all the way to the plane.

A startled chicken flew out of the aft cockpit as I climbed in, and then I tied myself in with a frayed rope that served as a safety belt, while Paco climbed down again from the forward cockpit, spouting a stream of Mexican obscenities because the batteries were dead. When the engine would not turn over even after he smashed the fuselage a few times with a heavy wrench, he called several men over to turn the prop by hand. Without waiting for the engine to warm up, Paco gunned the throttle and charged down the runway.

I had taken off the badly scratched Plexiglas windows for better visibility, and the moment we started down the runway I was bathed in gasoline. It was flying out of one of the wing tanks, which I noticed had not been closed properly. I leaned forward, tapped Paco, and pointed to the problem. There was still half of the two-mile runway ahead of us, but instead of slowing down gradually, Paco cut the engine off, and slammed down both foot brakes at the same time. Naturally the plane flipped up on its nose, sending sparks flying, and skidded to a stop on the grass apron skirting the runway.

We jumped out and ran like hell, expecting the plane to explode, but it didn't. Except for my bloody nose we both got off without a scratch. Chucho was grounded for a month by the general (Paco, I think, was demoted to private), but as soon as he could fly again, he came to beg me to forgive him for his little joke and offered to carry out his original promise. Since I was obsessed with finding those ruins, and since Chucho was really the best pilot on Cozumel—when he was sober—I accepted. This time, however, I carefully inspected the plane, especially the caps on the fuel tanks, while Chucho strapped on his set of pearl-handled pistols and tied a five-foot yellow scarf around his neck, so that his girl in San Miguel would recognize him when we flew over.

Chucho made a perfect takeoff, and after buzzing the town a few times, we headed across the channel. We flew over the jungle at treetop level for about an hour, then went up to two hundred, five hundred, and finally a thousand feet, but there were no signs of a clearing or the yellow rain poncho. There was nothing but unbroken jungle as far as the eye could see. After four hours we had to give up the search and head for Cozumel. Although the fuel gauge already registered empty, Chucho spent another ten minutes buzzing the town until his girl finally stuck her head out of a window and waved. Just then the engine started to cough, and he headed for the nearby airfield, but the landing gear would not go down. "Diver, we're going for a dive," he yelled back to me, and moments later we landed on the shallow inland lagoon just north of the town, settling gently on the soft mud bottom. It was a perfect landing, and it should have been, since Chucho confessed that it was the fourth time he had landed there. In less than two weeks the plane had been salvaged, and Chucho was flying again.

I made several more air searches over the jungle (with tourists who had come down to Cozumel in their own planes, not with Chucho), but all with the same results. I was beginning to wonder if I had imagined those "fresco ruins," but if I had it must have been mass hallucination, for some of the men who had been with me when we first stumbled across the site were still writing to ask me if I had relocated them yet. The only solution was to search for the site again by land, although more than a year was to pass before I was able to mount another expedition. My interest in the ruins did not fade, but the tourist business was becoming busier and busier as Cozumel developed into a popular resort island, and any spare time I did have was devoted to my main interest: the old wrecks around Cozumel and on the Quintana Roo coast.

During that year I became more and more convinced that there was something to the theory of pre-Columbian voyages to Mexico that Don Fernando Barbachano and I had discussed. First, Goggin had the potsherds from the "fresco site" analyzed by several experts, who all dated them around the twelfth century, which also agreed with the results of the radiocarbon dating of the two wooden lintels. I had also conducted trial digs around different ruins on both Cozumel and the Quintana Roo mainland, sending potsherds and photographs of pottery I could not identify to various museums. Several items were identified as being European and pre-Columbian in date.

Then one day, while leading a boatload of tourists around Tulum, I noticed that one of the walls of the largest temples had crumbled and fallen down since my last visit. On inspecting the damage, I discovered that the plaster covering the wall next to it had also fallen, revealing a large carving of a bull. Like horses, cattle were supposedly unknown in America until imported by the Spaniards. Tulum was inhabited when Cortés visited Cozumel in 1519, but it was abandoned soon after. Yet here was an unmistakable carving of a bull. The fact that it had been plastered over indicated that it dated from early in the city's history, for the Maya and other pre-Columbian peoples often refurbished their temples. Worship of sacred bulls, like the Minotaur of Crete, was well known in early Mediterranean cultures. By itself the carving could be passed off as a minor mystery; but the evidence, even if still circumstantial, was beginning to mount up.

I had not abandoned my intention of exploring the Yucatán's *cenotes*. They might produce more of the clues I was seeking, and, in any case, as Goggin constantly reminded me in his letters, the most interesting and best-preserved Mayan artifacts to date had come out of *cenotes*. But I had still received no answer to my petition to the Mexican government to dive at Chichén Itzá, even though it had Fernando Barbachano's full support. I decided to fly over to Mérida to check on the progress of my application and also to see Goggin, who was due down shortly to resume his study of Spanish colonial sites.

After landing in Mérida and checking into the hotel, I went directly to the office of the government archaeologist—let's call him Dr. Ricardo López—in charge of all pre-Columbian monuments and excavations in Yucatán. Dr. López was very cool when I entered his office; he asked me to excuse him for a few minutes and disappeared into anther room. I wasn't particularly surprised by his lack of cordiality: not only had I been pestering the man for over a year about diving permission, but also on my previous trip to Mérida, I had made some salty comments about bureaucratic efficiency in Mexico, with particular reference to Dr. López's department.

While I was waiting, however, one of his assistants, whom I knew fairly well, passed through the room and greeted me by saying, *"Que hubo, gran ladrón de antigüedades mexicanas,"* which translates roughly into "Well, if it isn't the great thief of Mexican antiquities." And when Dr. López still failed to appear after twenty minutes, it began to occur to me that something was up. I was just rising to leave when in rushed four policemen, who grabbed me and hustled me out to a waiting patrol car. Something definitely was up, but exactly what I could not find out. The four policemen just told me to shut up every time I asked what was going on. After a short drive to the outskirts of town, I was taken to a large, windowless building—apparently the local prison—and frisked, then deposited inside a dark, foul-smelling room crowded with about fifty other prisoners.

Looking around me after my eyes had become accustomed to the dim light, I spotted one of the *bandidos* from Barbanegra's camp. At first he refused to speak to me, claiming he had never seen me before, but after I started sharing my pack of cigarettes with him, he became positively friendly. It was fascinating to hear what had happened after Taolé and I escaped. The bandits had decided to move their camp farther inland even before the soldiers arrived. They apparently never suspected that Lola, the Chinese girl, had helped us escape, but I was sad to hear that she had died a few months later in childbirth. Barbanegra himself died shortly after from some fever, probably malaria, and then the gang broke up. This *bandido,* whose name was Gervasio, and two others became highwaymen. It was a very good line, he confided, although every once in a while some dope tried to play hero, and he did not really like shooting people.

Gervasio was awaiting trial on four charges of murder, which did not seem to bother him very much. What did bother him was the way he had been caught. He seemed happy to have a listener for his sad tale. A girl he had fallen for, the daughter of a white Mexican who was the fence for their stolen goods, had been sent off to a convent in nearby Valladolid, and Gervasio had gone to "release" her. It was bad enough that they had refused to let him in, even after he fired off a few shots, threatened to burn down the whole convent and the church, and told them who he, Gervasio, was. But those nuns had actually turned him in, and he had always been very religious —why, he had even once gone on a pilgrimage to Chalma, he protested. When he went back after spending a few hours in the local bar, the police were waiting in ambush and grabbed him before he could even draw his pistol.

I sympathized with Gervasio. It must be very embarrassing for a self-respecting *bandido* to have to confess that he was undone by a bunch of nuns. But at least Gervasio knew why he was in prison. Not knowing why I had been arrested or how long I would be there was worse than the prison itself, which was pretty foul. We slept on vermin-ridden piles of straw and twice a day were fed some indescribable mess that made pig slops a delicacy in comparison. Then, on the afternoon of the sixth day, I was suddenly released with no more explanation than when I had been brought there, and they even returned my watch and wallet.

Waiting outside the gate were the American consul and John Goggin. Good old Goggin. I probably would have rotted away in there if it had not been for him. He had arrived in Mérida two days after I was arrested and, paying the customary courtesy call on Dr. López, had learned that I was being held for several "serious offenses," which Dr. López was not at liberty to disclose. After failing to persuade Dr. López to have me released and obtaining the same results from the governor of Yucatán and other local authorities, Goggin remembered my having mentioned in one of my letters that I had been teaching the son of the president of Mexico to dive and that we had become good friends. Unable to reach him by telephone, Goggin had flown to Mexico City, where he finally located him. A few well-placed phone calls and a letter Goggin brought back to Mérida did the trick.

But we still did not know why I had been arrested in the first place, and without even stopping at my hotel for a badly needed shower and change of clothes, the three of us drove directly to Dr. López's office to demand an explanation. Dr. López was all smiles and handshakes this time, apologizing profusely.

His explanation was so absurd it had to be true. About a month before, an American yacht had arrived at an island called Isla de Sacrificios, an important pre-Columbian ceremonial center off Veracruz where the Spaniards first came upon the practice of human sacrifice in Mexico. The Americans produced faked documents authorizing them to conduct archaeological excavations there, and the caretaker, who most likely couldn't read anyway, let them go ahead. After three weeks, the island looked as if it had been blitzed; they even used dynamite and demolished several of the temples. Then they disappeared, carting off tons of priceless artifacts, many of which were already on sale in cities in the United States.

The furor in Mexico over this outrageous act of vandalism was tremendous, of course, and the government archaeologists, who had been caught napping, were pressed to take some action. As an American well known for my interest in pre-Columbian artifacts, I "naturally" came under suspicion.

The logic was almost irrefutable. "What do you mean, 'naturally'?" I yelled. "I haven't been off Cozumel in six months, except across to the coast, and you know it. Everyone knows I poke around ruins there, but keep me out of this other business!"

"Yes, of course," he apologized. "It has been a very grave

mistake, but I am sure that you understand my position." We left on friendly terms. I did not really hold it against him, although I hoped that the next time the politicians were screaming for his head, he would find another scapegoat. He even promised to hurry along the matter of my petition to dive in the sacred *cenote* at Chichén Itzá. But that was a laugh. When I eventually left Mexico three years after requesting permission, I still had not heard one way or the other.

I spent two valuable weeks helping Goggin on his colonial excavations in Mérida. Goggin was an authority on sixteenth-to-eighteenth-century Spanish pottery—the amphora-like olive jars, "blue-on-blue" tiles, Talavera ware, and other items that would help me date the Spanish wrecks I was finding off Quintana Roo. The Yucatán sun was hot, and we used to cool off in the evenings at the hotel bar, finding my recent run-in with the authorities more hilarious with every round of drinks. Goggin would shake his head at me in mock solemnity and say, "Bob, I was pretty wild in my younger days, but at least I never dynamited any ruins!"

I got an unexpected chance to dive in a *cenote* on that trip, but it was a dive that cooled my enthusiasm for *cenotes* for a long time. I ran into the American Maryknoll missionary from Cozumel, who was over in Mérida buying supplies, and he suggested I visit the new priest who had just taken over their mission at Peto. Remembering that there was supposed to be some interesting ruins around Peto, one of the few sites in Yucatán I had not yet visited, I arranged to go.

Peto is in nearly dead center of the peninsula, and the daylong bus trip was typical of public transport in rural Mexico. About a hundred people, in addition to a few dozen chickens and three pigs, were crammed into an ancient vehicle designed to seat about forty, with the overflow clinging to the back, sitting on the luggage rack overhead, and even sitting on the hood, blocking the driver's view. The passengers were Indians, friendly and generous like all the Maya, who produced a continual supply of highly spiced delicacies wrapped in banana leaves, which they pressed on the poor *gringo* who was obviously dying of malnutrition—I was very thin in those days.

Father Hubert, the young missionary at Peto, was glad to see me, especially since my visit gave him a chance to relax into English after having struggled along in Spanish or, mostly, Mayan ever since he had arrived at his new post. The next morning he had to ride over to another village to visit a sick woman, but he arranged for one of the local Indians to show me the different ruins around Peto.

About two miles from the village, on the way to one of the sites, I spotted a small hole, which on investigation turned out to be the top of an unusual *cenote*. Most *cenotes* drop almost straight down, but this one was like a crater in reverse, the sides sloping sharply away from a diameter of eight feet at the top to more than two hundred feet at the water level sixty feet down. My Mayan guide knew no Spanish, and my knowledge of Mayan was not much greater, but using sign language to indicate that this was a very bad spot, he insisted upon moving on.

Back in Peto that day, I inquired about the *cenote*. It was supposed to be haunted by spirits guarding a treasure, I was told, and at the word "treasure" my ears perked up. Legend had it that in the early days—apparently at the time of the conquest—some holy men were fleeing from the Spaniards with precious things from a temple, which they flung into this *cenote*. When the Spaniards caught up with them soon afterward, they too were flung into the *cenote* to drown.

I thought of the Sacred Cenote at Chichén Itzá in the center of the Yucatán Peninsula. It is considered one of the most important Mayan religious centers and is today one of the most frequently visited by tourists. In one of the *cenotes* at this site, known as the Sacred Cenote, virgin maidens and all kinds of offerings were flung into the well during religious ceremonies to appease Chac, the rain god, during periods of drought. In 1905, Edward Thompson, an amateur archaeologist, had directed a helmet diver over a period of several years and recovered a vast amount of gold and jade objects. In the 1950s, after I had been at Peto, an American treasure hunter named Norman Scott secured a permit from the Mexican government and undertook a more extensive excavation of the Chichén Itzá *cenote.* His team recovered the bones of nearly five hundred sacrificial victims, a large amount of gold and jade artifacts, wooden furniture, and hundreds of other interesting artifacts— almost everything dating before 1200 A.D., when the site was abandoned by the Maya. However, two of the artifacts created quite a stir in academic circles. Two wooden dolls bearing Latin inscriptions were recovered from the bottom of the *cenote,* dating earlier than most of the other finds recovered from the higher strata.

Thinking of Thompson's experience in the early twentieth century, I was eager to have a closer look at the *cenote* I had found. The only problem was that I had brought no diving gear, and there was naturally none to be found in Peto, a hundred miles from the sea. I finally managed to obtain goggles —tinted ones belonging to the blacksmith. They had holes in the frames for ventilation, but that was fixed with a few pieces of tape from Father Hubert's little office.

My guide agreed very reluctantly to return to the *cenote* with me. With the goggles hung around my neck and a metal bar for probing in the *cenote*'s bottom tied to my belt, I started cautiously down a strong hemp line we had tied to a tree several feet from the edge. I had not gone down ten feet when I was suddenly flying down to the water another fifty feet below, along with half the overhead roof, which had collapsed from my weight. Unable to determine the depth of the water from above, I had kept my heavy boots on, in case it turned out to be only a few feet deep. I have no idea just how deep it was, but weighted down by the metal bar and the boots, I plummeted down for what seemed like a hundred feet, after hitting the surface with a painful belly smack.

I remember in the Marine Corps some medic telling me my lungs were too large. Well, these "distended lungs," as he called them, came in handy in the *cenote*. Normally, in free diving I could stay under a little over three minutes without any strain, but it must have taken me almost twice as long to get rid of that bar, unlace my boots, and fight my way to the surface again, and that without any hyperventilation. After a good gulp of air, I quickly jettisoned my pants and shirt, which were also weighting me down, and began to shout for the guide. There was no sign of him above, and when I saw how much of the roof had come away, I thought that he must have fallen in also and probably drowned. As it turned out, he hadn't, but he thought I had. After seeing that I didn't surface, he figured that the *cenote* had claimed another victim and went back to Peto, with my watch and wallet, to announce my death.

Meanwhile, I began to appreciate how those Mayan priests must have felt when the Spaniards threw them in. I was accustomed to swimming in salt water, which is much more buoyant, and found that I could not keep afloat without treading water constantly. I swam around the *cenote* several times looking for some kind of ledge, but the sides were smooth. All I could do was hang on to one of the small crevices until the icy water started to cramp my legs, go back to treading water until I was exhausted, and then hang on again for a while. The worst of it was the many water snakes both in the *cenote* and on the walls. I didn't know whether they were poisonous or not, and when it got dark I could only feel them slithering around me.

Somehow I managed to keep from sinking that night and the next day, until, about five in the afternoon, I saw Father Hubert's anxious face peering over the edge. He looked surprised when I shouted up. He had remained in the outlying village an extra day to bury the woman, who had died soon after he arrived, and had returned to Peto only an hour before to find the guide and half the village mourning (or celebrating) my death over large quantities of *mezcal* paid for with the money in my wallet.

The only trouble was that Father Hubert had rushed

straight out to the *cenote,* forgetting to bring more rope, but he shouted down encouragements for the hour it took someone to run to Peto and back. Then they tied the new line to a tree, but at a safe distance from the rim, and when they saw I could barely raise my arms, let alone climb sixty feet up a rope, they lowered down one of the boys who had come along to watch. He tied the line under my arms, and they pulled me up slowly, since everyone, especially I, feared that more of the limestone roof would cave in. A few pieces did fall, but they weren't very large, and none of them hit me. By the time I was safely on the surface, I had spent more than twenty-four hours in the icy water of that *cenote* and cared little if the treasure from every Mayan temple in Yucatán was down there.

Back in Mérida, Goggin and I had another good laugh over my latest misadventure. After failing to persuade him to leave his dig and come to help me look for the fresco site, I returned to Cozumel.

It was another American archaeologist, Dr. Lowell Hemming, who joined me in the search for the fresco site. Hemming, who had spent a month every year for the past twenty years exploring Yucatán, had shown great interest in the frescoes, and I invited him along on my next expedition.

This expedition was much better equipped than my little jaunt with Taolé. Hemming brought most of the equipment from the States, while I contributed one of my boats, which was to stay over on the coast during the full month we had set aside for the search, as well as food supplies. In fact, the expedition was too well equipped. When I saw the mountain of gear Hemming arrived with, including everything from surveying equipment to a large direction-finder radio for marking the site precisely on the map, I realized that he would have to hire Indians to help us carry it.

I asked my friend Father Bob, the Catholic missionary stationed on Cozumel, to come along with us, since he was widely respected by the Indians, who ordinarily will not work for anyone. He agreed, especially because this would give him a chance to visit some of the villages on the mainland, which he had not been to for months. Communications were so bad that Father Bob rarely got to visit his mainland territory, which extended along two hundred miles of coastline, starting at the island of Holbox in the north, around past Cape Catoche, and down to Tulum, unless I took him. Hemming became very excited when Father Bob told him that the whole coast was dotted with ruins, and we decided to make a run along the coast before starting the main expedition.

We headed directly for Holbox, where almost the entire village crowded into dugouts to lead Father Bob ashore. Most of the people in his mission territory had never even seen a priest until the American Maryknollers started their mission work in Yucatán a few years before, yet they had retained a deep devotion to their religion. Every village had its catechist, usually the most influential man there, who somehow kept Catholicism alive from generation to generation, although, as Father Bob would indulgently point out, not in a form easily recognizable to any North American Catholic. We stayed there several days, while Father Bob performed several baptisms and one marriage, and then headed south for Isla Mujeres, where the same routine was repeated.

The next stop was the island of Contoy, which has a thriving population of about ten families. We were surprised when no dugouts came out to meet us and more surprised when the usual swarm of children failed to flock around as we stepped ashore. Hemming took off to the other end of the island to photograph some ruins we had passed coming in, and Father Bob and I headed for the village. At first sight it seemed to be completely deserted, but entering one of the huts, we were met by the grisly sight of an old man lying in a pool of blood with a large piece of wood piercing his chest and emerging from his back directly under the shoulder blade. We thought he was dead, and he should have been, considering the amount of blood he had lost, but there was still a feeble pulse beat.

As Father Bob knelt to administer the last rites, I went to

look for the other villagers and in the very next hut found another problem: a very pregnant woman who was moaning and thrashing around on a straw mat in the final throes of labor. Luckily she spoke a little Spanish, and I was able to learn that the other villagers, including the local *comadrona,* or midwife, had gone to the mainland the day before for a fiesta and would not be back for a few more days. The old man was her father. He had been chopping down a tree that fell the wrong way, and one of the branches had impaled him. She had not been able to do much to help him beyond getting him to his hut.

I ran back to the other hut, where Father Bob was still praying, and announced my new discovery. "You'll have to handle that, Bob," he said. "You probably know as much about obstetrics as I do." I flipped and threatened to run off and leave him with the job, but he persuaded me to try to help, saying that it would be inappropriate for him, a priest, to deliver a baby as long as there was someone else around. Several hours later, during which I drank all the homemade booze I could locate in her hut, the woman gave birth to a baby boy, in excellent condition, if I may say so. Mayan women are very hardy and brave, and this one seemed to fare better from the ordeal than her "midwife." She hoisted herself up and started to wash the baby, while I went outside to collapse.

By this time Hemming had returned. We carried the old man, who was unconscious but still alive, the woman, and her wailing baby out to the boat and headed back to Isla Mujeres, which has a small airstrip. The old man was flown out to Mérida within an hour after we landed, and I learned later that they managed to save his life. Mexican doctors are well trained; there simply aren't enough of them.

Two days later we dropped anchor off a mainland village called Playa del Carmen. Before going ashore Father Bob said, "Let's pray that everything will be normal here." It wasn't. There had been a feud raging between two families for some time, and only two days before one side had decided to put an end to it by burying alive four members of the opposing faction. Father Bob ordered the bodies uncovered and gave them a proper Christian burial, which all the villagers attended, including the culprits. They looked very repentant after the severe dressing-down they received from Father Bob, who had also told them they must cultivate the dead men's fields until their sons grew up. I know they obeyed, too, for Father Bob's word was law among the Indians.

After the burial service a woman asked Father Bob to visit her sick son. The boy had a raging fever, and Father Bob correctly suspected a ruptured appendix. We rushed him aboard and headed for Cozumel, abandoning our plans to visit the rest of the settlements and ruins on down the coast to Tulum.

This particular mission tour was longer but not much more eventful than the many others I took with Father Bob during my three years on Cozumel. The Indians accept suffering and premature death as a matter of course, very grateful for help but never expecting it. Father Bob and I (to a much lesser extent) did what we could, but the problems were overwhelming. There was malnutrition, for one thing. I thought the Indians could diversify their crops, and I sent up soil samples from around some of the villages to a friend of mine who owns one of the largest fertilizer companies in the world. His lab's verdict: a miracle that anything grew on that soil at all.

Hemming and I spent several days on Cozumel loading up with provisions and headed back to the mainland to find my fresco site. Father Bob had commitments on Cozumel, but he gave us a letter to the headman of Inah, the village closest to the spot from which I thought we should start our trek inland.

When we reached the little village we gave the letter to the headman. While he read it and then translated it from Spanish to Mayan for the other villagers, I glanced around. A patch of yellow in one of the huts caught my eye. Normally, nothing relieves the uniform drabness of the Indians' huts, and I walked over to have a look. My heart sank: inside was the yellow rain poncho I had stretched across the roof of the main temple at the fresco site, being used as a tablecloth. I grabbed it and ran out, shouting my discovery to Hemming. The villagers thought at first that I was accusing them of stealing it and would tell me nothing. I finally convinced them that I only wanted to know how it came to be in the village.

The headman explained. He had been hunting deer with bow and arrow and, after wounding a large stag, had followed it for more than a day before finally giving up the chase. On his way back to the coast, he had stumbled across our ruins, and seeing the colored markers tied to the trees, as well as the poncho, he had taken them all home. He then showed me the other pieces of cloth, which his wife had sewn together to make a dress. I learned that he had done this about the time that Taolé and I were starting out on our trek, so it was no longer a mystery why we had been unable to spot the markers during any of our treetop surveys. By the time I went searching from the air, two months had passed, and the clearing must have become completely overgrown by then.

There was one consolation. The Indian was sure he could easily find the site again. He not only agreed to lead us there but also persuaded three of the other villagers to come along. We found, however, that even with four Maya helping us, we had much more than we could carry, and we had to leave behind Hemming's surveying gear and a large part of our provisions. Although the headman, who was named Chumn, assured us that we would reach the site in a day, with each of the Indians taking turns blazing the trail, I made sure that we had at least a week's supply of food and water.

This expedition, as I said, was much more carefully planned than Taolé's and my fiasco, but it did not really make much difference. I am convinced that Yankee efficiency and organization, without either luck or the experience gained from being born and raised in that environment, is just not worth a damn in the Quintana Roo jungle. The first and second days, then the third and fourth, passed without any sign of the fresco ruins. Every time I questioned Chumn he was the picture of confidence, assuring us repeatedly that we would reach the ruins in no time.

Not that Hemming and I were entirely disappointed. On each of these four days we came upon a set of ruins. The first three sites had only a few buildings each, but the fourth was spectacular, a thrilling find. It was a real metropolis. We counted at least thirty buildings, most of which were merely bush-covered mounds, but several were large, stepped pyramids, topped by temples, whose outlines were only partially obscured by the undergrowth. We knew that these temples had not been visited by any recent explorers, probably not even by the Spaniards, because undisturbed artifacts of pottery, jade, and stone lay scattered all over the site, and on the altars in two of the temples we found large, beautifully decorated incense burners still containing the *copal* the ancient Maya used for incense.

It was still early in the afternoon of the fourth day when we found this extensive site, but we decided to camp there for the night and spend the rest of the day exploring and photographing the ruins. Our first move was to set up the radio direction finder to plot the site's position on the map. Either Chumn was leading us on a wild goose chase or I had been completely off in my estimate of the fresco site's location, for it turned out that we were now at least fifteen miles from where I thought that site should be.

Hemming and I photographed individual ruins, while the four Mayans cleared as much of the area as possible so that we could get shots of the female groupings. One of the Indians was bitten on the ankle by a fer-de-lance, a small but venomous snake. There was no antidote for its venom, or at least none we knew of. All we could do was make an incision over the bite and suck out the blood and, we hoped, the venom too. The man was soon unconscious despite our efforts, and since we had only a few days' rations of food and water left, I decided we should all start back for Inah. Chumn insisted that the other two men could make better time alone, and when they reached Inah they could get a few of the other villagers to help them bring back more supplies.

I agreed to this rather reluctantly. We would keep searching for the fresco ruins, but I had Chumn tell the other two Indians to follow the trail we would blaze from there. As a further safeguard we designated the present site as the rendez-vous point if either we or they got lost. Two long saplings and one of the pup tents made an excellent litter, and before dark the two Indians left at a trot carrying the unconscious snakebite victim. We were sorry to learn later that although they reached Inah in less than twenty-four hours following the trail we had blazed, the man was dead when they arrived.

We regretted having to leave this important site so quickly, but the fresco ruins were our goal. We set out early the next morning, leaving behind the supplies we were unable to carry at the site that was to be our base camp. Around noon we came out into a large clearing, which I recognized as one I had spotted from the air and marked on the map as being many miles from the fresco site. I told Hemming this, and we agreed that we were wasting our time. Chumn was too stubborn or too proud to admit that he no longer had the slightest idea where he had originally found that yellow poncho. We decided that we would return to the coast and try to find the site ourselves by using my original compass bearings. As was often the case, this clearing contained several mounds—three small ruins— and after pitching camp, we spent the rest of the day poking around the ruins, finding a few figurines and potsherds.

The following morning, while searching for dry wood for a fire, Chumn discovered the entrance to a cave on one side of the clearing. He would not go in himself, since Indians are afraid of cave spirits, but he led us there, and Hemming and I entered with flashlights. As usual, the bats went berserk from the sudden bright light, careening all around the cave, some of them smashing into us in spite of their radar. As soon as they settled down we started to move farther back and found that the cave was much larger than we had originally thought. The floor was littered with artifacts—intact clay pots of all sizes and shapes and at least twenty complete human skeletons. Mixed in with the bones we found nearly two hundred green jade beads, some of them from necklaces that had adorned the corpses, as well as many larger ones and earplugs of white jade, which the Maya prized very highly. There was also an assortment of ornately carved knives and axheads of obsidian, the black volcanic glass the Yucatán Maya must have obtained in trade from highland Indians.

From the vast assortment of potsherds we found all over the cave, dating from different periods, we surmised that it had been in use for many centuries. Hemming found some charcoal, which he started to collect for radiocarbon dating, while I walked back flashing my light along the walls to see if there were any frescoes. Suddenly my light was reflected off two emerald-green eyes belonging to a large jaguar (all jaguars seem large at a distance of ten feet) that was crouched on the floor of the cave. I was so startled I dropped my flashlight and only felt the animal brush past me as it bolted for the entrance to the cave.

I picked up the flashlight, but it didn't work. I yelled to Hemming to flash his light over my way, so that I could get back without stepping on any of the delicate clay pots that dotted the floor. But there was no answer from Hemming. I rushed over, pots or no pots, and found him lying unconscious on the cave floor. I dragged his 220-pound frame outside into the light and examined him. I could detect no injuries. He was breathing, and I loosened his shirt so that he could breathe more easily. Other than that I did not have any idea what I could do for him, except get him back to a doctor. But there was no sign of Chumn, whom we had left waiting outside the cave. By myself I could barely support Hemming, much less carry him (since I had arrived in Yucatán, malaria and amebic dysentery had brought me down from my usual 190 pounds to 130.) At first I thought of setting out alone for Inah to bring back help, but ruled out this plan when I realized that if the jaguar or anything else came nosing around, Hemming would be totally defenseless.

I sat there feeling pretty helpless and useless until Hemming finally came out of his coma four hours later. All he knew was that something had knocked him down. When I explained about the jaguar and its headlong flight out of the cave, he almost went back into his coma. Since he had suffered two heart attacks in recent years, he figured he had had another heart attack. He was very weak, barely able to stand, even with a crutch I made him from a tree limb and with my support on the other side. I had to leave everything behind but my machete and a few canteens of water. I wrapped our rifles and cameras in a tent and buried them under a mound of bat guano in the cave, hoping to reach the base camp with the rest of our supplies in a day's time.

From then on it was almost a repeat performance of Taolé's and my ordeal eighteen months before, only more arduous, because I had to half-carry, half-drag poor Hemming. Even though we went on all that night, stopping only briefly to rest at hourly intervals, we didn't reach the base camp until late the following afternoon. I almost lost heart when we discovered that all the supplies we had left were gone—purloined by another mysterious jungle thief, since Chumn swore later that neither he nor the other villagers had taken them.

Hemming by this time had lapsed into semiconsciousness. I was so worn out I simply dragged him up the steps to one of the low temples and fell asleep myself next to the altar. The next morning I found some of the vines Taolé and I had quenched our thirst from with no apparent ill effects. I forced some of the liquid down Hemming's throat, drank some myself, and started out again.

I remember little of what occurred during the next four days and nights it took to reach Inah, except Hemming's dead weight. He would awaken on and off, but mostly he was unconscious, and the last two days I was so weak myself that I had to drag him by the arms. It is a wonder that this alone didn't kill the man, and in fact he did end up with a dislocated shoulder, but it was either that or leave him behind in the jungle.

I had hoped to get Hemming on board my boat as soon as we reached Inah and head straight for Cozumel. But when we emerged from the jungle, I was startled to see the boat lying heeled over half up on the beach, with neither of the boatmen in sight. I headed for the village, still dragging poor Hemming. The first person to see us was Chumn's wife, who took one look and ran off shrieking. Eyes peeped cautiously from huts, but no one would come out until one brave soul sneaked up behind me and prodded me cautiously with a machete. When I jumped, it was decided I was not a ghost. Chumn, it seems, had seen the jaguar come flying out of the cave and had fled immediately, telling everyone in the village that the jaguar had eaten both of us and letting his imagination supply the details of the gory scene in the cave.

While I attacked some beans and tortillas, Chumn explained what had happened to my boat, and I wish it had been as fictitious as his tale about the jaguar. Soon after we left, the two boatmen broke into one of the lockers they knew contained a good supply of scotch and brandy and started on a roaring drunk that lasted five days. During that time they made several raids to capture two of the village woman and carry them back to the boat, all unsuccessful. Each time the Indian men had driven them back with machetes, and the last battle had ended in total defeat, after one drunken boatman lost his left ear to a machete stroke and the other shot himself in the foot with one of my spear guns.

The Indians did not know what to do with their captives, fearing reprisals from Cozumel if they killed the men, and finally decided to send them back to Cozumel via a boat that was loading copra from the nearby plantation of Acumal. The two Indians had returned with the dead snakebite victim in the middle of the fracas, and in the excitement they had forgotten all about taking the rest of the supplies back to the base camp. The village simply returned to normal—that is, until Chumn came running in a few days later with the story of our being devoured by the jaguar. With this news they all set about stripping my boat bare, even to the portholes and parts of the engine. They also took the anchors, leaving the boat tied to a hunk of coral, so that when a squall hit the coast the next night, the wind and heavy seas threw her up on the beach.

Chumn and his villagers were basically kind people and honest. They were maddeningly unreliable, but not thieves. They had taken property that they thought no longer had an owner, and while I slept they worked the whole night putting everything back. Not a thing was missing the next morning but the contents of the liquor chest my boatmen had stolen. They then helped me refloat her and get Hemming aboard, considering themselves generously paid with the food supplies I left. The engine, of course, was a dead loss, at least for the time being; the Indians had replaced all the parts, but without remembering which parts went where, and I was not much better as a mechanic myself. I hoisted sail, and with a favorable wind we actually made it across to Cozumel in less time than is usual even under power.

Hemming had regained consciousness before we left and was even able to talk. He was in pain from his dislocated shoulder but considered that a much lesser evil than being left back in the jungle. He was flown out to Mérida, where he spent the next few weeks in a hospital. There was nothing wrong with me that a few good nights' sleep and some solid food could not cure. A week later I headed back to the cave, before the trail became completely overgrown again. For a change, nothing went wrong. The jaguar had probably decided the neighborhood was getting crowded, and I retrieved the rifles and cameras, and also collected some charcoal as well as artifacts from both sites for dating, all without incident.

During the next twelve months before I left Cozumel for good, I made five other expeditions to search for the fresco site, all without mishap but also without any success. That part of Yucatán must have been very densely populated at one time, for on each of the expeditions I came across at least one unknown site of ruins, sometimes two or three, but not the one I was looking for. The jungle had swallowed it up again, apparently without a trace.

I departed from the land of the great white gods knowing that someday I would return again to search for traces of Quetzalcoatl, who had left untold centuries before.

5

The Voyage of the Niña II

fter leaving Cozumel I spent a year exploring just about every island and islet in the Caribbean. The goal of this grand exploration was twofold: to search for traces of the great white gods and to find the most likely site for a treasure-laden shipwreck, settle near it, and salvage it. During my years on Cozumel I had recovered several million dollars' worth of treasure from the *Matanzero* and other Spanish shipwrecks under an agreement with the Mexican government entitling me to half of what I had recovered. However, I was completely naive about the ways of the world and the way of Mexican officialdom in particular. Consequently, I ended up with nothing but great memories. A clause in the agreement stated that the government had the right to keep everything of "artistic, historical, or archaeological value to the nation." I had been assured that this was to cover unique items only; nevertheless, government officials ultimately declared that everything I had recovered fitted that description.

So it was time to find more treasure—and keep some of it.

From the secondary sources I had researched, I selected a hundred targets. Of these, I managed to locate only two, and neither yielded anything of interest. This was not surprising. I was as naive then about shipwreck sources as I had been about Mexican politics. I was to learn later, in the course of intensive primary research in various European archives and libraries, that almost every one of the hundred wrecks I searched for was merely the figment of a romantic author's imagination. However, the year of roaming those sunstruck islands was time well spent. I located more than seventy-five shipwrecks and gained a great deal of knowledge and experience. Unfortunately, I found no traces of the past presence of the great white gods.

I then went up to Washington, D.C., to spend a month with Clay Blair, Jr., an old friend who was a writer for the *Saturday Evening Post*. Clay had visited Cozumel several times and written articles about his experiences with me chasing after sunken treasures and exploring the dense jungles of Quintana Roo. He convinced me that if I was to have success in finding shipwrecks in the future, I needed more reliable information. The only way to get it was to do research myself from primary sources. There are many repositories in Europe and elsewhere that contain material from the Spanish colonial period, but most of the centuries-old documents relating to Spanish galleons are housed in the great palace of the Archivo de las Indias in Seville. The archive contains more than fourteen million handwritten documents. Spain, then, was the logical place to go. It would also enable me to get back to my underwater museum in Cádiz Bay, and I might even be lucky enough to find some documentation relating to the great white gods.

To prepare myself for the challenge of research in the Seville archive, I holed up in a lonely cabin in the Canadian wilderness for several months with thousands of pages of old documents on microfilm. I studied the archaic Spanish as if my life depended on it, with a bit of time off for diving in the icy lakes and some romps with curious bears and moose. I emerged from the woods bearded and scrawny but able to decipher old

Spanish, something experts had cautioned me normally took a couple of years.

I arrived in Seville at the beginning of Holy Week, 1961, to find the Archivo de las Indias, and everything else except the cafés and churches, closed. For seven days and nights the entire population jammed the narrow streets to watch processions of robed and masked penitents, each led by a jewel-bedecked Madonna. The sight was impressive, especially at night when the Madonnas seemed to float along on a wave of candles, but I was itching to see what was waiting for me in the archive.

Several hours after the heavy, brass-studded doors of the archive swung open on the Monday after Easter, I had a case of document fever that made my previous bouts of treasure fever seem like the sniffles. There was everything I had dreamed of and more. I do not know how the Spaniards found time to colonize an empire, because from the look of things they must have spent every waking minute scribbling documents. Port officials didn't just record the departure of a treasure fleet from Cartagena or Veracruz; they listed every nail that had been driven into every ship that cleared port. A governor did not just write back to Spain that a ship had run aground on the coast of, say, Florida; he gave the exact location whenever possible, eyewitness accounts of the disaster by the survivors, and detailed reports on the salvage attempts.

I found such a wealth of material that I was soon forced to hire several research assistants. Within a few months I had to find a larger apartment, having been squeezed out of the first one by the crates and sea chests of notes I was accumulating. For I was gathering data not only on shipwrecks, but also on the whole system of *flotas,* the Spanish treasure fleets that sailed annually from Spain to the New World and back for several centuries. During my months of library work trying to identify the wreck of the *Matanzero,* I had become as disillusioned with the published sources on Spanish maritime history as I was with the popular books on sunken treasure. It was not so much that the information was false as that there simply was none, or at least nothing solid and detailed, based on original documents. So Clay Blair and I decided to fill the gap ourselves by writing a two- or three-volume work on the treasure fleets.

Shortly after my arrival in the archive, the director, Dr. José de la Peña, invited me to lunch. He was a friend of my old rescuers and acquaintances the two Don Manuels. Apparently they had told him of my obsession about other Old World cultures reaching the New World before Columbus, whether accidentally or by intention. The director was cordial but made it quite clear that if I was hoping to carry on any research in his archive relating to this topic, he would expel me. I encountered similar feelings from almost everyone I ran into in Spain, so I had to conceal my enthusiasm for the subject.

One day I ran across a German historian who was working briefly in the archive and discovered to my great joy that he shared my belief about the early discovery of America. He went into great detail with me about what had occurred with Columbus's descendants. Columbus had been promised that he and his heirs, in perpetuity, would receive 10 percent of the value of everything shipped from the New World. They received nothing. For centuries the descendants periodically sued the Spanish Crown, always to no avail. With a gleam in his eye, the German suggested that I might enjoy reading the court records of these numerous cases.

After months of work I drew a blank. No one I asked professed to know anything about them until I mentioned my search to one of the Don Manuels. He told me that all of the court records were in the Archivo Colombino, which happened to be located adjacent to the Cathedral of Seville, just a hundred yards from the Archivo de las Indias. This archive had been closed since the beginning of the Spanish Civil War in the thirties, but a token of appreciation to the caretaker finally gave me access, and it was like discovering a gold mine.

I lost track of time and place as I deciphered the faded writing on fragile parchment leaves. What I read was dynamite. I understood why the documents had been sequestered. The

Spanish Crown itself contended that Columbus had not been the discoverer of the New World. Each of the Crown defenders in the court cases used the same argument as his predecessor: Columbus had not discovered the New World and thus neither he nor his descendants had any right to a percentage of New World treasures. In their arguments the legal wizards credited just about everyone from the Phoenicians to the Norsemen with having reached the New World before Columbus. They emphasized that Columbus's real goal was to find a new route to the East Indies and Cipango (Japan) and not to rediscover places that already were known to exist.

On the first day I frantically took notes for eight straight hours until my fingers almost fell off. I had never been so excited in my life. History was about to be rewritten because of this fantastic find—or so I ingenuously thought at the time. The next morning when I got to the archive I found Dr. de la Peña and a rather sad caretaker waiting for me. I was informed in no uncertain terms that unless I turned over all of the notes I had written the previous day I would be barred from doing any further research in any archive or library in Spain. The archive director went back to my apartment with me so I wouldn't have a chance to duplicate my information. I had no choice in the matter. Either I complied or I would lose access to all of that valuable shipwreck data in the archive. So for the time being I had to forsake my great white gods.

After working only a few months in the Archivo de las Indias, I realized that something essential was missing in the material I was gathering—the human element. If I was going to write a really interesting history of the *flotas,* I reasoned, I ought to include what life aboard the galleons was like and who the men were who set out on them. I found countless ship's logs and even narratives written by passengers, but they rarely mentioned the things that we thought readers would want to know—how the crews and passengers felt during the long, tedious ocean crossings; what they did to while away time during calms; what their reactions were to the violent storms that came up without warning; how it felt to eat weevily biscuit and drink the putrid green water. These and many other things were lacking from the documents.

How I solved this problem is a long story, and the best place to start is on a hot August day in Seville. I was sitting in the hushed reading room of the archive, sweating blue blazes in the requisite jacket and tie, when a familiar voice boomed out: "My God, look who's turned scholar. Pirate Marx himself." The pince-nez perched on the nose of the wizened old man in front of me fell to the glass-topped table with a clatter at this infringement of reading-room rules. I looked up. Standing at the door with a broad grin on his face was—who else—John Goggin.

Goggin and I just could not seem to shake each other. We quickly adjourned to the nearest sidewalk café, where Goggin explained he had come to Spain to do some research on Spanish ceramics and pottery. I had told him that I was going to Seville, but he hadn't taken me seriously and was just as surprised to see me as I was to see him. We spent about a month touring southern Spain from Seville to Gibraltar, photographing every old jar and pot we could find and looking for private collections of documents that might have material for my *flota* book. We even photographed a large clay jar (and its skeletal contents, probably the bones of Christopher Columbus) dug up from the crypt of an old Carthusian monastery outside Seville. Columbus had in fact been buried in that monastery, and although many people claim that his bones were moved to Santo Domingo, there is no documentary evidence to prove it. But my roll of film, unfortunately, was confiscated, and Goggin was refused permission to carry back a small sliver of bone for spectro-analysis. There is a big Columbus monument in the Cathedral of Seville, supposedly containing the bones of the "Admiral of the Oceans" (there are also similar "tombs" in the cathedrals of Santo Domingo and Havana), and there are a lot of people who would look awfully silly if that lowly clay jar turned out to contain the real thing.

I believe those were the bones of Columbus, and I'll tell you how the old admiral come to repay me for accidentally stepping on one of his thighbones after Goggin had laid out the contents of the clay jar for me to photograph. Goggin was as responsible as anyone else for the episode that follows. I was telling him one day about my problem with the history of the Spanish treasure fleets—the missing human element in all the material I was finding—and he replied, "Of course, you can't really know what a toothache is like unless you've had one."

"Who's talking about a toothache? I'm talking about seventeenth-century Spanish galleons," I said.

"So am I," Goggin replied. "What I mean is that you can't know how those people lived aboard the old galleons unless you've sailed on one yourself. Why don't you build a replica?"

Now that was exactly the kind of advice I wanted to hear. After being ashore so long, I was restless for some action, and here was a man I admired suggesting something I had often dreamed about but thought was too crazy to attempt. I would build a replica of a seventeenth-century galleon, sail it to the West Indies, and then sail it back again to Spain. I kept poor Goggin up half the night, spilling out ideas about the voyage: how it would have to be absolutely authentic, with no modern navigational aids, radios, or survival gear; everything from the food and cooking equipment to the sails would have to be the kind carried on an old galleon. Goggin agreed. The only thing he would not agree to was to come along for the ride. Digging and diving were his lines, he said, not teetering around on a yardarm fifty feet above a pitching deck.

I wrote Clay about the idea immediately. He thought it was great and signed up for the voyage. He also persuaded the editors of the *Saturday Evening Post* to help back the venture in return for exclusive magazine rights. Clay's only suggestion was that I finish my research before taking off, and I agreed, since it would take at least that long to construct the vessel and make all the preparations. So, in addition to my regular research, I set about gathering all the information I could for the voyage, especially material on early navigational methods and the rigging and handling of old square-sailed ships. I checked out shipyards and persuaded a good friend who was a naval historian in Madrid to draw up the plans for the two-hundred-ton galleon I would build.

What I did not know was that someone else had a plan very similar to mine. News of my project eventually spread all over Spain. One day in June 1962, when I was in Madrid researching in the Naval Museum, I received a call from a Spanish naval lieutenant from Pamplona named Carlos Etayo Elizondo, who said that he was building a replica of the caravel *Niña,* the smallest of the three vessels Columbus used on his voyage of discovery. He asked if I would be interested in joining him. My galleon was still only on paper, he said, but his caravel was already in the water. He had a point there, and we arranged to meet several days later in Madrid.

Carlos was not the rough-and-ready sea dog with a rolling gait I had expected. Shy and slight, he confessed that his sailing experience consisted of a brief cruise twelve years before on a four-masted Spanish navy training schooner. But what he did have was a contagious determination to sail his vessel to America. He had been working quietly, almost secretively, on the project for almost ten years, but only six months before, after receiving a modest inheritance, had he been able to start building his caravel. By the time of our meeting, the bare hull had been launched, and the shipwrights were then working on her masts and rigging.

Carlos offered me the job of pilot-navigator, and I accepted—as he had said, my galleon was still only on paper. But there was one hitch. There would be no point in making the voyage, as far as I was concerned, unless we duplicated the conditions under which Columbus and his crew had sailed. I insisted on using fifteenth-century victuals, clothing, navigational instruments, charts, and equipment—otherwise one might as well sail across in a modern yacht. Carlos balked at the idea, claiming that it was all very well for us to endure those rugged conditions for the love of history, but we would never find any seamen willing to sail without a radio, life rafts, and other safeguards. I argued for hours, saying that he underestimated his countrymen's love for adventure and stressing the contribution we would be making to naval history. Finally, after I made it clear that I could not participate otherwise and would go ahead with my own plans to build and sail a galleon, Carlos agreed to duplicate fifteenth-century conditions, and the bargain was sealed.

The following day, I canceled all work on my galleon and started to help Carlos prepare for the voyage of the *Niña II*. A theatrical costuming firm was contracted to design and make fifteenth-century clothes for us. The Madrid Naval Museum agreed to make replicas of the charts and navigational instruments used in Columbus's time; and the Artillery Museum set to work making replicas of fifteenth-century cannons, swords, and other period arms. I spent several weeks combing the Rastro (the Madrid flea market) and antique shops for original fifteenth-century items, such as bowls and cutlery, flints for making fires, candlesticks, and sand-filled hourglasses, and whenever originals were not for sale, I had reproductions made.

As soon as all these preparations were completed, I drove to the north of Spain to meet Carlos, who had been supervising the work on the *Niña II* at Pasajes, a small port on the Bay of Biscay close to the French border.

My first glimpse of the ship was a shock. No pictures or models of any of Columbus's three ships have been preserved, but a lot of clues about their size and design have been uncovered from other sources, and none of these clues tallied with what I saw lying at anchor in the Pasajes shipyard. The common opinion of naval historians is that the original *Niña* was between seventy-five and one hundred feet in length with a capacity of about sixty tons. There may be room for slight disagreement, but the *Niña* Carlos had built was barely forty-two feet long, with a capacity of about fifteen tons (an estimate given later by several naval architects, although Carlos believed that his ship was thirty tons burden). But she was not even a pint-size version of the original; there was nothing in the *Niña II*'s squat shape and deep draft (eight feet) to suggest the graceful lines of a fifteenth-century caravel, a vessel noted for its speed of up to eighteen knots and its ability to sail close to the wind.

I had spent weeks fretting over the authenticity of the cooking implements we would use and other minor details without even thinking about the most important item—the ship. I had assumed that Carlos had followed the commonly accepted opinions of naval historians, among whom some of the foremost are fellow Spaniards, but he had done his own research, and he countered my criticisms with the claim that the experts were wrong. Even Columbus was wrong, he contended. Columbus had stated clearly in his log that the original *Niña* carried three masts, but the *Niña II* was fitted with only two, the mainmast and the mizzenmast. I had a momentary urge to make tracks back to Madrid and take up where I had left off on my galleon project; but by then I felt as deeply committed to the Columbus voyage as Carlos. I consoled myself with the thought that at least we would be sailing under the same conditions as Columbus and his men, even if the vessel was somewhat modified in design. Closer inspection of the *Niña II* brought an added consolation; if nothing else, she was solid, built by hand from the keel up with the same careful workmanship and even with the same type of tools as the original *Niña*.

There was still plenty of work ahead to prepare for the voyage. One of the main tasks was to select a crew. Carlos and I had been swamped by hundreds of applications from adventure-seeking men, and women, too. Surprisingly, most of them had never been to sea before. Instead, Carlos signed on three Basque seamen from the Pasajes area. The first was José Valencia Salsamendi, who had spent most of his thirty-eight years at sea and turned out to be the best seaman on the voyage.

The next was Nicolás Bedoya Castillo, a white-haired man of sixty-nine who had seen nearly fifty years of service in the Spanish navy. (However, all but two of them, we learned after setting sail, had been spent ashore tending lighthouses.) And the third to sign on was a powerfully built fisherman, Antonio Aguirre Oróñoz, forty-two years old, who had formerly been a professional boxer. Antonio was a good cook and an excellent harmonica player in the bargain.

Carlos and I stayed in Pasajes trying to rush the finishing touches on the *Niña:* rigging, sails, anchors, hatch covers, caulking, ballast, and a million odds and ends. The tasks seemed endless, especially with the almost daily fiestas (all attended by our crew, sailmakers, and ships' carpenters) and the throng of curious spectators who came over from the big summer resorts in San Sebastián to have a look at both this odd craft and the lunatics who were planning to cross the ocean in her.

Finally, on July 28, she was ready for her first sea trial. Under the skeptical gaze of hundreds of onlookers, we cast off our moorings and started to row out of the sheltered harbor, only to discover that our long oars, called sweeps, were not long enough and barely reached the water. Yet they were so unwieldy that we couldn't maintain a steady beat and did little more than bang them together and curse each other for being so inept.

Meanwhile, a strong incoming tide began to carry us toward a mudbank. We managed to keep off the mudbank, but that was our only triumph of the day. After three hours of rowing we found we had covered only three hundred yards, with a thousand more to go before clearing the entrance to the harbor. Carlos decided to call it quits. We rowed back to the dock, smarting under the jeers and catcalls of the laughing spectators, who had enjoyed the entertainment immensely. José summed up my feelings perfectly when he asked, "How are we going to sail this crate across the Atlantic when we can't even get her out of port?"

Three days later we made another attempt, this time with longer sweeps and several more men to help us. We had about the same success as on the first try, until I convinced Carlos to try a new method of moving the *Niña*—by warping, or towing her with a skiff. There was nothing ignominious about this, since it is the way sailing ships were brought into and out of port in the old days whenever the winds were not favorable. Once outside the harbor we hoisted sail, and the unbelievable happened. The *Niña* could not sail, at least not in a straight line. She staggered and reeled like a drunk on his way home after closing hours. Then to top it off, our mizzenmast, improperly stepped in the quarterdeck instead of the keel, came crashing down on the deck, and with the loss of our mizzen, the most important sail to help steer, the wind and current started to carry us toward shore. We manned the sweeps again, but the wind was too strong, and only the timely arrival of a fishing boat, which took us in tow, saved our *Niña* from a premature end on the rocky coast.

The fishing boat took us to the small port of Guetaria, east of Bilbao, where we quickly set about making essential repairs and alterations. Having a new mizzenmast constructed and stepped in the keel was only the beginning. We had to find a way to make the *Niña* sail. The rudder was enlarged and lengthened and ballast moved aft to bring the bow higher out of the water. These and other minor alterations did the trick. When we took her out for new sea trials on August 12, we were elated to find that the *Niña* could now actually sail—not very fast, but at least in a straight line. She would not sail at all with the triangular lateen sail Columbus had first used on the original *Niña,* because the mainmast was too far aft, but the large square mainsail he had replaced it with in the Canary Islands for the main part of his voyage did work, and at this point we were not prepared to be fussy over details.

We were very pressed for time, since we had hoped to duplicate Columbus's voyage exactly, leaving the port of Palos in southern Spain on the same date he had, August 3. It was already too late to do that, but Columbus had spent nearly a month in the Canary Islands before setting off on the last leg of his voyage across the Atlantic on September 6, and we figured that we could catch up with him there. This meant that we had to get down to Palos and then on to the Canaries with a minimum of delay.

There was the expected last-minute panic. The official permission to sail that we needed from the Spanish government had not come through yet, and I shuttled back and forth between Guetaria and Madrid to hound every influential contact I had. Carpenters had to be urged on to complete repairs, and supplies had to be rounded up and loaded on board. Even on this preliminary leg of the voyage down to Palos, we would carry exactly the same kind of food stores as Columbus: vinegar, olive oil, biscuit, lard, chick peas, rice, beans, almonds, raisins, sugar, salt, garlic, onions, sardines, wine, brandy, and water. Since tobacco was not known in Europe at the time of Columbus's voyage, we tried to talk the crew, who were all heavy smokers, into giving up cigarettes until we reached America (no problem for either Carlos or me, since we don't smoke anyway), but they protested that this was carrying authenticity just a little too far.

In Guetaria we signed on two more crew members. The first was a twenty-nine-year-old Frenchman, Michel Vialars, a veterinarian who had recently completed an army hitch in Algeria. He had no sailing experience, but he did very well in the *Niña*'s second sea trials and signed on as ship's doctor and apprentice seaman. Since no Spanish ship would be complete without a chaplain, the Reverend Antonio Sagaseta, a forty-six-year-old Catholic priest from Carlos's hometown of Pamplona, was signed on to oversee our spiritual well-being. Father Sagaseta, or Padre, as we called him, had served as a gunnery officer during the Spanish Civil War before being ordained, so he was also put in charge of the *Niña*'s four artillery pieces. Padre brought along a decrepit one-eyed cat, which I named Circe, as ship's mascot. But Circe, with that strong sense of self-preservation possessed by all animals except man, took one look around the Niña and jumped ashore. We fetched her back over and over, and after the tenth escape we had to keep her tied up to the mast until we got to sea. That cat obviously had more brains than the rest of us put together.

Finally, on the morning of August 23, everything was ready—everything, that is, but the weather. Shortly before we were to leave port, a strong northwest wind, diametrically opposed to what we needed, began to blow. It was predicted to last ten days. Carlos and I decided to swallow our pride and arrange for a tow that would take us around Cape Finisterre, the northwest tip of Spain, where we could pick up more favorable winds and make the rest of the 950-mile trip to Palos under sail.

The towship arrived the next evening, August 24, and by seven o'clock we were underway. The three hours that followed were a nightmare, for the Niña wallowed on her towing cable in the huge seas like a seasick whale. A few times we swung so far to one side of the towship that the Niña was pulled sideways through the water and almost capsized. Two and sometimes as many as four men had to man the tiller. One minute fighting the helm was like an hour on a bucking bronco, and all of us were covered with bruises before the night was over.

The tow continued for two more days and nights. Carlos and I averaged about three hours of sleep each day, we were all so exhausted from the work at the helm that no one even attempted to cook a hot meal. When the towship finally left us, we had passed Cape Finisterre and were only a few miles north of the port of Vigo near the Portugese border. It would be smooth sailing south to Palos, we thought.

It was smooth, all right. About the same instant we cast off the towing cable the wind disappeared, and for the next fifteen days we literally drifted to Palos, a trip we had estimated would take no more than three days. Only on two occasions was there enough wind to use the sails. Most of the time we were lost in fogs so thick that we could barely see a hundred feet, even in the middle of the day. We were in constant danger of collision with passing fishing boats and freighters, and one of us had to keep watch on the bow constantly, beating on a metal pan with a spoon to warn off approaching vessels.

We finally reached Palos on September 11, looking as if we had been at sea for years—bearded, covered with fleas (thanks to Circe), and badly in need of a bath and change of clothes. This unofficial leg of our voyage had been nearly catastrophic. All our drinking water had spoiled after a few days out, and we had had to stop several boats to get fresh supplies. Then the ship's biscuit (a type of hard bread), which had been specially baked according to a fifteenth-century recipe and was guaranteed to keep for a year, turned so moldy that it looked like a solid mass of penicillin. To me the greatest problem had been the lack of discipline on board. Everyone did as he pleased, working and following orders if he felt like it and disregarding them if he didn't, which meant that the burden of work fell on a few. Little did I suspect that all the calamities and problems that arose then were to set a pattern for our long voyage across the Atlantic.

At Palos we found quite a welcome waiting for us, even though the newspapers had claimed for the past week that the *Niña* had sunk with all hands lost. For eight full days we were wined and dined in a continuous round of fiestas, with hardly a free moment to attend to work needed on the *Niña*'s sails, which we had found were improperly made, to clean the rotten barrels that had caused our water to go bad, and to do the countless other essential tasks. We met many of the descendants of Columbus's original crewmen from the Palos area. We stayed at the thirteenth-century Franciscan monastery of La Rábida just as Columbus had. We even had our new supply of ship's biscuit baked in a massive old brick bakehouse that Columbus's biscuit probably had been baked in almost five centuries before.

At Palos we took on two more crewmen, who brought the ship's complement up to nine. The first was Manuel

("Manolo") Darnaude Rojas-Marcos, thirty-three years old, the scion of a prominent Andalusian family, a keen amateur sailor, and the holder of a navigator's degree from a Spanish merchant marine academy. None of us, except perhaps José, had much experience handling sailing vessels, and we thought Manolo's skills would be very useful. The ninth addition to our crew was made purely by accident. We had found a comical little guy named Pepe Robles (aged thirty-nine) hanging around the dock at Palos and hired him to guard the *Niña* while we were all ashore living it up. Soon after leaving Palos, I went below to consult a chart and found, instead of one of the crewmen holding the tiller, Pepe. I asked what in the hell he was doing there. He seemed to think it made perfect sense that since we had not paid him, he had decided to stay on board until we did. Carlos wanted to hail a passing boat and send Pepe back to Palos, but I persuaded him that we could use Pepe. As it turned out, he was one of the best seamen we had, even though his normal occupation ashore was goatherd. Maybe scrambling around the rocks after his charges is what had made him so agile; nobody else could scurry up the mast like Pepe.

At sunrise on September 19, we started down the river leading from Palos to the open sea, to the accompaniment of Gregorian chants sung by the Franciscan friars of the clifftop La Rábida monastery. As we crossed over the bar at the mouth of the river, dozens of Spanish air force planes buzzed us, and we waved goodbye to all our friends aboard the scores of yachts and fishing boats that had escorted us out to sea.

Padre was eager to fire a parting salute, and Carlos gave permission to fire the falconet, one of the four small cannons the Artillery Museum had made for us. But there is a big difference between fifteenth-century falconet and the modern artillery Padre was used to. He used too much powder, and in the explosion part of the charge backfired through the fuse hole right at José, who had lit the fuse. For the duration of the voyage, he was busy digging tiny scraps of metal and powder from his face, chest, and arms.

This accident was a fitting curtain-raiser for a voyage that was plagued with bad luck from beginning to end. For three straight days the wind blew strong from the west, nearly carrying us through the Straits of Gibraltar into the Mediterranean. Then the unfavorable wind died down and was followed by a period of calms, although fortunately the current was running in the direction of the Canaries. On the sixth day out, while we sat eating our noon meal of rice and beans and watching a school of porpoises play around our drifting hull, the dead calm was broken by a sudden gust of hot wind straight from the African desert. It felt as if someone had opened a furnace door. Bowls, cups, pots, and people smashed against the lee gunwale as the *Niña* heeled over to a 65-degree angle, the tips of her mast almost touching the sea, and within seconds the wind had risen to sixty knots. The sky became dark, and huge seas curled over the tilted decks, to which we were all clinging for dear life.

All the sails had been set during the calm in order to catch any chance puff of wind, and we realized that unless they were lowered or cut away the *Niña* would soon capsize. José saved the day. Grabbing a knife, he scrambled out on the almost horizontal mainmast over the churning seas and started to slash the lines holding the mainsail in place. Manolo and I then followed suit with the smaller mizzen, and when both sails had been loosened, releasing the tremendous pressure of air trapped in them, the *Niña* righted herself. But our problems were far from over. For thirty miserable hours the gale raged on, and the storm sail we rigged could not persuade the *Niña* to ride the huge seas stern to the wind. She preferred to face them broadside on and took such a terrific pounding that we all marveled that she did not fall to pieces. She did leak a great deal, however, and during the entire thirty-hour period one of the two hand pumps had to be manned constantly. Our small cabin was a shambles, with mattresses, clothes, and gear sloshing around in the water that covered the deck. A ten-gallon jug of olive oil had broken loose and smashed, making it impossible to move around the cabin at all except on all fours.

When the gale finally abated we went below to inspect the provisions and were met by a disheartening sight. It looked as if a tornado had passed through the hold. Nearly all the clay jars containing water, wine, vinegar, honey, and brandy were broken, as well as many of the barrels and crates containing our other stores. While several of the men repaired our tattered sails, others tackled the sticky, slimy mess in the hold and cabin.

Carlos and I had agreed that I would navigate with only the fifteenth-century instruments, such as the astrolabe and quadrant, that the Naval Museum had reproduced for us. Both of them work on the principle of measuring the angle of the sun's zenith at midday to determine latitude. But during the voyage he insisted upon double-checking my calculations with a modern sextant he had brought along as a precaution when we left Palos. After the storm had ended on the seventh day out from Palos, both of us took sun fixes and placed our position at about two hundred miles west of the nearest point on the North African coast. Later that night we spotted the blinking light from a lighthouse, which meant that we could be no farther than thirty miles from shore and that Carlos and I were unbelievably bad navigators. Manolo, who had no navigational instruments and had not even consulted the charts, had told us earlier in the day that our estimated position was at least 150 miles off, and now he was proved correct, much to our embarrassment.

As we gradually moved south into lower latitudes, the temperature naturally grew warmer. In a way this made life more comfortable, but it also intensified a problem that had been with us from the start—hygiene. My biggest headache during this phase of the voyage, aside from trying to master the science of navigation, fifteenth-century-style, was the sanitary conditions on board the *Niña*. Few of the crew saw anything wrong with discarding cigarettes butts, leftover food, and any other trash on the decks and in the cabin, and only Michel and Manolo shared my views on the subject of bathing, taking daily sea dips with me. Nicolás swore that bathing caused rheumatism, Antonio claimed that it led to scurvy, and the others had similar excuses. At times, especially during calms, when no dissipating breeze entered the cramped cabin, the stench inside was so unbearable that I would resort to throwing buckets of seawater over the deck and dousing the walls with sweet-smelling brandy, of which we had an abundant supply.

One would have thought that after the experience we had on the voyage from Guetaria, special precautions would have been taken with water and victuals in Palos. They were not. Instead of replacing the fouled barrels that had caused the water to spoil, Carlos had decided to use some chemical to keep it drinkable. Not only was the chemical an unauthentic, twentieth-century innovation, but also we forgot to put it in the barrels until we were a week out of Palos, by which time the water had spoiled again and we had to depend exclusively on wine. This meant nothing to José, since he never drank water anyway, even when we were in port. I can attest to the fact that during the six months I lived in close contact with the man, he never touched one drop of water; he even used wine to brush his teeth. All the rest of the crew, although not as exclusively wine-drinking as José, had been brought up on wine since early childhood, but I never got used to it as a substitute for water and always found that it only increased my thirst.

Like the water, our specially baked biscuit once again went bad only a few days out. I do not know what secret the old-time sailors had to keep it fresh, but I suspect that their biscuit was much dryer and less like regular bread and was also stored better than ours, which was kept in the damp, unventilated hold. As a substitute, I began to make a kind of Mexican tortilla out of moldy flour, olive oil, and seawater. They looked like mud pies but tasted very good, or at least my customers said so, and I never seemed to be able to keep up with the demand.

On October 3, we reached the Canaries, although we missed our intended landfall by seventy miles. We were supposed to put in at the island of Gomera, as Columbus had done, where about fifty members of the press were waiting for us, but Carlos decided to put into Las Palmas on the main island of Grand Canary instead. We were welcomed by thousands of cheering islanders and tourists, and after a series of speeches from local officials and clergy, we were bustled off to a fantastic banquet at one of the main restaurants. Hours later, with bulging stomachs and swirling heads—I lost count of the toasts proposed to us and by us after about twenty-five—we were deposited in palatial rooms at the Hotel Metropole. Several of the crew, especially Pepe, who had known little more than the harsh life of a goatherd, and José, who had endured the even more rugged life of a Spanish cod fisherman on the Newfoundland Banks, were dumbfounded at the sight of such luxury. But all of us (including Manolo, who I later found out was Spain's answer to Beau Brummel) looked like nine ragpickers among the elegant clientele of the hotel's dining room that evening.

There is nothing to beat Spanish hospitality (except, perhaps, Mexican): our whole stay in Las Palmas was a duplication of the week-long fiesta in Palos. One fiesta ran into another, and there was not a moment's attention given to the *Niña*'s sails and rigging, which were both badly in need of repair. Here, too, was an opportunity to replace our rotten water barrels and accomplish a few hundred other tasks, but I had finally met someone who beat me at trusting to luck and endurance rather than careful preparations.

Sometime between banquets and cocktail parties I managed to find time to draw up a list of provisions, which the local authorities had offered to supply gratis. During the voyage from Palos, the *Niña*'s top speed under the most favorable conditions had been four to five knots. I had no reason to believe she would be transformed into a contender for the America's Cup on the crossing from Las Palmas to San Salvador in the Bahamas, and I calculated our provisions on the basis of a forty-day voyage with a reserve supply for another thirty days. Carlos was more optimistic. Columbus had made it in thirty-three says, he said, and he cut down my list by more than half. Columbus had sailed across on three ships, not drifted on an oversized barrel, I argued. Carlos finally agreed that we would take on more provisions at Gomera, but even so, I made some silent prayers for favorable winds on the crossing.

Praying was very big on the agenda in Las Palmas. Almost every church in the area claimed the distinction of being the scene of Columbus's last Mass before he set out on his voyage of discovery, and in order to keep peace, we too attended Mass at all of them in between fiestas.

We had long before given up the hope of duplicating Columbus's sailing date. As it was, we barely got away from Las Palmas before the date on which Columbus *arrived* in America —the 12th of October. On the morning of the 10th, we staggered down to the dock, nursing bad hangovers, and began to load on provisions and water. Our plan was to leave at noon, but after everything was aboard, Manolo noticed that we had neglected to obtain any firewood for cooking, and most of the crew took off in taxis to scour the island for firewood.

I took off on my own, having remembered that the *Niña* had no mascot. Circe had finally jumped ship in Palos; she leaped overboard the minute we dropped anchor and swam ashore, never to be seen again. I returned with a fluffy, flealess little kitten, which Antonio promptly named Linda, meaning "pretty" in Spanish. Linda soon made friends with Pinzona, the other new addition to the *Niña,* a nanny goat Michel named after a girl he had met in Palos.

Accompanied by the fanfare of a brass band and the cheers of thousands of spectators crowding the docks, we cast off late that afternoon and started to row for the open sea against a strong wind. After we had almost smashed into several anchored vessels, we shamefacedly accepted a tow. Once we were out of the harbor and our towlines had been cast off, we hoisted sail. The wind promptly died down, but we were all relieved

to be at sea again after the hectic round of fiestas ashore, and we drifted lazily for the rest of the day, grateful for the much-needed rest.

That night a good breeze sprang up and we headed in the direction of Gomera, 150 miles to the west. We were supposed to make a brief stop there for additional stores and also to appease the irate islanders and members of the press who had been waiting there for weeks. For all I know they are still waiting. We overshot the island, and Carlos, reluctant to waste time beating back to windward, ordered me to set a direct course for the island of San Salvador, 3,360 miles away. I thought he had to be joking: the *Niña* was already leaking badly and her rigging was in sorry shape. Our food and water supplies had been inadequate in any case, and two of the nine water barrels had leaked dry since we left Las Palmas. But he was serious, and even though the rest of the crew were also against this plan, I did not fancy myself in the role of Christian Fletcher. San Salvador it would be.

Our original plan after leaving Gomera was to sail nearly due west with the northeasterly trades, as Columbus had done, since San Salvador is in almost the same latitude as the Canaries. But even the steady, dependable trade winds played fickle with the luckless *Niña*. For fourteen straight days we either drifted or were forced to sail due south, because a square-rigged vessel cannot sail very close to the wind, even less so when her crew are as inept as we were. We moved farther and farther away from San Salvador each day, and at one point we were so close to the Cape Verde Islands that several of the crew claimed they could sight the high mountain peaks from the top of the mainmast.

From the start our main worry was the dwindling supply of food and water. By the end of the first week we found more than 40 percent of our water had leaked out of the faulty barrels; the fresh fruit, stored in the hot, damp hold, not surprisingly rotted, as did the fresh supply of biscuit (our third batch, also guaranteed to last for years) that had been baked in Las Palmas.

The whole food situation was beginning to seem like a recurrent nightmare. Carlos ordered immediate rationing of water, but discipline on board the *Niña* was lax, and water continued to dwindle at an alarming rate. I tried drinking small amounts of seawater. Michel and Carlos soon joined me, and by the end of the voyage the three of us were downing about a quart of seawater daily, usually mixed with a small amount of wine. We never noticed any ill effects, even though it is a common belief among sailors that drinking seawater will drive one mad; but then we had to be half crazy to have started on this venture in the first place.

Fishing, which the sailors of Columbus's day (and before and since) depended on heavily to supplement their shipboard fare, was for us a pitiful farce. Between Guetaria and Palos, we caught only one small shark, even though fishing lines were out and tended around the clock. The catch during the Palos–Canaries run was even less impressive: one small amberjack, caught as we entered Las Palmas Harbor. After Carlos's decision not to stop at Gomera, we doubled the number of fishing lines trailing from the *Niña*'s stern, using a different kind of bait on each one. But for some mysterious reason we caught nothing, although the ship was constantly surrounded by hundreds of fish, including porpoises, sharks, and even whales.

Finally, on our ninth day out, Antonio hooked four small amberjacks, which we ate for supper along with two undigested squid found in the stomach of one of them. Then, three nights later, the Padre, who had never fished in his life, hooked a ten-foot tiger shark. It was full of fight, and chaos ensued when several of the others tried to help him pull it aboard. The powerful shark thrashed around the deck as Nicolás tried to tie its tail to the mainmast, Antonio stabbed it with a large harpoon, and Carlos chopped away at its head with an ax. Carlos, the deck, and everything else was drenched with blood. Pinzona bleated in terror, and Linda scampered up to the very top of the mainmast, refusing all efforts to coax her down again for hours. Still the shark fought on, and soon all nine of us joined

in the battle, adding sledgehammers, a spear gun, and clubs to the ax and harpoon. Even so, it took us nearly an hour to finish off the shark, and just when it seemed we could all get back to sleep (except the two men on watch), Manolo hooked another shark, probably attracted by the first one's blood, which was draining out through the scuppers. This one was only an eight-footer, but the same mad scene was repeated, and after polishing off the second shark, we were all too keyed up to sleep. Antonio broke out his harmonica, and we spent the rest of the night celebrating our good luck over a bottle of brandy.

This fresh meat came none too soon. The next morning we discovered that our remaining supply of salted meat was full of worms, and all of it was flung overboard (a hasty decision we were to regret later; worm-ridden food is better than no food). The cheese and dried fruit were in the same condition, but we wisely decided against chucking them overboard with the meat and eventually we ate them, worms and all.

Even though we plowed along at an unbelievably slow pace, this was no leisurely cruise with time to loaf around. The sails needed constant attention, unless we hit an absolutely flat calm. Any time the breeze stiffened, the bonnet on the big mainsail had to be taken in, only to be let out again when the wind decreased. This operation, which was repeated at least several times a day, required the whole crew, since the heavy yard and sail had to be lowered partway and raised again. The sheets, as well as the smaller mizzen and jury-rigged spritsail, could generally be handled by one or two men. Even in a flat calm two men had to be on watch, one at the tiller and one as a lookout on the quarterdeck, although, strange as it seems, we sailed for over two months before we sighted the first passing vessel. The helmsman's job was never easy—in the low cabin, less than five feet high, he had to stand bent over for hours at a time—but in strong winds it was hell, and sometimes as many as four or five men were needed to hold on to the bucking tiller to keep the *Niña*'s stern into the wind.

There was always some task for those not on watch:

pumping out the bilges, caulking the leaks below deck, tending the fish lines, and airing out the already putrid provisions, to name a few. Repairs were unending, especially on the rotten rigging and sails. We had brought no spare set, but the useless lateen sail was steadily cannibalized until there was nothing left at all. Nicolás was excused from watches, being too nearsighted either to serve as lookout or to keep a steady compass course, but he was a wizard at splicing lines and patching sails. Some of the rest of us had special chores also. Pepe, our ex-goatherd, was delegated to milk and tend Pinzona; Antonio did most of the cooking, except for my mouth-watering tortillas; and I had the self-appointed job, assisted by Linda, of keeping down the fly population that had accompanied us all the way from Palos. But they seemed to breed faster than we could kill them (my record was 203 in one hour), and by the end of the voyage there were more flies than when we started.

I had brought along a chessboard and a set of dice, which I knew the sailors in Columbus's time had used to while away off-duty hours, but only once during the whole voyage did our crew have time to use them, and that was when I staged a chess game in order to shoot some photographs. I suppose we could have played in the evening—we had candles, and later, when they ran out, rags dipped in olive oil—but the men preferred to relax by singing, accompanied by Antonio's harmonica, or engaging in the favorite pastime of Spaniards: arguing, about politics, religion, women, the relative merits of *tabaco negro* and *tabaco rubio* (dark versus light tobacco), anything. Most of the men slept in the cramped, foul-smelling cabin, but there was room for only six at a time, and some of us preferred to stretch out on the open quarterdeck in all but the foulest weather.

For the first two weeks everything went fairly smoothly, even though we were sailing south, farther from our destination each day. Then, around sunset on our sixteenth day out, a bad gale struck, again without any warning. Seasoned mariners might possibly have sensed it coming. I don't know; all I know is that a sudden gust of wind struck the large mainsail with such force that the mainmast cracked in several places and was wrenched loose from its step, or socket, on the keelson. Again the *Niña* heeled way over, taking on the large seas and threatening to capsize any minute.

I was at the helm at the time, and because all the other hands were needed to lower the torn and flapping sail and to man the pumps, I had to continue holding the tiller alone. It was a tug-of-war between a man already weak from malnutrition and the powerful seas that crashed against the ship with increasing violence. The *Niña,* as usual, was bent on self-destruction; sometimes only by lying almost prone across the tiller and bracing my feet against the bulkhead could I keep her from turning broadside to the waves. After about an hour I collapsed from exhaustion, but luckily Manolo was nearby and quickly ran to grab the tiller.

The gale died down the following morning, but worse was to come. Pepe went below to fill the wineskin and reported that the hold already had four feet of water and was filling rapidly. Both hand pumps were broken by then, so we quickly formed a bucket brigade to keep the vessel from sinking. For two full days we bailed continually, stopping only long enough to grab an occasional piece of dried shark meat and a swig of wine, and all this time we simply drifted at the mercy of the wind and current with no time to repair the tattered sails and rigging. Finally, realizing that we were fighting a losing battle—Nicolás, Padre, and Carlos had already dropped out of the chain from sheer exhaustion, and the rest of us were not far behind —I decided to try one last ace in the hole. Although it was not authentic, I had brought along my set of snorkeling gear for use in the Bahamas. I went over the side secured by a lifeline and searched the submerged hull for the source of the leak, which none of us had been able to find from the inside. After nearly an hour I located a hole, only about an inch in diameter, where a wooden peg (called a "treenail") joining a plank to one of the ribs had worked loose. While Antonio and Nicolás were busy shaping a wooden plug for me to insert, I remembered the story of the Dutch boy and the hole in the dike, and like an idiot I put my thumb in the hole as a temporary plug. Each time the ship rolled and my head came above water I got a quick gulp of air. Then suddenly the *Niña* caught a particularly heavy sea and I was pulled way under as the vessel heeled over on top of me. I held my breath, waiting for her to roll back, but she did not—the vast amount of water in the hold prevented her from righting herself—and when I tried to pull my thumb out I found that it was stuck. I reached for my knife, and was just ready to cut my thumb off (it was either that or drown) when the vessel rolled back enough for me to gulp a precious mouthful of air. I quickly enlarged the hole with my knife and extracted my swollen thumb, and a few minutes later the plug was ready. Three hours later we had bailed the hold dry.

The gale had pushed us even farther south, and by the evening of the eighteenth day we were wallowing along within insect range of Africa. By this time Columbus was better than halfway across the Atlantic, while we were actually seven hundred miles farther away from San Salvador than when we first left the Canaries. We had two choices ahead of us: continue on to San Salvador with the risk of running completely out of food and water before we reached there, or head east to Africa and safety.

That night I called a meeting of the whole crew. Carlos was opposed to the idea at first, but I argued that everyone had the right to help make a decision on which all of our lives might depend. Michel reported on the woefully small supply of verminous food and putrid water, Manolo did the same on the state of our leaking vessel, and Carlos and I admitted that we did not know our exact position, but were fairly sure we were now some four thousand miles away from San Salvador. The voting was to be secret. Each man was given a sliver of wood: if he wanted to head for Africa, he was to place the sliver in Pinzona's empty water dish, and if he wanted to keep on for San Salvador, he was to throw the sliver overboard. It was very dark. One by one the men filed out, cast their vote, and returned to sit wordlessly on the cabin deck. I was the last to vote and found the water dish as I had expected—completely empty. It would be San Salvador or bust!

Whether it was our vote of confidence or just plain luck, the next morning we finally hit the long-awaited southeast trades, and for the first time since leaving the Canaries we were able to sail toward, instead of away from, San Salvador. That first day the *Niña* fairly clipped along, covering 117 miles, which for her was amazing. The winds became lighter the next day and we averaged only fifty miles in each twenty-four-hour run—a snail's pace, but at least it was in the right direction. The favorable wind really worked wonders with everyone's morale. Nicolás, who had sworn that both of the hand pumps were beyond repair, got one of them working; Michel helped me improvise plankton nets so that we could supplement our diet; and Manolo and José made hand spears for spearing fish. I was even able to bring all the crew around to my ideas on shipboard sanitation. We scrubbed out the cabin with vinegar, and for the first time on the whole voyage everyone—except the diehard Nicolás—took a sea bath.

Food was still our principal concern, since rations were now down to starvation level. We had devoured the raw, dried-out shark meat much faster than anticipated and were back to a daily diet of one hot meal of rice and beans plus several of my tortillas, a few cloves of garlic, a quarter of an onion, and about an ounce of worm-ridden cheese per man.

We tried every method of fishing possible, but with scant success. Even though we knew that the porpoise is a sailor's best friend and should never be killed under any circumstances, this rule meant little to starving men, and each of us took turns at the bow throughout the daylight hours, trying to harpoon one of the many porpoises that constantly played around the vessel. But these creatures are so intelligent that the moment anyone lifted an arm to throw the harpoon, they would sense it and scoot out of range until the arm was lowered again.

Manolo and I had both bought spear guns in the Canaries, but neither one saw much use. One night Michel shot a large dolphin from the deck with my gun, but the line broke, and the fish got away with the spear. Several days later I grabbed Manolo's gun when a school of yellowtail appeared around the *Niña,* but, unknown to me, the line connecting the spear to the gun was untied. I fired and actually hit a fish, only to see it swim away with the spear through its middle: so much for our unauthentic gear. We then made several hand spears from our Columbus swords, and whenever it was fairly calm both Manolo and I would dive under the hull and try to spear some of the hundreds of fish that lurked in the shade, feeding on the heavy marine growth that covered the bottom. This was the most frustrating method of fishing ever devised. We had no file aboard to make barbs on the ends of the spears, and so for every hundred fish we speared, ninety-nine managed to wriggle free before we could grab them with our hands.

About the only really happy creature aboard the *Niña* was our little kitten, Linda, who received constant affection from everyone, including a couple of men who claimed they hated cats. Linda had grown plump and frisky on her diet of fresh milk, courtesy of Pinzona, but then Pinzona, as undernourished as the rest of us, ceased to give milk, and Linda began to grow thin too, until she developed a taste for raw shark meat. Pinzona had even more adaptable tastes: after her supply of alfalfa ran out, she started to nibble on her wooden water bowl, and in fact she ate everything within reach, including parts of the canvas mainsail, the anchor cable, and the deck planking. As our own food supply ran lower and lower, our hungry stares increasingly fixed on Pinzona. We had grown fond of her, but we knew there would come a day when hunger would override any feelings of sentiment.

The prospect of a slow death by starvation was always with us, but on November 1, our twenty-third day out, all thoughts of hunger were pushed into the background by a much more immediate danger. What we had thought were bad storms before were little summer squalls in comparison to the monster that hit us that day. This time we had sufficient warning: menacing dark patches on the horizon grew steadily larger until by nightfall the sky was totally black; then lightning flashed all around us as the seas rose to immense size in a matter of minutes and violent gusts of wind filled the sails to the bursting point.

The only sensible thing to do was to lower the sails immediately (actually we should have taken in canvas long before) and either set a storm sail or put out a sea anchor. But we were not sensible men; we were madmen obsessed with the idea of reaching America before our food ran out completely, and the powerful wind coming from the east was pushing us toward our destination at a speed we had never thought possible on the *Niña*. Whereas her top speed had been four, possibly five knots, we were soon doing ten, and the *Niña*'s bow crashed through the seas like a half-submerged torpedo. But the feeling of exhilaration was short-lived. The wind steadily increased in force, and as I watched our two quivering masts bend forward like archer's bows under the strain, threatening to snap in two, I was sure the end was coming. For the first time in my life I felt real fear.

It was too late to lower the sails properly. Instead, we slashed them with harpoons and hand spears to release some of the tremendous wind pressure, then pulled down the spars and gathered in the tattered, billowing canvas. Sailing under the bare poles, the *Niña* was now almost impossible to steer. We threw out a hastily improvised sea anchor, but even several men hanging on to the tiller could not hold her steady. The waves seemed to come from every direction, twirling the ship like a cork or engulfing us in tons of water as they crashed right over her decks. If I had had time to think about it then I would have been grateful that the *Niña,* ungraceful in design or not, had been built like a watertight barrel filled with air, for I am sure that this is the only thing that kept us from going under.

The night seemed endless, but the next day was even

worse. It was so dark that only my watch told me that it was daytime. If anything, the storm increased in fury, the wind reaching at least seventy knots. We all huddled like zombies in the cabin, which protected us from being washed overboard but nothing else. The strain on the masts before the sails were cut down had loosened the deck planking overhead, and seawater and rain poured down on us through the many openings. Inside it felt as if the whole vessel were being tossed like a basketball and pounded with battering rams all at the same time. No one even thought of eating. Antonio lapsed into a feverish coma that was to last for six days. Nicolás crouched in one corner of the cabin, not talking or even moving for two full days, and the rest of us sat almost as silent, wondering how long the *Niña* could stay in one piece.

During this second day of the storm, I was on tiller watch when suddenly the tiller shaft broke off the rudder head, whipping my left wrist against the bulkhead. Luckily it was not broken, only painfully sprained, but now we were in serious trouble. Both sea anchors had been carried away, and since we had no means of steering the ship to keep her bow headed into the heavy seas, the danger of capsizing was added to that of being pounded to splinters. At times the *Niña* would be turned over a full 90 degrees, with her keel above water and the tips of her masts awash. Fortunately the crates and barrels of provisions below had been securely stowed, for with the slightest shift of the cargo in her hold, she would have turned turtle.

The next morning, the third day of the storm, we decided we had to do something about the rudder. There seemed no end to the storm, and we knew that our vessel could not stand much more pounding before one of her sides was stove in. We ripped out one of her rowing benches, cut it in two, and made a sling on which Carlos and Manolo lowered me down the stern, so that I could assess the extent of the damage. I found it even worse than we had expected: not only had the tiller broken off from the rudderpost, but also the rudder itself had split in two and was barely hanging on to the ship, so that the next heavy sea crashing against the stern could easily have wrung it loose.

The first task was to mend the rudder. It was far too heavy —more than a quarter of a ton—to lift onto the deck, and the only solution was to mend it in place. This turned out to be the most desperate and frustrating piece of underwater work I have ever attempted. One moment a fifteen-foot wave would lift the stern high and dry, and the next most of the vessel, and I along with it, would be underwater. I was continually smashed against the barnacle-covered hull, and the blood flowing from the numerous scrapes and cuts inevitably attracted several sharks. Manolo and Michel stationed themselves on the fantail with harpoons, ready to strike if any came after me, but fortunately they kept their distance. Just to drive the first nail into the hard oak rudder planks took over an hour. Both the rudder and my sling seat heaved up and down in the water, but never in unison, and all I could get was passing swipes at the nail; sometimes in thirty swings I only hit the nail once, although I averaged much better on my own fingers. It took nearly six hours to drive in the eight nails necessary to hold the broken rudder together. We still had the problem of the rudderpost and tiller, but I was too exhausted to tackle that chore, and it had to wait for the following day.

It took two more full days to repair the rudderpost and tiller, but since this involved less underwater work, Carlos, José, and Michel were able to take turns relieving me on the wildly pitching sling seat. By this time the storm, which we later learned was a full hurricane, had died down, although the seas were still heavy. But everyone was so feeble that another full day was spent mending the rigging and sails before we could get underway again. Then, only a few days later, just as it seemed we had everything squared away, we were hit by another gale, but it was less severe and this time we were pre- pared for it. We had several sets of storm sails Nicolás had worked steadily to finish and four well-constructed sea an- chors. Twelve days after we had ridden out this storm, still another storm struck us, but by then we were such old hands at weathering gales that the damage, both to morale and the vessel, was minimal.

After recovering from this last gale, we found our hunger so great—aggravated by not being able to cook our daily hot meals of rice and beans during foul weather—that the end finally came for our goat. Poor Pinzona was already half starved and would have died soon anyway, so that we looked upon it as a mercy killing. Michel, the veterinarian, had the job of slitting her throat after José had stunned her with a sledgehammer. She was so skinny that she yielded only six pounds of meat, but nothing was wasted: the intestines made a good soup, and the blood was fried with onions. For days afterward Linda moped around sadly, probably thinking that she would eventually meet the same fate.

After weeks of dragging the plankton net, we finally caught a substantial amount of the stuff. Michel, José, and I scooped out spoonfuls of the gelatinous mess from the net and began to eat it, claiming that it tasted like caviar. The rest of the crew were not convinced, and their skepticism was justified. José suddenly dove for a *bota* of wine, yelling that his mouth and throat were on fire. Then Michel and I felt it too, and within minutes the three of us were hanging over the gunwales retching violently. As soon as we recovered we examined the net closely and found that the glop we had thought was plankton was actually hundreds of tiny stinging jellyfish.

We gave up on plankton after that. We had better luck with sargasso, a type of seaweed that floats on the surface of the sea and is so thick in a certain zone of the mid-Atlantic that the area is called the Sargasso Sea. It tasted like iodine, but it was very filling, and I was later told that the sargasso was probably what saved us from any serious cases of scurvy, since our fresh fruit had gone bad only days out of Las Palmas. Manolo and I also began to collect barnacles and other marine growth from the *Niña*'s hull, which, together with rice, beans, and seaweed, made a passable soup. The worst problem for everyone, except José, was thirst. We had almost unlimited supplies of wine, which curiously enough never leaked or spoiled like the water, but wine is not a real thirst-quencher, and because of our meager rations of food, most of us found that even small amounts of wine made us as drunk as a quart of brandy would under normal circumstances.

On our forty-eighth day out, a violent squall struck us. It was over in less than two hours, but its sudden appearance and violence made up for its short duration. Once again our sails were torn, and the splits in the mainmast opened more, wide enough in some places for us to stick a knife straight through the middle of the mast.

Even worse than the gales and squalls, though, were the long periods of calm that followed. During the crisis of a storm, we were usually so intent on the immediate problem of saving the ship that we had no time to brood about food and water, but morale sank to its lowest point in these deadly calms. Days would pass without a breath of wind to move us closer to our destination. Everyone lay on the blistering deck getting thirstier, more pessimistic, and more quarrelsome by the hour. It was almost a blessing that we were all so weakened by hunger, for senseless arguments broke out constantly, but rarely did the men have enough strength to do more than trade insults. Not all of us scrapped and argued. The Padre kept pretty much to himself, and Carlos and Nicolás brooded in their own private purgatories, sometimes going for days without speaking a word to anyone. Nicolás was not too bad as long as we could keep him busy caulking the deck and the skiff, splicing lines, or repairing the sails, but Carlos had nothing to do during the calms but stare at the chart, as if by doing so he could move us closer to our destination. The only consolation, if one could call it that, was that these mid-Atlantic calms, or doldrums, were a common curse of old sailing ships whenever they passed through the area called the Sargasso Sea, and it meant at least that we had covered more than half the distance to America.

On the morning of November 30, the fifth day of a calm, a heavy swell started; there were light, erratic puffs of air that changed direction every minute or so, and a long line of storm clouds darkened the horizon. It seemed certain that another hurricane was brewing, and we prepared for the worst, doubting that the *Niña* could survive another battering like the last one. The heat was even more oppressive than usual, and by midafternoon we all lay sweltering on the deck or in the cabin, almost looking forward to the storm—anything seemed preferable to that terrible heat. Nicolás, who had spoken hardly a word to anyone in the last two weeks and who usually could not even see our makeshift bowsprit if he was standing on the fantail, suddenly shouted that he had sighted a plane and that it was heading straight for us.

We had mixed reactions at the sight of the plane, a U.S. Navy P2V hurricane hunter. Manolo and I knew it was a hurricane hunter and thought it had come to warn us of the hurricane we were expecting; Carlos and Michel thought that the plane's appearance was accidental and that the crew had no idea who we were; the rest figured that it had come to help us, and as it turned out, they were right. Unknown to us, the *Niña* was believed to have gone down somewhere in the middle of the Atlantic. We were long overdue and had not been sighted by any passing vessels since leaving the Canaries, so that the world press had reported us lost at sea. Clay Blair had then contacted some friends high up in the Navy and convinced them that an air search should be mounted. The British, Spanish, Portuguese, and French air forces had joined in the search, which began on November 24, and for six days planes scoured the Atlantic for thousands of square miles, but all to the north of us, since we had originally planned to follow the exact route taken by Columbus. On the last day of the search, one U.S. Navy P2V, piloted by Commander Vernon F. Anderson, ventured farther south and, after searching for six hours, was heading back to its base on Puerto Rico when the radar operator reported a contact, which turned out to be the *Niña II*.

After making several terrifyingly low passes over us, the plane dropped three bundles. None of the parachutes opened, but José and I jumped in the leaking skiff we were towing behind and retrieved them. One package contained a rubber life raft, but the bottle of compressed air had been triggered on impact, blowing the raft, which was tied in a bundle, to shreds. The next package contained a Gibson Girl emergency radio that had been smashed into an accordion shape on hitting the water. But the third package, with emergency rations and survival gear, was intact and very welcome, especially the two cartons of cigarettes it contained. Our supply had run out weeks before, and the men had resorted to smoking the dried-cornhusk stuffing of our sleeping mats.

The Navy plane next dropped a one-way sonobuoy, which enabled me to speak to its crew, and they answered by wagging the plane's wings or dropping notes in sealed tins. We were relieved to learn that the storm we had been preparing for was not headed our way, but the next item of information was shattering: our true position was latitude 19 degrees 41 minutes north and longitude 51 degrees 20 minutes west, more than four hundred miles to the east of our estimated position. Without a chronometer, which had been invented long after Columbus's time, or even a good watch on board (mine had been smashed when the tiller broke), we could not have expected to measure our longitude with any great accuracy, but even so it was a shock to discover that we were so much farther from our destination than we had thought.

Nevertheless, this brief contact with the outside world after so many weeks was the high point of the voyage, perhaps even more of a relief than our final landfall at San Salvador. That night we celebrated accordingly. Michel broke out several bottles of warm champagne he had been saving for a special occasion, and we sang and joked late into the night.

Three days later two more Navy "Bluebirds," as I had baptized them, arrived and dropped another sonobuoy along with a list of questions. The main one was whether we planned to head for the nearest land, which was Puerto Rico, about six hundred miles due west, or would still try to reach San Salvador, fifteen hundred miles to the northwest. We made a quick vote and the answer was San Salvador: we had already struggled along for fifty-five days and 2,750 miles and we were not going to give up now. Fresh fruit, canned goods, more cigarettes, and a bunch of magazines and newspapers were parachuted down to us and quickly retrieved in the by now half-submerged skiff (it leaked faster than we could bail it). We pounced on the newspapers and magazines, eager to learn what had been happening while we were cut off from the world. We were surprised to read that the sighting of the *Niña* was big news—we had not considered ourselves lost, merely delayed. The magazines were mainly copies of *Playboy*. They had a short life. Padre found the photographs scandalous and, before we could stop him, dumped them overboard, much to our consternation.

This same day, the steady easterly trade wind started up again, and instead of drifting toward our destination, we began to sail at a fairly good clip—good for the *Niña,* that is, for if she had been built and rigged like a proper caravel we would have been averaging 160 miles a day instead of only sixty. We were still faced with the problem of water, since even with an emergency reserve of 160 quarts we had somehow overlooked and found again, we still had barely one quart per person per day to last us the thirty days we calculated as the minimum time it would take us to reach San Salvador. But it was no longer a question of reaching our destination or dying of thirst; in a dire emergency we could always signal for water from either the U.S. Navy and Coast Guard planes that came to check on us nearly daily or passing vessels that for the first time in the whole voyage we began to sight. Now our main concern was to preserve the authenticity of the crossing and reach San Salvador as we had planned, without any modern aids.

Then tragedy struck the *Niña*. One morning we awoke to find Linda missing. All of us searched frantically in every con-

ceivable place she could have been sleeping, although she usually spent the night in the cabin nestled against one of the crew.
There was no sign of her, and we finally had to assume that she
had fallen overboard sometime during the night, since she was
quite a daredevil, forever climbing the masts, out on the spars,
and along the handrail. She had become our talisman, and we
had all grown so fond of her during the long voyage that her
disappearance sent us into a glum state again.

A few days later we had another mascot, but it failed to
replace Linda in our affections. It was a thirty-foot whale,
which we decided thought the *Niña* was another whale of the
opposite sex and had fallen in love with her. Whatever the
reason for the attachment, the whale stayed with us constantly.
During the day it cruised around the vessel, and Manolo and I
both swam with it a few times, holding on to its fins and even
touching one of its huge eyes. At night it would lie right under
the ship, snuggling against the keel and keeping us in constant
fear that the *Niña*'s thin hull would be crushed. The animal's
heartbeat was so strong that the whole vessel throbbed, and it
was like trying to sleep right on top of an African tom-tom: a
very strange sensation. Then, on the third afternoon, José flung
one of our harpoons at our mascot. Whether he actually
thought we could catch and eat the animal I don't know, but
that was the end of the short love affair between a whale and a
ship. The startled beast swam off, easily snapping the harpoon
line, and we never saw it again.

Even though we were making fairly good progress toward
San Salvador, it seemed that our tempers grew worse every
day. Finally Carlos had to order that no one bring up matters
of religion, politics, or food, which seemed to be the three most
explosive topics. Discussion of them invariably resulted in a
bitter argument and occasionally even a fistfight. One time
when I was speaking into a sonobuoy microphone to one of
the Navy planes, José and Pepe got into a loud and violent
discussion right next to me—over what, I don't know. I tried
to shut them up so that I could speak into the mike, and when

that failed, I gave them both a shove to separate them. Pepe instantly went berserk, but instead of attacking me, he started to pound his head against the mainmast, opening a large gash before the others could restrain him. On another occasion, Antonio and José went for each other with knives out on the deck, and only the quick action of several of us prevented bloodshed. As I look back, the fact that tempers flared up more and more as we came closer to the end of our voyage is not surprising. Up to then we had been engrossed in the business of just keeping alive. Arguments stopped short of physical violence when you reasoned that a storm might hit the next day and your opponent might be the only one near a lifeline if you were washed overboard. But now that these dangers seemed past, we turned on each other.

Several minor storms struck us, but the trade winds remained faithful, and so did the planes. They appeared nearly every day to drop badly needed fresh water, small supplies of food, and notes giving our positions, which were invariably different from the ones we estimated. We were getting closer and closer to San Salvador, and on December 23 we established a round-the-clock lookout from the mainmast, fearful of missing our landfall. We had a dozen false alarms, and nobody paid much attention when, at around 1500 hours (three in the afternoon) on Christmas Eve, José announced that he saw something on the horizon. But within an hour even those of us on deck below could make out the low, dark shape on the horizon —San Salvador, our first sight of land since we had left the Canaries seventy-six days before. We all broke into cheers and then joined Padre in singing the *Salve Regina* and reciting prayers of thanksgiving.

By sundown we were off the southern end of San Salvador, but found ourselves unsure what to do, since in our desire for authenticity we had declined to take any charts of sailing directions for the island. Manolo and I were for anchoring until morning, but everyone else sided with Carlos, who favored heading around to the western side of the island for the town of Cockburn, which is supposedly the site of Columbus's landing. By midnight we had gotten within half a mile of the town's pier, but, unable to beat to windward against the strong easterly trade wind, we got no closer. We lit a lantern and waved it frantically, but we had made such good progress in the past two days that we had arrived a full day before we were expected, and no one was on watch for us. We lowered the sails, set out the sea anchor, and settled down to a sad Christmas Eve within full sight of the town lights ashore.

A few hours later Manolo shook me awake to report that a very strong current was pulling us away from the island. We roused the others, raised the sails again, and tried to beat back to windward toward the island. It was fruitless. By dawn we were fifteen miles from San Salvador and being blown steadily west toward the dangerous reefs surrounding Cat Island. At noon I signaled a passing Bahamas Airways plane with a flare from the survival kit the Navy had dropped; in about an hour a U.S. Coast Guard plane appeared, circling overhead, and several hours later a small Navy boat came out from San Salvador and took us in tow.

It was a humiliating end to our seventy-seven-day voyage. After covering the 4,250 miles from Las Palmas on our own, we had to do the last fifteen miles behind a towline. But at that point, pride was the farthest thing from our minds. For weeks we had been set on reaching San Salvador by Christmas, and we did, although just barely: when we finally staggered ashore, it was a few minutes before midnight on December 25. A large welcoming party was there to greet us with a calypso band and a feast that lasted for hours. Manolo has since told me, and everyone else he meets, that he is not sure which was the most amazing moment of the whole venture: when I calmly attacked my third platter heaped with spaghetti or, on finishing that, when I started on a half-gallon serving of ice cream without a pause.

Was it really worth it? Up until that point it was, for I gained what I had sought from the voyage. Not that I learned very much about how the old sailing ships were handled; I am sure that Columbus and the other skilled mariners that followed up his voyages of discovery would have had a good laugh at our fumbling attempts to imitate them. But I had learned how it feels to cross an immense body of water, completely at the mercy of wind and current; to face the constant threat of violent storms; to be so hungry and thirsty that you will eat maggot-infested meat and drink water that smells like a cesspool without turning a hair. There were the moments of joy, too: when the sails filled with a stiff breeze after days of calm, and, most of all, that first sight of land after months of nothing but ocean.

Most important, the voyage served as further proof that it was possible for the great white gods to have made the voyages from the Old to the New World in just about any kind of small vessel, even though they had much larger and far better built ones available. If nine non-seamen could make it across the Atlantic in a half-size caravel with only a minimal knowledge of seamanship, I think the ancients would certainly have been able to make the same voyages. Shortly after our voyage an Englishman attempted to cross the Atlantic in a large wooden wine barrel. He managed to drift over eight hundred miles before oversetting in a storm and being picked up by an accompanying boat.

If I have any misgivings about the voyage, they concern only its aftermath, a disgraceful squabble over money and pride that received almost more coverage in the Spanish press than the voyage itself. I ought to know, for I was cast as the villain of the piece. The hero? Who else but Carlos? Some of the allegations were laughable. I had a good chuckle over one article in which I was said to be such a bad photographer that none of my photos of the voyage came out; the article, of course, was illustrated with a few of the over eight thousand photos that had come out. Others were not so funny. The reports that I had made a fantastic fortune from the *Niña* voyage (estimates went as high as $150,000), all of which I kept for myself, are easily disproved by a few little scraps of paper: receipts signed by Carlos for his 65 percent share of all proceeds from my articles, my movie of the voyage, and my radio and television appearances, plus the 20 percent of my share that was to go to the crew. But it saddens me to think that the other men, except Manolo, with whom I have stayed in close contact, believe I cheated them.

The other main issue—my accounts of the voyage—is less easy to resolve, since it involves personal opinion. My statement that we were all frightened during the worst hurricane that struck us is a case in point. I believe the others were frightened: *I know I* was, and I'm convinced that anyone who failed to feel some fear under those circumstances would have to be either insane or a fool. Maybe I was wrong, but all I could do was write what I saw, thought, and recorded in my daily log. There is nothing to keep anyone else from writing his own version, even if no one else bothered to keep a log. In fact, several of the crew members have written their own accounts. Nicolás claimed in his book, for example, that I talked incessantly about women during the whole voyage. I don't think I did; I was usually too hungry to think about much besides food, and the main daydreams I recall involved huge plates of spaghetti. But if he remembers it that way, that is his prerogative.

The ludicrous hubbub over the aftermath of the *Niña* voyage eventually died down, after raging on for more than a year alongside news of world-shaking international events. It is a shame, though, that a basically idealistic venture that could have been remembered with pride by those who participated in it should have turned into such a sordid mess.

Two months after the termination of the voyage, while I was still trying to regain some of the many pounds I had lost in the crossing and was enjoying the delights of being back in civilization, another adventure beckoned. The World's Fair was to be held in New York City in 1964, and a full-size replica of Columbus's *Santa María* was being constructed in Spain to be displayed at the fair. The group having the vessel built asked if I would skipper the replica from Spain to New York City. Here I had an opportunity to make another voyage across the Atlantic, this time in a vessel of the correct size. I accepted and set about raising a new crew and obtaining all of the necessary supplies and victuals to make another completely authentic voyage. Then the fly landed in the ointment. The insurance firm covering the replica, which cost more than $600,000 to construct, refused to let us sail unless we carried an engine and were escorted during the entire crossing by a tugboat. Nothing could change their minds, and in the end I refused to make the voyage under those restrictions, so the *Santa María* was carried to New York as deck cargo on a large cargo vessel. Throughout the crossing in the *Niña II* I had been mentally formulating plans to construct a Viking ship replica for a transatlantic crossing, so failing to sail the *Santa María* wasn't too much of a letdown.

6

The Voyage of the Long Ship

I n early 1963, a few months after the end of the *Niña II* voyage, I appeared on television in Spain and expressed my opinion that Columbus had not been the first to discover America. The next morning headlines in Madrid's largest newspaper thundered: "Robert Marx is a disgrace to history." The writer of the front-page article went so far as to suggest that the government withdraw the knighthood it had granted me several months before. I was pretty much *persona non grata* in Spain until the following year, when my voyage in a Viking ship replica turned out badly, cheering the Spaniards, who interpreted my failure as vindicating Columbus and proof that the Vikings and others couldn't have discovered America.

The saga of the replicated Viking voyage began after I left Spain with a heavy heart. I love the country and its people and was hurt that they interpreted my desire to investigate history as maligning Spain. I had been planning the Viking voyage for a long time, and I headed for Scandinavia with the intention of constructing a Viking ship replica and making an authentic crossing from Norway to New England. I already knew, and experts in Denmark, Norway, and Sweden only confirmed, that there was a great deal of information about how certain Viking vessels were constructed, but these were warships, not the type of vessels that Norsemen would have used to cross the Atlantic. Three intact tenth-century Viking ships, found in graves of Viking kings at Gokstad and Oseberg and in the canton of Tune, are displayed in Oslo's Viking Ship Museum. These vessels were completely open to the harsh North Atlantic elements, with no enclosures or decks. From historical documents we knew that the Norsemen did have vessels with cabins and holds that were decked over to protect crews and provisions. However, we had no data to use in construction of an authentic replica of a Norse vessel.

In 1956, sport divers in Roskilde Fjord, Denmark, chanced upon five shipwrecks, which were initially identified as Viking warships. In 1962, archaeologists placed a large cofferdam around these wrecks. They removed the seawater and began slowly and systematically to excavate them. In 1967 they published preliminary findings that indicated that only two of the wrecks were Viking warships. The others were two merchant vessels and a fishing boat, and they were decked and had cabins. This information was too late for my first Viking replica voyage, and although I learned of it shortly before the second voyage, I could not afford the cost of remodeling my replica into an enclosed Norse ship.

A Portuguese scholar, Dr. Armando Cortesão, had been the most knowledgeable and helpful of all the academicians I had been corresponding with about pre-Columbian voyages. Dr. Cortesão had dedicated his life to the study of this subject and in 1954 had made a cartographic discovery that rocked the skeptics back on their heels. In an obscure Portuguese library he found the Chart of 1424, which shows many Caribbean islands, labeling "Antillia" those islands that even today are called the Antilles. The publication of the chart caused a great deal of excitement. It also provoked charges that it was a fake, but the chart was put to every available test and declared authentic, substantiating the many legends that Portuguese seamen reached America in the fourteenth or fifteenth century.

From Norway I went to visit Dr. Cortesão at the University of Coimbra in Portugal, and I spent several delightful weeks with him. I proposed constructing a Portuguese caravel and making another transatlantic crossing. He said, however, that I had already proved that Portuguese mariners could have accomplished this feat with the *Niña II* voyage, since Spanish and Portuguese caravels were almost identical in construction. We both believe that the Phoenicians were the first to reach the New World from the Mediterranean and decided that duplicating a Phoenician voyage would be more valuable to history. But Cortesão pointed out a snag, one that had been bothering me for some time too. Very little is known about the construction of early Mediterranean vessels; there are a few drawings and seals showing their overall design and most significant features, but no plans or scale models to show exactly how they were put together or even which woods were used in their construction. He suggested that I give up the idea of a Phoenician vessel altogether and build a later type, say a Greek ship, about which more is known. I balked at this, since there is scant indication that the Greeks reached the Americas. He feared that if I attempted to build a Phoenician replica with insufficient data, my efforts would be in vain, because skeptics could claim that my vessel was not authentic and charge that my voyage proved nothing except that I could navigate like the ancients.

While researching construction on all types of ancient vessels I had noticed how little the design had changed over the centuries. I was struck by how similar the drawings of ancient Mediterranean ships were to the Viking ships of the Middle Ages: shallow draft, little or no deck, steerboard instead of stern rudder, a single large square sail, and high-swept bow and sternpost. The details of construction of Phoenician and Greek ships may still be debatable points, but not those of the Viking ships, for three original ones exist in Oslo. The great white gods seemed to be whispering to me again.

I thought, Why not build a Viking ship instead, since it is known that they evolved from the earlier Mediterranean vessels? At any rate, a Viking voyage would prove that this type of ship could make it across the Atlantic in the lower latitudes that the Phoenicians would have used. Even though a Viking ship was not suitable for a North Atlantic crossing, it could make it across the southern route. It was also possible that the Vikings, during their numerous piratical sorties into the Mediterranean regions, could have been blown across the Atlantic by inclement weather after passing through the Straits of Gibraltar on one of their return voyages.

Anyone would think that the *Niña II* crossing would have put me off even rowboats for the rest of my life. In fact, most of my friends, who suspected I was slightly loony anyway, decided I definitely ought to be locked up when I announced my plans for the new voyage in a Viking ship. Before this next adventure, or misadventure, was over, I was beginning to think they might be right.

In May 1963 I was able to start work on the ship itself. I consulted various authorities on Viking ships in Denmark, Norway, and Sweden and looked for a shipyard that could make a precise replica of the original Gokstad ship, using the same types of wood, fittings, and techniques. I finally located one in Bergen, Norway, that agreed to do the job for an estimated $10,000, at the most. Three weeks later, when I returned to New York from my European trip, I found a letter from the owner of the shipyard informing me that the yard had miscalculated the costs, which were now estimated at $35,000. I blasted off a sharp reply, saying I would try to raise that amount but was not sure I could, and instead of assuring me that this estimate would not be exceeded, the shipyard sent another letter raising it to $50,000. I canceled the contract and went on a week's drunk.

That seemed the end of my Viking voyage, but a month later I ran into an old friend who was working in the publicity department of Columbia Pictures, and when I told him about my bad luck with the Viking vessel, he said: "Marx, you lucky dog, you can call me Santa Claus, because I'm going to *give* you a Viking ship."

I thought at first he'd had too many martinis, but he explained that Columbia was making a Viking movie in Yugoslavia called *The Long Ships,* for which they had had three Viking ships built. My friend said that they would probably be destroyed after the movie was finished anyway, and he was sure that Columbia would sell, lend, or maybe even give me one of them. But I was dubious. These ships were movie props, I protested, probably just pieces of junk, and certainly not seaworthy enough to make an Atlantic crossing. He said he would check into it and let me know in a week or so.

I couldn't wait that long. After two sleepless nights I decided to go and check for myself. I obtained a visa for Yugoslavia in the record time of two hours (it normally took two weeks) and that same day was on a plane heading for Belgrade. Arriving at Budva, a village halfway down the Adriatic Coast of Yugoslavia, where the movie was being made, I was pleasantly surprised to see what looked like three faithful replicas of the Gokstad ship lying at anchor, instead of the overgrown canoes I had half expected.

My eyes hadn't deceived me. The three ships, I learned, had been built in Yugoslavia (Yugoslavian oak, according to the Bergen shipbuilders, is the best in Europe) under the supervision of Danish and Norwegian Viking experts, following the exact plans of the tenth-century Gokstad ship I had seen on display in Oslo. After inspecting all three of them carefully and testing their sailing qualities, I selected the one I liked best and rushed back to New York to convince the directors of Columbia Pictures to donate the vessel to me. They agreed (not pure altruism, of course; they would be receiving their share of publicity from the voyage), but only on condition that I sign a statement releasing them from any liability in connection with the voyage. A routine precaution, no doubt, but too bad I didn't take it as an omen of things to come.

Just about this time it was announced to the world that the Norwegian archaeologist Dr. Helge Ingstad had uncovered the indisputable remains of a large tenth-century Viking settlement in Newfoundland. After centuries of controversy, even the die-hard skeptics had to admit that other mariners had preceded Columbus to America. The time was ripe for me to prove the possibility of pre-Columbian voyages across the mid-Atlantic. The season was too far advanced for a crossing that year, so I planned to leave the following spring instead. But this time I was determined to make careful preparations, instead of scurrying around at the last minute and leaving undone half of the essential tasks, as had happened with the *Niña II* voyage. I resigned from my job at the *Saturday Evening Post* in October 1963, about ten months after I was hired as an adventure editor, and headed for Europe.

The first step was to plan my route. Finding the Portuguese very interested in the voyage, probably because they too have consistently disclaimed Columbus's discovery of America, I made Lisbon my point of departure. I would sail down to the Cape Verde Islands, across to Yucatán, and then back to Europe via the northern route, all without the aid of an astrolabe or even a compass. The trip from Yugoslavia to Lisbon would be a shakedown cruise with a skeleton crew to test the ship's sailing qualities and seaworthiness. At Lisbon she would be completely overhauled, new sails and rigging would be fitted, and the bulk of the crew and provisions would be taken on. Then on to America.

I was busy making preparations throughout the winter. I discovered that people were extremely interested in the voyage —everyone except the Italians and the Spanish, who undoubtedly felt that it would steal some of Columbus's thunder—and received letters from hundreds of volunteers. Out of these I selected a crew of twelve men from ten European nations. The second-in-command was a Portuguese naval officer, a direct descendant of Ferdinand Magellan, the first circumnavigator of the world. Many countries also volunteered supplies: the Danes offered mead, an alcoholic drink made from yeast, malt, and honey; the Dutch sent half a ton of goat's-milk cheese; the Portuguese offered dried fish and fresh provisions. Other sources offered a variety of foodstuffs, all of which had to be items that were common fare in the tenth century.

Finally, in mid-February of 1964, everything seemed ready. After a last-minute check with the Columbia Pictures people, who informed me that all three ships had been taken for safekeeping to the shipyard where they had been built, I packed my duffel bag and headed for Punat Island, not far from the Yugoslav border with Italy, near Trieste, to take possession of my vessel, which I christened the *Long Ship*. I rushed straight from the ferry down to the shipyard, eager for a glimpse of her. Instead all I saw was the high mainmast and the two elaborately carved figureheads on the bow and stern; the rest was submerged in a fathom of water, flanked by the two other vessels, which had suffered the same fate.

I scoured the island in search of someone who knew some English and finally located the foreman of the shipyard, who unraveled the mystery. Someone along the line had neglected to mention the donation to the Yugoslavs, and all three ships had been brought to Punat not for safekeeping but to be stripped of all valuable materials and then destroyed. The ship I had selected was the least damaged, but even so, her sides were stove in in several places, some of the supporting ribs and knees had been removed, her sails were serving as an awning over the village marketplace, and the location of her carefully constructed, authentic Viking rigging was a complete mystery.

The shipyard foreman thought I was a first-class crackpot, arriving unannounced at this isolated spot to take possession of a vessel he had been ordered to destroy and then coming up with some crazy joke about sailing the ship to America. Unable to convince him that I owned it, much less that I was serious about having it raised and prepared for sailing, I decided to make my way to the nearest telephone, which was at Rijeka, on the mainland, to call the Columbia Pictures representative in London. When I finally got through to him, I dug up every forceful expression I could remember from my days as a Marine Corps sergeant and added a few juicy ones of my own invention. I must have gotten my point across, for the next day a three-man delegation of VIPs from the Yugoslav state film company arrived from Belgrade with an interpreter and ordered the shipyard foreman to raise and restore the vessel under my supervision.

The wheels left, and my interpreter, named Dragon, and I got to work. The shipyard's planned method of raising the vessel was to pull it up on a beach with a team of oxen, but I put a stop to that: the ship, her structure weakened by the loss of several ribs and many planks, would have fallen to pieces. The whole shipyard then went on strike, demanding that I be kept off the premises until the vessel was ready, but the strike was short-lived. Dragon, like most official interpreters, turned out to be a member of the Yugoslav secret service, and since the shipyard was state-owned, the boys were back at work within hours. In the meantime I decided that I would have to raise the vessel myself, since it was really a job for a diver.

It was bitterly cold, even in the Adriatic, but luckily I had brought along a rubber diving suit, as well as my snorkeling gear. On my first dive I discovered the ship was much more seriously damaged than I had thought. I should have given up the whole idea of the voyage right then and let the Long Ship stay there as a home for octopi and moray eels, which was about all she was good for. But setbacks and hopeless cases only have the effect of making me more determined than ever. Sometimes I like to call it persistence; in this case it was sheer lunacy.

My plan for refloating her by pumping air into large oil drums attached to cables slung under her keel had to be ruled out, since I couldn't find enough drums, or any valves at all.

Pumping air into the ship was out of the question, since there was nothing to pump it into—she was a giant version of an open rowboat, with no deck or hold and only a minuscule cabin in the bow. My efforts were a constant source of merriment to the shipyard workers, who sat around drinking slivovitz while I scurried around the yard.

Then I thought up a new plan. Dragon and I managed to collect about a dozen ordinary car jacks, which we put to work after I covered over all the holes in the hull and nailed reinforcing planks over the weak spots. At each low tide I was able to raise the vessel a little farther off the bottom, and after four days, when her gunwales were above water, we started to pump her out. This rather haphazard engineering feat so amazed the hecklers that they decided I was not such a bad guy after all, and they all offered to cooperate fully in repairing the ship.

The following morning we pulled her carefully up on the ways, and the men went to work, sometimes as many as forty or fifty at a time. We had to replace the forty-five-foot mast, which we found cracked in several places, and more than a third of the hull planking. We needed a number of new ribs and knees and completely new rigging. Dragon retrieved the sails from the marketplace; they were badly stretched, but new sails were being made in Lisbon, and I had also decided that for the Punat-Lisbon shakedown cruise I would have the film company's engine reinstalled as an auxiliary. The engine, like almost everything else, had been removed; it had been sold by the foreman to some fishermen, but we were able to buy it back.

As the repair work neared completion, I sent word to the five crew members who were to make this leg of the voyage to join me at Punat. Three weeks to the day after I had arrived to find the ship under water, she was ready to sail (Dragon more than anyone else deserves the credit for this feat), and right on schedule my five crewmen arrived on the evening ferry. They were five good men: an Englishman, Bill Holmes, a chemist on land and a real sailor at sea; two Norwegian descendants of

the Vikings, Knut Adeler and Per Christiansen; and two Yugoslavs, Jevtic Slobodan, an artist and sculptor, called Jumbo
because of his size, and Plavsic Slavoljub, who had fortunately
been nicknamed Bell for short when he worked as a stuntman
on the movie for which the ship was built. They ranged in age
from twenty-two (Per) to thirty-one (Jumbo), a real change
from the venerable crew of the *Niña,* of which I had been the
junior member by a wide margin. There was one problem:
neither Jumbo nor Bell knew a word of English, which was to
be our *lingua franca.* I was afraid I would have to take a quick
course in Serbian from Dragon but discovered that Jumbo
knew some Italian, and then they both started to pick up English words very quickly from the rest of us—but not the sort
of words they would have learned at a Berlitz school, I'm
afraid.

    After dropping their bags off at the local inn, they all
trooped down with me to see the ship. A bitter snowstorm was
blowing at the time, and the ship looked ghostlike, covered
with ice and snow, but at least she was afloat and ready to sail.
They set to work with a will, sweeping the snowy shroud from
the deck and examining every inch of her structure. Neither
Jumbo nor Bell had had much sailing experience, and both had
heard the local fishermen and even the shipyard workers remark that the vessel was only a movie prop and not fit to paddle
around a lake in, much less sail across thousands of miles of
open sea. Her lines were graceful—seventy-six feet from stem
to stern and eighteen feet across the beam—and with a draft of
only three feet, she appeared to be built for speed. But could
she withstand heavy seas? The huge Jumbo started to jump all
over the gunwales to test their strength (someone had told him
they were the ship's weak point), and Knut inspected the planking with a critical eye. I was hurt that the boys should doubt
her sturdiness, for at that time I considered her the soundest
vessel ever built. Later I was to recall that scene with bitter
amusement.

    That night, as we sat drinking the potent slivovitz to warm

ourselves against the cold, I went over my plans for the voyage again, warning them that this would be no pleasure cruise. They all knew the conditions. To save time on the voyage to Lisbon, we would have the auxiliary motor, charts, and a compass; but from then on our only means of propulsion would be the one large square sail, our only navigational aids the sun and stars, and our only food the kind that would have been carried by tenth-century mariners. And of course we would have no radio or life rafts. But I wanted to make sure they understood and to give them a chance to back out if they wanted to. Not one of them did. Bill Holmes said, "Chief, we'll get there if we have to paddle this canoe across." I wondered at the time how much of their enthusiasm depended on the slivovitz, but I never had cause to wonder again: although the ship let me down, the men never did.

The snow melted the next day, and we made the final preparations—checked out the engine, filled the fuel tanks, and loaded the decks with gear and supplies. We were ready to cast off when the second stroke of bad luck occurred. (Looking back, I can't decide whether the first stroke of bad luck was the scuttling of the ship or my raising her.) The port authorities and customs officials suddenly announced that we couldn't leave without changing the ship's registration and paying 20 percent export duty. When I discovered that the ship had originally cost $30,000, I was panic-stricken. Anxious to be away before the next snowstorm began, I persuaded them, with Dragon's help, to let us leave, on the condition that we leave the ship's papers behind. I was sure that the ancient seamen had not bothered with such petty matters as owner's papers, registration, and national flags and was almost happy to be sailing without them.

Around noon on the 9th of March we were underway at last. The old sea dogs in the port of Rijeka, where we had to go to receive official clearance, could not dampen our spirits, in spite of their warnings that March was the worst month for sailing those waters and their advice to make for the nearest sheltered cove the moment the barometer started to fall. We planned to sail around the clock and hit port only when we ran low on food and water. I set up continuous watches and calculated that we could make the 2,400-mile trip to Lisbon within fifteen days, twenty at the most: the least we could do was six knots using the engine, and under sail with a good breeze we could do ten. But our first day out established a pattern that was to repeat itself with frustrating monotony during the three weeks that followed—an unending struggle to keep our flimsy ship afloat and headed toward Lisbon.

That evening, as we were running south at more than eight knots along the Yugoslav coast, a violent squall struck without warning. The problem I had feared most, heavy seas breaking over the gunwales (which cleared the water by only three feet) and swamping the ship, was only minor. The Vikings had known what they were doing when they designed their ships: she could ride the big tail seas as easily as a gull bobbing on the waves of the bay. But if the design was good, the construction was not. Whenever we were hit by head seas, which plagued most of our journey, the whole frame shook and the sides heaved in and out like bellows. Instead of being held together by the heavy spikes, wooden treenails, and walrus-hide thongs the Vikings had used, this ship was joined by short nails with spike heads soldered on to give the appearance of solidity that had deceived us. We could have minimized the damage by never venturing out unless we had a perfect tail wind, but in that case we never would have left port, since we had head winds 95 percent of the time. Also I wanted to put the ship through the severest tests possible; if she was going to fall apart, better in the Mediterranean than in the middle of the Atlantic.

Lowering the sail, we quickly started the auxiliary engine, and as the crew made frantic efforts to keep up with the small geysers sprouting from bow to stern (made worse, if anything, by the vibrations of the motor), I steered for a small cove. There we sheltered until dawn, plugging leaks most of the night and dining on canned tripe and raw-onion-and-ketchup salad prepared by Jumbo, the ship's cook.

Anyone superstitious, and most sailors are, would say that our bad luck was only natural. In the movie the vessel had been a funeral ship, stolen by a renegade band of Vikings who then suffered a series of disasters that culminated with the ship's wrecking on the coast of North Africa. Bill had warned me that I was making a big mistake in using the black "death sail" from the movie, but I had no choice. The ordinary Viking sails were being made in Lisbon, and we had to test the ship's sailing ability on this part of the voyage, bad omen or not. Per and Knut, who both knew the old Viking myths, had said jokingly that the only way we could break the curse on the death ship was to sacrifice a maiden to the Norse gods. We all had a good laugh over that one, but we soon began to think we might have made better use of our time in port by hunting around for a suitable victim.

Fair weather returned with daybreak. The wind was perfect and we raised the sail again, averaging slightly over nine knots that day—over twice the best speed that the *Niña II* ever averaged. Bill eyed the billowing black death sail suspiciously, suggesting that we should at least paint it another color as soon as we made our next port. "Chief, you're entirely too superstitious," I answered. "It'll be a breeze reaching Lisbon."

Yet that evening I began to wonder if we were not really cursed. We were hit by a sudden squall that caused a large tear in the sail before we could haul it down, a fire developed in the propeller shaft when I ordered the engine started, and a fuel line snapped moments after we put out the fire.

The next morning produced fair weather again, and I decided to cross the Adriatic to the Italian coast, where we could make repairs and rig a tarpaulin over the forward deck for shelter from the heavy spray that had drenched everything and everyone on board. There was no doubt that our ship had been designed for speed. With a fair wind we covered the 125 miles across to the Italian port of Vieste in eleven hours, an astonishing average speed of over eleven knots. At that rate and without any prolonged calms, we could cross the Atlantic in fifteen days!

From Vieste we made our way down the Italian peninsula, taking refuge in several ports along the way whenever a particularly bad sirocco blew up, bringing blasts of hot wind straight from the North African desert. We were completely unaware that we were the objects of a massive sea and air search mounted by the Yugoslav government. Our failure to put in at Vis Island, south toward Dubrovnik, which had mistakenly been reported as our next port of call after Rijeka, had started a rumor that the ship and all hands were lost. The story reached the press as far away as London and New York and sent our families into a needless panic. We were the only ones who didn't know we were missing. We learned of the search a week later when we were passing Crotone and a police launch came out loaded with reporters and photographers to congratulate us on our "miraculous survival." Even the Italian navy and air force had joined in the search, and it is still a mystery to me how the rumor continued for so long when we had reported to the harbormaster each time bad weather drove us into a port. It isn't as if a seventy-six-foot open-decked Viking ship could be mistaken for a fishing trawler.

The almost constant siroccos, the innumerable leaks, and the other mishaps did not deter us from our original plan. We thought there would be no problem once we reached Lisbon for a complete overhaul, removed the motor, which was the main cause of the damaging vibrations, and started across the Atlantic with a good tail wind filling our sail. Hugging this rockbound coast was really more dangerous than crossing open water, and we suffered one particular mishap that never could have occurred in the middle of the Atlantic. Around noon on the fourth day out, a dense fog suddenly blanketed us, reducing our visibility to a bare twenty yards. Bell, who was always interested in how I plotted our course, asked me, "Chief, do you really know where we are in this fog?

"Bell, I have a built-in radar. There's nothing to worry about."

Then Per, who was stationed at the bow as a lookout, said, "Your radar isn't working so well, Chief. I can see bottom."

At the same moment we heard voices, which I thought came from a passing fishing boat, but seconds later a large truck appeared out of the fog and hurtled across our bow. We were almost aground, no more than ten yards from a coastal highway! I yelled for Bell to throw the engine into reverse as Bill, who was on helm watch, made a 90-degree turn to port, but as we swung away from the shore we became entangled in a fishing net suspended from several buoys. After freeing ourselves from the net and sacrificing all the cigarettes and a good portion of the slivovitz aboard to placate angry fishermen, we headed seaward. Losing our position entirely and colliding with other boats in the dense fog were risks we could expect, but not a head-on collision with a truck.

Luckily we did not lose our position (my radar was working again), and six hours later we put in to Bari, the next port down the coast, to take on fuel and make more repairs. But even in port we never had a moment's relaxation. We usually entered without the harbor pilot's help, and always without the proper papers. The port captains were invariably incensed that we flew a large Viking pennant with a dragon insignia instead of the compulsory Italian flag. We had nothing against the Italian flag, but we always arrived after nightfall when all the stores were closed and we couldn't buy one. Things got so bad in Otranto that the harbor police confiscated our rudder, refusing to let us leave until we flew the Italian flag. Per and Knut offered to pull a Viking raid and steal one from an Italian navy boat in port, but a quick reconnaissance stroll down the pier revealed that security measures were too stiff, so Bill had to sew one together out of different items of clothing. It wasn't very pretty, but it had the right colors and it was more or less rectangular.

There were plenty of other annoyances. Throngs of curious locals scrambled all over the ship, staring at the disheveled crew and interfering with our work of caulking and patching. That was when we were lucky enough to find a place to tie up that was neither a restricted naval zone nor already jammed with other boats taking shelter from the foul weather. About the only good thing about putting into port was that we were able to get some decent food. I had made the grave mistake before leaving Rijeka of assigning Jumbo to buy all the provisions. It wasn't until we were well underway that I found out what his idea of a well-balanced shipboard diet was: canned tripe (eight cases of it); six cases each of very hot peppers, pickled cauliflower, and ketchup; three sacks of onions (but no cooking oil; he liked them raw); one sack of garlic; and a small amount of crackers and cheese. While Jumbo and Bell gobbled down these Yugoslav delicacies, the rest of us munched on cheese and crackers until we could buy some cans of sardines and other more palatable food in Vieste. "Very good *mangiare,* Chief," Jumbo would say, looking very hurt when I refused a plate of tripe and raw onions. In fact, he liked the stuff so much that most of the time in port he would volunteer to guard the ship while the rest of us trooped off to stuff ourselves with antipasto and lasagna.

We never could get a reliable weather forecast in port. Whether in Monopoli, Otranto, Crotone, Reggio di Calabria, or any of the other places we stopped, the story was always the same: the radio gave storm warnings, the harbormaster predicted a flat calm, and fishermen prophesied everything from a hurricane to a hailstorm. It made little difference; no matter what the weather was when we left port, it always became foul or fouler within a few hours out. Not that foul weather is unusual in the Mediterranean at that time of the year. In fact, March is considered the worst month, so bad that fishing and sailing practically come to a standstill until April or May. However, the gale that hit us in the Gulf of Taranto our seventh day out was unusual even for March.

We left Otranto at daybreak and headed around the heel of Italy's boot, intending to cut across the 120-mile-wide Gulf of Taranto and to make Malta, or, if luck held out, some port on the coast of North Africa, our next stop. Everyone was in high spirits as we bowled along before a good tail wind for the first time in days. But the stiff breeze soon became a twenty-, then a thirty-knot wind, and while we were lowering the huge spar to put on a small storm sail—Viking sails have no bonnets—it veered around almost 90 degrees, and before long a seventy-knot gale was upon us in full force. "The hell with the storm sail," I shouted. "Start the engine."

The seas became enormous. Whipped up by vicious cross-currents, they swamped the ship in spray and foam so that she seemed more like a torpedo than a floating vessel. After several hours in which we made absolutely no headway, I decided to run for the port of Gallipoli. The chart showed a large rocky bank near the surface and about a mile offshore halfway up the east coast of the gulf. My plan was to get sea room and pass on the outside, but the seas had other plans. They lifted the ship, thrusting her forward like a surfboard no matter which way we tried to steer her. I decided that we would have to pass between the bank and the shore, but moments later even this choice was impossible. Suddenly we found ourselves on the bank in water so shallow that when the trough of a wave passed over, we could see the jagged rocks all around us.

Only the courage and resourcefulness of the crew pulled us through. Throwing everyone a life jacket, I grabbed the helm and sent Per to the bow to guide me through the labyrinth of murderous rocks. Bill and Knut smashed open several drums of diesel fuel and began throwing bucketfuls over the weather side of the ship to prevent the high seas from breaking and smashing us down on a dry bottom. Jumbo and Bell heaved over ballast rock at breakneck speed to reduce our draft. Jumbo was thrown against the mast and sprained his shoulder, but he never let up for a minute. Several times we crossed over rocks with barely a few inches of water to spare, but the death-ship curse seemed to spare us at the right moment, and each time a big sea lifted us high and carried us across. After three hours of this strain on nerves and muscles, we had zigzagged our way safely out of the rocky bank into deep water. Looking back, all we could see was a solid mass of foam.

I had been afraid that the crew would all desert the moment we reached Gallipoli, and I could not have blamed them if they had. But I had chosen my men well. In spite of what they had just been through, they vowed to stick with the ship and even joked about the danger we had faced. We soon learned how narrow our escape had been: several fishing trawlers, whose distress flares we had seen while we were battling across the bank, had foundered in the same area and been smashed to pieces on the rocks. Fortunately most of their crews had been rescued by larger vessels, but six men had drowned.

We stayed in port the following day, caulking, pounding back loose nails, and driving in new ones to replace others that had fallen out altogether, while we waited for the gale to blow itself out. We finally crossed the Gulf of Taranto the next day, even though the weather was still rough and became steadily worse as we made our way south along the Calabrian coast and the eastern shore of Sicily. For four days and nights the ship was battered by heavy seas and drenched by continual rain-squalls, while we bailed unceasingly and even resorted to plugging leaks with honey-soaked rags. I had hoped to reach North Africa without another stop, but the men had gone without sleep since we left Gallipoli, and I decided to put into Sciacca to give them a rest before we set out across open water for Tunis.

Some rest they had. The little Sicilian port was so jammed with sheltering fishing boats that the only place for us to tie up was against a twenty-foot-high mole enclosing the harbor, and after a few hours of being lifted and pounded against the wall —the seas were so rough that occasionally waves came right over the mole to break over us on the other side—we headed seaward again. About four hours later, as we approached the southwestern tip of Sicily, an Italian naval vessel came along-side and signaled a gale warning, suggesting that we put into the nearest port, which was Mazara del Vallo on the south-western tip of Sicily. It seemed as if the weather was deter-mined never to give us a break.

The familiar radio forecast of *mare agitato* kept us in Mazara del Vallo for four full days. We had arrived there on March 21, our thirteenth day out from Rijeka, when according to our original plan we should have been within landfall of Lisbon. As we waited for the weather to improve we were entertained royally by Big Shot Tony, a retired Chicago gangster who had been deported from the United States a few years before and was eager to show off his knowledge of English and his wealth to the people in his hometown. He was very happy to have a chance to talk with an American and besides wining and dining us while we were in port, he loaded us down with enough food and wine to reach America.

We almost lost Per in Mazara del Vallo. He fell in love with a local girl and had a hard time deciding between the voyage and his Sicilian beauty. In the end we made up his mind for him by getting him drunk and carrying him aboard just as we were leaving. When he finally woke up with a horrible hangover a few hours later, we were well out to sea, and there was nothing he could do but threaten to murder the lot of us. Actually we probably saved him from being murdered himself, for the few times he had been able to talk to the girl, by waiting outside the local church where she attended daily Mass, about a dozen glowering brothers and cousins had gathered around to protect her from our Norwegian lover boy.

Although we enjoyed Big Shot Tony's hospitality, we were anxious to press on to Lisbon, and each day we delayed in port was agony, except for Per. We seized the opportunity of the first favorable weather forecast, and at midnight on the fifth day in port we waved goodbye to Tony, thanked him for all the cigars and delicious dinners, and set out for Tunis. The weather was perfect; calm seas, a light but steady tail wind, and the skies so clear that for the first time we were able to navigate just by the stars and without a compass, in practice for our Atlantic crossing.

I don't think I'm particularly superstitious, but that black death-sail definitely had some kind of attraction for gale-force winds. About five hours out of port, only minutes after Knut had remarked, "Maybe Mediterranean weather isn't as bad as

Norway's after all,'' another sirocco hit us, this time bringing particles of sand as well as blasts of hot air all the way from the North African desert. This storm was even worse than the one in the Gulf of Taranto, but at least we were in open water, which any sailor will prefer in a storm to a rock-stewn coast. Mazara del Vallo lay only twenty-five miles to our stern and Tunis over 130 miles ahead, but I decided to strain our luck and head for Tunis under power. Per wanted to go back and see his girl, but all the rest of the crew were as sick of lying in port as I was and preferred to keep on, even if it meant battling this granddaddy of a sirocco.

Fighting a storm in the *Long Ship* demanded the utmost in skill, nerve, and backbreaking work. In other types of vessels, deck hatches could be battened down and the ship made fairly safe unless it capsized. Ours was completely open, so that every drop of rain, spray, and breaking wave had to be bailed out, even if she had not leaked like a sieve as well. Just when we had bailed out most of the water and thought we could collapse for a moment of rest, another large sea would break over the gunwales and we would have to start all over again. The long narrow hull made the helmsman's job particularly nerverack-ing. He had to judge the speed and direction of each wave, because a direct hit amidships from a heavy sea would have swamped us and possibly overturned the ship completely. For the next forty hours all we could do was pray and force our aching arms to keep bailing.

The gale diminished in force as we entered the Gulf of Tunis. Exhausted, but thankful that we had made it, we crept slowly along the channel toward the faint lights of La Goulette, Tunis's seaport. After tying up at the first empty berth we saw, we all fell asleep as if drugged.

Although we were only halfway to Lisbon at this time, it never occurred to any of us to give up. The delays and dangers only made us more determined to reach Lisbon as quickly as possible, to make the major repairs the ship needed, fit a tar-paulin over most of the deck, change our black death-sail for the more cheerful red-and-white-striped one, and set off for America. From the newspapers I learned that most of the other seven crew members were already in Lisbon—all the more reason for our impatience to reach there ourselves. When the harbormaster gave us permission to leave, after extracting a heavy fine for our having entered, as usual, without a pilot, proper papers, or a flag, we eagerly pored over the charts, checking distances and calculating that with no trouble we could reach Morocco, three quarters of the way to Lisbon, in a few days.

At sunup on March 29, Good Friday and the twentieth day out of Rijeka, we set out for Algiers. The weather was good (rarely did we start under bad conditions) except for an unusually heavy swell running from the northwest. I knew this could not be the aftermath of the sirocco we had just battled through, since it was coming from the opposite direction, and we stopped off briefly at Bizerte on the Tunisian coast to get a weather report. Although the forecast was favorable, just to be on the safe side we did not even attempt to use our jinxed sail. It made no difference. About half a day out of Bizerte a strong wind started to blow from the northwest. I just could not believe that another storm could hit that coast so soon after the last one, but it did, the only difference being that this one was an icy cold mistral sweeping down from the mountains of France, instead of a sirocco. Once again our ship was lifted high on the crest of one wave, dashed into its trough, and pounded by the next sea. We began to hear sharp cracks and snaps: she was breaking into pieces like a handful of twigs.

By then we were nearly halfway between Bizerte and the next port, Tabarka, on the Tunisian-Algerian border. I made up my mind to continue on, but soon regretted my decision. The sky became pitch-black, and the seas enormous. Per, seeing the strain on my face, offered me a cigarette. I don't usually smoke, but I snatched that one up. "The way things are going," I said, "I'd better smoke three at a time."

One by one the planks separated from the ribs, and the nails flew out like bullets. Frantically we hammered in more nails, trying to fasten the planks back on the ribs, but in places there were six-inch gaps, which Jumbo stuffed with more honey-soaked rags to keep out the gushing water. As the seas hit us, the entire hull began to twist and squirm like a snake, the mast worked loose from its base on the keel, and the gunwales heaved in and out as much as eighteen inches. My *Long Ship* was now like the branches of a tree shaking in a strong wind: she resembled a ship only in outline.

Realizing now that we had no hope of making port before the full fury of the storm was unleashed, I had two choices: either run her ashore on some beach, or find a safe anchorage. Ahead lay a rocky headland running north and south, and I made for the small cove on the lee side to shelter from the gale. As soon as we dropped anchor I put on my diving gear to patch the hull underwater, since we could not locate most of the leaks from above. I got a shock when I saw that many of the spikes holding the planks to the ribs below the waterline were missing, while others were pulled in as far as half the thickness of the wood. But the crusher was the keel. Instead of being made of one solid piece of oak, as on the Gokstad original and all other Viking ships, it had been laminated. The two inches of special resin covering the bottom, topped by thick tar, had hidden this fatal flaw from me when I had dived to inspect her in Budva and again when she was up on the ways at Punat. The keel, the vessel's backbone, was now broken in many places and whole sections were missing altogether.

When I climbed aboard to spring this thunderbolt on the crew, who were all bailing furiously, the wind had increased to gale force. The ship was now beyond repair; without a solid keel, not even a complete overhaul could make her fit for an ocean crossing. I felt like abandoning her right there, but the nearest town was more than thirty miles away, and between it and our cove lay a rugged mountain range and a desert, both of which we would have had to cross on foot. I decided that we would have to keep the vessel afloat and try to hail a passing vessel to carry us to some port. We had been relatively protected at this anchorage, but the huge seas began to swing around the point and enter the cove, increasing as the storm continued. Swells of fifteen to twenty feet passed under the ship, straining our anchor cables, then broke on the shore only twenty yards away, throwing spray as high as fifty feet, which the wind blew back over us.

By dawn the next day, the situation was even grimmer: our anchors had dragged, the seas entering the cove had increased in force and size, and although we had been bailing constantly, the water level, if anything, was higher than the night before. Jumbo said to me, "Chief, you have to do something or we'll be lost."

I said nothing. What could I say when there seemed no chance of saving either the ship or ourselves?

"Where's your Viking spirit, Jumbo?" Per asked.

"Spirit? Huh. We'll all be spirits soon. Dead ones," Jumbo retorted.

I had to make the most difficult decision of my life, and quickly, before the ship broke up under us or we were driven onto the shore. I knew that the expedition was finished and that my main responsibility was the lives of my crew. My worries increased when Knut reported that both anchor cables were frayed and would soon snap. The breakers smashing against the rocky shore of the cove ruled out abandoning the ship and swimming ashore there, but remembering that about two hundred yards to the east we had passed another cove with a sandy beach, I called the men together and explained my plan to drive the ship aground there.

I was surprised to find that Per, Knut, and Bill were dead set against destroying the ship (Jumbo and Bell, neither of whom could swim, accepted the plan as the lesser of two evils), even though they knew it was beyond repair. Bill took the news the hardest, saying bitterly, "Is this why we've been killing ourselves for weeks, to wreck our own ship? Why not just stay here and let the storm do it for us and save ourselves the shame?"

After a while he too realized that going down with the ship would be little consolation for ourselves and our families, and he joined in the preparations. We lashed empty fuel drums together to make a raft, loaded it with a cask of water and a sack of canned food, and placed map and compass in a plastic bag so that we could find our way to civilization. Even though we all wore life jackets, Per and Knut were assigned to get Bell ashore if we capsized, while Bill and I would handle Jumbo. Per tried to cheer him up by saying, "Jumbo, with all that blubber, you couldn't sink if you tried."

Unable to raise either anchor, we tied the cables to floats, a fortunate precaution, for when we reached the other cove all we could see was a solid mass of white foam and spray for twenty feet from shore, where the immense waves were breaking with a thunderous roar. Sandy beach or not, to run aground there would be suicide. We turned about quickly and reentered the first cove, where Bill dove overboard, retrieved the anchor cables, and had us tied up again, safe for the moment at least. Things are really bad when you can't even abandon ship or run her aground—the sailor's two last resorts.

The storm continued the rest of the day along with a steady downpour. Cold, wet, and exhausted, we kept on bailing and plugging leaks. By that time all the rags had been used, and we had to stuff the tarpaulin, sleeping bags, and even spare clothes into the gaps. Somehow the anchors held, and by the following dawn the wind had died down considerably. By noon the seas had decreased enough to permit us to weigh anchor and head seaward in hopes of finding a passing ship. But perversely, ships seem to appear only at nighttime or in a dense fog, when you fear a collision, and never when you are adrift, out of water, or about to sink. Finding that the ship was still hanging together and that the seas became even calmer, I decided to take her back to Bizerte.

It was a slow and tedious return. For three full days we inched along, hugging the coast in case the ship should suddenly go under and we should have to swim for shore. Once safe inside the harbor, I chose a sandy beach next to the abandoned French yacht club and ran her aground.

Our final task was to dispose of the hulk that had once been a ship. I wanted to sell the valuable motor and other gear, all still in good condition, but the Tunisian authorities demanded an 80 percent import duty, which, added to the compulsory 20 percent commission for the agent, would have left me with exactly nothing. I was forbidden to give anything away to anybody but the Tunisian merchant marine, and the American consul in Tunis urged me to make such a gift, which, he said, would promote goodwill between our countries. I might have accepted this official twist of my arm if it had not been for the ill treatment the police inflicted on my crew. First they ordered us to pull the ship off the beach and tie her up at a pier, which meant that we had to bail constantly; then, even though I was permitted to go ashore, the men were kept prisoners on board, with an armed guard stationed on the dock who constantly searched the ship to make sure nothing was being sold to the locals.

The customs officials were almost as bad, threatening arrogantly to keep us all in Tunisia until we had disposed of the ship to their satisfaction—that is, donated everything to the merchant marine, since I was also forbidden to abandon the ship there or take her out and scuttle her. News of our difficulties reached the international press, and the well-meaning articles that appeared, blasting the Tunisian government for harassing us, did not make the authorities any more cooperative. In the end these sympathetic articles were to be our indirect salvation, but we did not know it at the time and cursed the press for making matters worse.

By this time, more than a week had passed, and it looked as if we might spend the rest of our lives imprisoned on board that leaking wreck. Fed up with Tunisia, even more fed up with the ship, I decided to destroy her, valuable motor and all. If the Tunisian merchant marine wanted it, let them dredge it off the bottom of the sea. The crew pledged their support, with the exception of Jumbo, who had signed up for the voyage in order to visit his brother in America and, determined to reach there if he had to hitch a ride with an albatross, chose to go ashore rather than risk a lengthy stay in a Tunisian prison. The scheme was aided by official incompetence and the obligatory Tunisian siesta hour. I went ashore, wandered around town for a while, and returned, announcing to each guard that his superior had given me permission to move the ship to another berth. While they all scurried off to telephone their napping chiefs—harbormaster, head of customs, superintendent of police—for confirmation, we were able to cast off and slip out of port. On the way out we hailed a passing fishing boat and persuaded her crew to accompany us and take us back to shore in return for any equipment they could salvage.

The *Long Ship* was dead. All that was left was a skeleton, straining and creaking with the mere effort to reach open water again. She had failed us, but she still deserved a funeral in proper Viking style. We knew we could not reach the twelve-mile limit before the police discovered our trick and caught up with us, and we dropped anchor about two miles out. Avenging all the frustration and disappointment we felt at the failure of our grand plan to cross the Atlantic, we all took axes and sledgehammers and smashed everything in sight—motor, planks, decks, and mast—while the fishermen scrambled to grab anything of value they could find on board. Then we drenched her in diesel fuel and set her afire. Quickly we jumped aboard the fishing boat. We had already heard the siren of the police launch, and as the fire spread, the launch, along with other fishing smacks and three large freighters, sighted the blaze and made for us. The ship was burning too slowly, and fearing that our pursuers would arrive in time to douse the fire, Bill and Knut leapt back on board amid the flaming timbers, defying the risk of an explosion from the fuel tanks, and smashed more holes in her sides. By the time the police launch pulled alongside, only a small part of the bow remained above water, and in minutes there was nothing left of the *Long Ship* but bubbles and thick, tarry smoke.

During the trip back to port, escorted by the police boat and the harbormaster's launch, both filled with angry officials, we were sure that our jinxed expedition would end in a Tunisian prison. However, a fairy godmother in the person of the wife of a friend was waiting for us on shore. Her husband, a wealthy French industrialist with business interests scattered all over North Africa, had read the newspaper accounts of our difficulties and, unable to come himself, had sent his wife to help us out. From the president of Tunisia, a family friend, she had obtained a safe conduct for all of us. She handed it to the chief of police, who read it with a scowl and reluctantly ordered his men to release us. For Per and Bell this meant being let off the ground, where they had been pinned down after taking swings at two policemen. As her reward, our rescuer received enthusiastic embraces from five sweaty, none-too-clean sailors, and just as she thought the worst was over, from Jumbo, who arrived with two taxis. While the officials cursed us soundly, we piled into the taxis and sped off to Tunis and the freighter that was to take us to Marseilles.

The Columbus fans felt secure when they read the news that our *Long Ship* had gone down, but they haven't had the last laugh. No matter what the skeptics say, we know the Vikings made it a thousand years ago, and the Phoenicians more than a thousand years before that, and, with a sturdy ship, so would we.

Our Viking voyage had failed, but our determination had not. Toward the end of the expedition, especially during those frustrating ten days in Bizerte, I had decided that maybe I was not cut out to be a sailor and that I had better stick to diving for old shipwrecks instead of creating new ones. But that did not last for long. Even before we docked in Marseilles to scatter to our various destinations, we were making plans for another voyage. This time it would be on a Phoenician ship of the type built from 1000 to 500 B.C., and it would be built under my personal supervision, with every spike and every plank of the best material—and with a solid keel.

I was still faced with the same problem that had originally

obstructed the Phoenician voyage: no one knew exactly what Phoenician ships looked like, much less how they were constructed. But several months after the voyage a new discovery was made that changed the whole picture. My friend Elisha Linder, the Israeli marine archaeologist, wrote to tell me he and a team of divers had located several Phoenician shipwrecks off the Mediterranean coast of Israel, near Caesarea, and he believed that there were still others in the area. They planned to make a thorough search and to excavate the wrecks as soon as the funds and equipment could be assembled, and the evidence they hoped to recover would enable me to build an authentic and, I hoped, seaworthy replica.

7

Back to Columbus Again

fter the ill-fated voyage of the *Long Ship,* I returned to underwater archaeology again, this time taking on the most ambitious project of my career—excavation of part of the sunken city of Port Royal. During the second half of the seventeenth century, Port Royal, located near present-day Kingston on the island of Jamaica, was one of the richest cities in the Western Hemisphere. Known as the "wickedest city in the world," it was a den of pirates and privateers, as well as the main contraband center for European nations illegally trading with the Spanish colonies. On June 7, 1692, a devastating earthquake, followed by several tidal waves, toppled most of Port Royal's three thousand stone and brick buildings into the sea. More than five thousand people perished in the disaster. This site is the seventeenth-century equivalent of Pompeii and is the most important underwater archaeological site in this hemisphere.

When I arrived on the scene, plans were afoot to dredge the area and construct a deepwater port. The entire site was in danger of obliteration. I prevailed upon the Jamaican government to delay dredging, and my team and I worked feverishly on a portion of the extensive site for three years, seven days a week, with each diver averaging more than fifty hours underwater per week. Working on the sunken city was extremely challenging, because there was nil visibility and we perpetually risked being buried under tons of mud and the walls of fallen buildings. During the course of the project we excavated over two million artifacts—more than have been recovered from all other Western Hemisphere shipwreck sites combined.

Among the myriad artifacts we recovered were some of particular interest to me. It has long been known that the Maya used vessels of some type for coastal trade. However, there was no evidence that they made sorties across open water into the Caribbean. Underneath the layers of sediment that contained the materials associated with Port Royal, we recovered numerous intact ceramic pots that were definitely Mayan, as well as many objects of obsidian that could only have come from Mexico or Central America. This indicates that the Maya traveled at least as far as Jamaica, if not all over the vast Caribbean. Another interesting find was a large stone pedestal with a Latin inscription, which proved to be Roman. It probably had been picked up somewhere in Europe and served as ballast, which was then jettisoned at Port Royal. However, it might possibly have been brought over on a Roman vessel.

Fortunately, as a result of our successful excavation of the sunken city, the Jamaican government moved to prevent any future dredging operations on the site. We had covered only about 5 percent, and there is still a great deal more to be done on the sunken city. While my excavation at Port Royal was still underway, I once again got involved with Columbus.

Years earlier, I had met Dr. Harold Edgerton, the renowned physicist and electronics wizard, who died in 1990. Over the years we worked together many times in far-flung locations ranging from Brittany to the Bahamas and Brazil. Dr. Edgerton was at MIT for many years and invented the electronic strobe for photography, as well as many devices used in oceanography, including two types of bottom-penetrating sonar units called the "boomer" and "pinger."

He came to a lecture I gave in Boston about my work at Port Royal. I talked about the period in which I made a preliminary exploration with the metal probe and metal detector. After the lecture, Edgerton said I had done it the hard way. I should have used his boomer or pinger. I explained that I knew of his equipment, but that lack of money had kept me from using it. I had unsuccessfully searched for funds with which to rent one of his units so we could make a complete survey of the underwater city. With the primitive method I used at the time, I know I missed many objects hidden beneath the seafloor. Nor had I been able to plot those I did find as accurately as I should have. "Doc" Edgerton, whose enthusiasm and appetite for adventure were legendary, magnanimously offered to come to Port Royal at his own expense and make a complete sonar survey of the site, but it was nearly a year before I could get permission for him to do it from the Jamaican government.

Edgerton arrived in January 1968 with two assistants—Dr. Tsuneyoshi Uyemura, of the University of Tokyo; and Dr. Louis Wolfson, a medical specialist from Boston, who had worked with Edgerton on several marine archaeological sites in the Mediterranean. The first two days were lost because of problems with customs involving bringing his equipment into the island, this despite the fact that he was doing the survey for the government. Fortunately, one of the senior officials in the Jamaican Survey Department was an active member of the Jamaican Historical Society and was very interested in my work at Port Royal. He was able to provide a team of surveyors to assist us and even provided us with a small survey boat, the *Chart*. Ivan, my watchman, and another man worked from a skiff, setting and picking up the buoys we needed for the survey. For a week we worked from sunrise to sunset every day, completing the survey sooner than expected.

Running between buoys offshore and markers set up by

the surveyors ashore, we made more than three hundred runs at right angles to the shore, each spaced ten to fifteen feet apart and each between five hundred and eight hundred feet in length. The surveyors had the hardest job of all. In addition to plotting the position of each shore marker used on each run, they had to plot the position of each offshore buoy used, so we would know the precise course we had run and the area surveyed. Aboard ship, I ran the *Chart* while Doc and his assistants operated the boomer and recorded the exact time that each run took, which was essential to establishing the position of each object we located.

The runs gave us a graph showing the water depth, bottom contours, and geological information to a depth of about 150 feet below the seafloor and indicated the presence of solid objects that were either protruding above or hidden beneath the seafloor. They didn't identify the type of object, though. That would come later. By the time we completed the survey, we had located more than four thousand solid objects of considerable size. The easier part of the survey was over. All of the data obtained on the sonar graphs now had to be transferred and plotted on four large charts of the site, which was a ticklish undertaking, because we had made the runs at varying speeds to counteract winds and currents; in addition, the length of each run varied considerably.

On the afternoon that we finished the sonar survey, Doc said he still had several days left and asked if I wanted any other sonar surveys made on Jamaica. Immediately St. Ann's Bay, on the north coast of the island, came to mind. After I told Doc what I hoped to find there, he was raring to go.

I reminded him that in April 1502, Columbus sailed from Spain with four small caravels on his fourth and last voyage of discovery. It turned out to be his most dangerous and least profitable voyage. He spent almost a year in the Caribbean, cruising along the Central American coast but discovering little of importance. Meanwhile, teredo worms caused such damage to the hulls of his ships that two had to be scuttled on the coast of Panama. With his two remaining ships, *Capitana* and *San-*

tiago, in deplorable condition, he finally had to admit failure and start for home, heading first for Santo Domingo, where he hoped to repair the caravels before making the long ocean crossing. By the time he was between Cuba and Jamaica, not only was he suffering from an acute shortage of water and food, but both vessels were leaking so badly and were so near sinking that his son Ferdinand, who chronicled the voyage, wrote: "Day and night we never ceased working three pumps on each ship, and if any broke down, we had to supply its place by bailing with kettles while it was being patched up."

The vessels were so full of water that they made slow progress, and when the wind swung around to the east and blew against them, it was too much. On June 25, 1503, they were forced into St. Ann's Bay, which Columbus had visited on his second voyage and had named Santa Gloria. There both vessels ran aground, "about a bow shot distance from shore." There was fresh water nearby and an Indian village from which Columbus hoped to obtain food for 116 men. With only the fore and stern castles protruding above the water, there were insufficient accommodations aboard for everyone, so many of the men camped ashore.

Soon after his arrival, Columbus bartered for a dugout with the local Indians and sent it to Santo Domingo to notify the authorities there of his plight. But because the governor of Santo Domingo was his enemy, Columbus and his men spent a year and four days on the island before being rescued. Things went well at first. The Indians were glad to trade food for hawks' bells, glass beads, and other items, but after they had accumulated a substantial quantity of these items, they began bringing less and less food to the marooned Spaniards, and conditions deteriorated. When months passed and there was still no aid, several of the expedition's leaders enlisted a majority of the men in mounting a mutiny. They blamed Columbus for all of their problems and plotted to assassinate him. But Columbus, though bedridden with arthritis, was able to quell the mutiny.

By the time a rescue ship finally arrived on June 29, 1504,

and picked up the Spaniards, who left behind the two now worthless caravels, Columbus was a discouraged, heartbroken man, and he died not long after reaching Spain.

From the book written by Ferdinand, as well as other contemporary accounts, the location of the two wrecks is well known, unlike that of most Spanish ships lost in the West Indies. In 1940 an expedition sponsored by Harvard University and led by Admiral Samuel Eliot Morison, one of the world's leading authorities on Columbus, used this information in attempting to establish the location of the wrecks. Morison's Pulitzer Prize book *Admiral of the Ocean Seas* has a chart of St. Ann's Bay with the position where he thought the wrecks lay marked. We found both wrecks within a hundred feet of where he estimated they were.

One person who helped Morison when he visited St. Ann's Bay was a Jamaican plantation owner, Charles Cotter, who for half a century has been conducting land excavations at the site of New Seville, the Spaniards' first settlement on the island. New Seville was situated on the shore opposite where Columbus's ships were abandoned. For years Cotter dreamed of locating the site of the wrecks, but until I arrived, he had been unable to get anyone interested in diving to the site, including the Smithsonian Institution. He was overjoyed when he learned I was interested in searching for the wrecks.

I was especially interested in these two wrecks because, unless someone finds a Viking or Phoenician shipwreck in the New World someday, they are the oldest that will ever be found in this hemisphere. Although Columbus lost other ships during his four voyages, all were lost under conditions that make it highly unlikely that any trace of them will ever be found. A good example was the *Santa María,* which was wrecked on Columbus's first voyage off Cap-Haïtien, Haiti. The wreck was stripped of its timbers and other items and was used to build a fort ashore for the men from the ʼreck who were left behind when Columbus sailed for home.

On the other hand, the two wrecks in St. Ann's Bay were

so heavy because of the vast amount of water in them that most of the lower sections of their hulls were pushed deep into the silt and mud, thus preserving them from the ravages of the teredo worms. If I was right about this, the wrecks could furnish invaluable information, including data about the construction of ships of that period.

Although my primary work was at Port Royal, I considered these wrecks of even greater archaeological and historical importance and repeatedly asked permission to mount a small expedition to find them. Government officials showed no interest, especially when I told them there was no likelihood of finding treasure or valuable artifacts. I finally convinced Edward Seaga, my boss, who later became prime minister of Jamaica, to let me spend one day searching, and I went to the bay one Sunday in March 1966 with my wife and Stan and Louise Judge, English friends who worked in Jamaica.

About a month earlier, I had asked a friend to help me take some aerial photographs of the bay. I knew that even if Morison and Cotter were wrong in their location of the wrecks, there was only one small area in the entire bay that fit Ferdinand's description and where the water was shallow enough for the ships to have run aground. A series of charts of the bay, some dating as far back as the middle of the seventeenth century, showed that the coastline and shape of the bay hadn't changed over the centuries, except at the opposite end of the bay from where the wrecks lay, where a massive landslide had occurred during the 1692 earthquake.

As we were preparing to dive that Sunday, several residents stood by, warning us that this part of the bay was a mating ground for large sharks and that it would be suicide to dive there. Just the night before, they told us, a fisherman had caught a fourteen-foot tiger shark, and he was there on the beach skinning it when we arrived. But nothing would deter us.

With ten-foot metal probes we swam along in a line underwater, forcing the rods into the bottom sediment, trying to locate solid objects that might indicate a wreck. Using this method, by which we located several large, dead coral heads, we spent five hours before finally striking pay dirt. My wife motioned to me that she needed help. Her probe, which was about eight feet down in the sediment, was stuck in something solid. It took three of us to pull it out and six hours of excavating by hand and with buckets to reach the solid object, which turned out to be a wooden beam. When we relayed this information to Charles Cotter, who was pacing up and down the beach in anticipation, he said it was probably a piling from an old wharf that had sunk in a hurricane in the area over twenty years before.

I thought we should forget about it and continue searching, but my wife said I might be making a mistake, that it could be part of a wreck. She was right. Feeling around in the pitch-black hole in the sediment, I discovered treenails in the beam. Treenails—wooden pegs—were used to fasten ships together in the old days. The hole was large enough for only one person to squeeze into, and because of the danger of a cave-in, we began enlarging it. My wife, who was the smallest, got the honor of probing the bottom of the hole. When she came up with several pieces of obsidian, I was elated, sure we were on the verge of the most important marine archaeological discovery ever made in the Western Hemisphere.

Even though dark was fast approaching, I decided to see what I myself could find in the hole. Besides some more obsidian, I recovered several pieces of Spanish pottery that dated from the time of Columbus's shipwreck. Then, as I was about to call it a day, the dive came to an abrupt and dramatic end. Stan Judge, who was above me, grabbing the objects I handed up from the hole, was bitten on the neck by a two-foot-long sea snake, reportedly often deadly. In twenty years of diving, I had never seen one, nor did I know of any other diver who had seen one in the Caribbean. As luck would have it, we had just encountered the first one during what could be the most important dive of my life. Stan was in considerable pain, so we rushed him to a hospital, where he was given an injection of serum. By the next day, he had recovered and was laughing about the experience.

During the next month, while awaiting confirmation from various experts concerning the identity and date of the sherds and the origin of the obsidian, I petitioned Seaga for permission and money to do more work in St. Ann's Bay. When the confirmation came, I took it to him, sure he would be excited by the reports. But all he would promise was that sometime in the near future he would send me back up there. I was convinced that I had found one of Columbus's wrecks, or at least a section of it, and it was damned frustrating not to be able to do anything about it.

Doc Edgerton was excited—as I had been two years earlier when we first dived in St. Ann's Bay—at the prospect of discovering the *Capitana* and the *Santiago,* so the morning after finishing our work at Port Royal, we met with Seaga. He was quite satisfied with our sonar survey of the sunken city but not very happy when we asked for permission to search for Columbus's wrecks. Only when we promised to spend no more than a few days searching and not to undertake any excavation work did he reluctantly grant us permission.

I lined up a boat by telephone, and we drove to the coast the same day. There we found Charles Cotter, who thought I had given up my search for the wrecks. The next morning, we got off to a poor start. It was pouring rain, and the boat I had engaged was nowhere in sight. After several hours, however, the rain stopped, the sun came out, and the boat finally appeared.

Doc and his Japanese assistant had the boomer operating in a few minutes, and within an hour we had two positive sonar contacts. From the sonar graphs, we knew they were shipwrecks. More important, they were in the right area—that is, where the documents said they should be and where we had found the wooden beam, obsidian, and sherds—and were about the size we knew the wrecks should be. To be on the safe side, after marking both sites with buoys, we made a complete sonar survey of the other areas in the bay where the wrecks could possibly lie. When there were no contacts, I was certain we had located Columbus's wrecks.

We returned to Kingston the next day happier than if we had found a million dollars in gold. Doc and his two assistants caught a plane for the States, and I notified Seaga of our discoveries. Although he had shown no interest in the wrecks so far, he now became very excited and wanted to hold a press conference and announce the find. I talked him out of it, convincing him that more work had to be done before we were sure of the discovery. He instructed me to mount a major expedition to excavate the site. When I told Mrs. Hart, the secetary of the National Trust Commission, about our discovery and Seaga's instructions, she chuckled and said it was just like him to do that without making provision for financing the project. She promised to find the money somewhere.

Before we returned to the site of the shipwrecks, there was planning to be done; many factors had to be taken into consideration. First, since the wrecks were of such great historical importance, the best scientific methods of excavation would have to be used, and at the moment I had neither the best equipment and personnel nor the money to obtain them. Furthermore, every sliver of wood from the wrecks would be of immense importance. Without an adequate preservation laboratory I could go down in history as the man who destroyed the Columbus shipwrecks, because the wood, once exposed to the air, would disintegrate and be lost forever if not properly treated. Seaga came to understand that it would take a lot of money to excavate the wrecks properly and build a good preservation lab, and that we would have to seek funds from outside sources such as UNESCO or a foundation. I pointed out that before any foundation would give us the money, we would have to establish beyond any doubt that these were the Columbus wrecks, and to do this I would have to recover a substantial amount of material from the sites for identification and scientific dating.

For a project of such importance, I decided to enlist the help of experts in my field. They agreed that we should disturb the sites as little as possible. Rather than excavate a large hole to recover the sample material for testing—which would not only disturb the archaeological context of the wrecks but might expose the wooden timbers to the teredo worm, from which they had been protected in their muddy grave—we should use another method. Dr. George Bass of the University of Pennsylvania suggested that we use a coring device and found one that had been invented by Dr. John Saunders of Columbia University. Saunders offered to lend it to us and to send one of his assistants down to help us use it.

I expected daily to leave for St. Ann's Bay but did not get there at all in February. I was told that no money could be found to finance the project. After several weeks, I offered to pay all the expenses myself, but Seaga refused. Dr. Saunders's assistant, Bob Judd, had his bags packed and was ready to come at a moment's notice, and I had to phone him every few days to tell him to wait a bit longer. News of the find leaked to the press, and worldwide attention focused on the Columbus ships; but even this did not produce the funds for the job.

We were scheduled to leave for St. Ann's Bay on March 1, but a few days before that, I was told that we would need a special permit from the Beach Control Commission. I groaned, knowing all too well the snail-like pace at which the Jamaican bureaucracy functioned. I spent an entire day sitting in the office of the permanent secretary of the Beach Control Commission until he was so tired of my face that he finally issued the permit. He told me to come back the next day to pick it up. But when I did, it hadn't been signed yet, as I should have expected. In fact, it took three weeks just to get the chairman of the Beach Control Commission to sign it, despite the fact that I was actually working for the government; had I been requesting the permit as a private citizen, I might have had to wait months or even years for a signature.

I had invited Dr. Bass to come to Jamaica in early February and work with me on the site, but he had to decline the invitation. He never flies, and thought it would take too long to get there by ship. As it turned out, he could have sailed around the world and still had plenty of time to arrive before we finally got permission to start. He said he would send one of his assistants, Larry Joline, who, like Robert Judd, had to wait for word to come. Then, after nearly two months of waiting, when I phoned Joline and told him that we would be starting the next day, he had the flu!

On March 21 our permit from the Beach Control Commission was signed, and I made plans to leave immediately for St. Ann's Bay. I had requested a minimum of $500 to finance the project, which would last one to two weeks. I was given only $168. This called for a drastic change in plans. I couldn't put up five or six people in a hotel, feed them, pay for the rental of a boat, and meet the other expenses with that paltry amount.

Coral and Alphonso, my diving assistants, were on vacation. When I told Coral that we would be leaving the next day and asked him to find something to sleep in on the beach, at first he refused to go, saying: "In all my years of poverty, I've slept between white sheets and with a girl. I refuse to sleep on a beach and leave my girl behind in Kingston." It took a lot of convincing to get him to go, especially when I wouldn't let him bring his girl along. When seventeen-year-old Alphonso showed up, wearing a patch over his eye like a pirate, because of a bee sting, he gave me an even stranger reason for not wanting to go. "I don't like Jamaicans. I don't want to live around them, because they are bad people." Like so many other inhabitants of the modern town of Port Royal, he considered himself not a Jamaican but a Port Royalist, and the only other place on the island he had ever been to was Kingston.

We planned to set up camp on the beach near the wreck site. I borrowed three tents and some other camping equipment from the local chapter of the Boy Scouts. When Alphonso heard that Coral was refusing to sleep in a sleeping bag, he too refused. So from a junk pile on the grounds of the police training school at Port Royal I got six rusty beds and filthy mattresses, which Ivan covered with canvas before Coral and Alphonso could see the condition they were in.

We were scheduled to leave at seven the following morning, but the Public Works truck that was to carry us and our equipment—which included an aluminum skiff, since I couldn't afford to rent a boat—caused an unexpected delay. While we were loading the truck, the driver and his two assistants, all of whom appeared to be drunk, disappeared, and it took me two hours to get them out of the Buccaneers' Roost, the local rum shop. The driver careened over the narrow, dangerous mountain roads like a lunatic, managing to force a dozen or so vehicles off the road before we somehow reached St. Ann's Bay. My draftsman, Walter, jumped off about halfway there and hitchhiked the rest of the way.

We spent the rest of the day setting up camp and putting markers on the beach. Alphonso had been right about Jamaicans being bad people—or at least one of them. Hundreds of curious people from the nearby town came up the beach to see what we were doing, and by the end of the day two of my cameras and several tools had disappeared. Charles Cotter found someone to stay with us and serve as watchman, and the man took the job seriously. Every time someone approached the camp, he would fire a shotgun over his head. Not surprisingly, nothing else was stolen.

I was delighted when Bob Judd arrived and amazed when I found out what a voracious appetite he had. He was six feet eight and weighed 260 pounds. During his first meal he consumed seven huge sandwiches and four soft drinks. We named him the Jolly Green Giant. When we went into town everyone gazed at him as if he were the eighth wonder of the world.

We had planned to start making the cores first, but Judd's luggage, which included the coring device, had been lost and didn't turn up until late that night. So instead we took turns using the water jet to blow away a few feet of overburden around the area of the two wrecks. The next morning, all of the overburden was back where it had been before, because of strong winds (and therefore currents) during the night. My plan was to get core samples from the sites of both wrecks, but we were able to work on only one site before the money ran out. We started off using ropes—which were easily visible in those waters, where the average underwater visibility varied from ten to thirty feet, depending on how much we had stirred up the muddy bottom—and laid out a grid pattern on the bottom. We also circled the area with buoys that rose to the surface. With this system, we would know exactly where we had gotten each core.

The coring device was simple and ingenious. It consisted of a steel tube four inches in diameter, made up of four detachable sections, with an overall length of sixteen feet. After this had been forced into the seafloor as far as possible by hand, another small section of thicker tubing, which had a steel rod projecting upward for three feet, was placed on top. The tube was pounded into the sediment with a fifty-pound, two-handled hammer that rode up and down on the steel rod. It sounds easier than it was. Because divers are almost weightless underwater, trying to manipulate that hammer while hovering in the water was quite a feat.

Once most of the tube had been driven into the sediment, it was a bit easier. The diver could stand on the bottom and wrap his legs around the tube, gaining more leverage for working with the hammer. After all but about a foot of the tube had been driven into the bottom, the heavier section of tubing and the hammer were removed and a rubber plug was screwed into the top of the tube to maintain suction (otherwise everything would drop out of the tube as it was being pulled up). Then came the hardest part. It usually took an hour to pound the corer into the sediment, but sometimes twice that long to pull it out. For the first few days, Judd and I worked on the bottom, twisting and pulling on the tube, while Coral, Alphonso, and Walter worked from the skiff, pulling on the lines. The work became easier when Stan Judge brought one of my portable lifting bags from Port Royal. Attached to the top of the tube

Aerial view of one of the many sunken buildings located off northern Andros Island in the Bahamas.

Marx with diving assistant Louise Judge examining some of the ceramic sherds recovered from one of the Columbus shipwrecks in St. Ann's Bay, Jamaica.

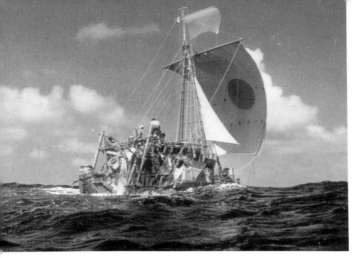

Thor Heyerdahl's Ra II, a replica of an Egyptian craft, which he attempted to sail across the Atlantic.
PHOTO: FOUL ANCHOR ARCHIVES.

Thor Heyerdahl's raft Kon Tiki, which he sailed across the Pacific.
PHOTO: FOUL ANCHOR ARCHIVES.

Thor Heyerdahl sitting on a section of his papyrus craft Ra I.

The Niña II, which Marx sailed across the Atlantic in 1962.

Eight of the nine members of the crew of the Niña II after reaching San Salvador Island, Bahamas, in 1962. Marx is third from left.

One of the crew of the Niña II,
Father Antonio Sagaseta,
readying a cannon for firing.

Marx diving in a Yucatán
cenote (sinkhole) and
recovering a pre-Columbian
Mayan jar. Other person is
archaeologist Dr. Wylie Andrews.

Marx with his wife, Jenifer,
recovering a Mayan skull and
clay figurine from a cenote in
Yucatán in 1971.

The replica Viking ship Alfie *being used in the Hollywood movie* Alfred the Great.

The replica Viking ship Long Ship *being used in the film* The Long Ships *in* Yugoslavia.

Marx aboard the Alfie studying the best method to sail her.

*Marx waving to writer-
adventurer Milt Machlin,
during the test runs of
the Alfie.*

*The original tenth-century
Viking Gokstad ship in the Oslo
Viking Museum.*

The Long Ship *under sail in the Mediterranean.*

The *burning of the* Long Ship *off Bizerte, Tunisia, in* 1969.

Archaeologist examining a stone statue, found in Yucatán in 1923, believed to be a sphinx of pre-Columbian manufacture. A Mayan ruin lies buried in the background.

Typical Mayan ruin in the jungles of Yucatán, one of hundreds discovered by Marx in the 1950s.

This bronze axhead, made in the western Mediterranean, probably in present-day Israel, about 1000 B.C., was found on a Mayan archaeological site on Cozumel.

In 1957 a French archaeologist claimed to have found this carving of a non–New World sailing ship, most likely of Oriental origin, on the walls of an Inca ruin in Peru. He died in an automobile accident soon afterward, and the ruin has not been rediscovered.

Piece of sandstone, nine inches square, found at Fort Benning, Georgia. The strange script that covers it shows similarities to Minoan writing dating back to 1000–2000 B.C.
PHOTO: LAWRENCE SMITH.

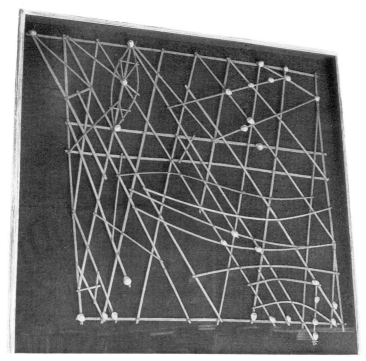

Polynesian stick chart. The shells are islands and the curved bamboo rods indicate wave patterns as they relate to the islands. In the trade winds, the effects of land can be seen more than twenty miles away.

Stone lintel of a sixteenth-century church in Tihosuco, Yucatán, with Phoenician inscriptions on it.

Marx in front of door of ruined church in Tihosuco, Yucatán; lintel above door has a Phoenician inscription.

Roman stone pedestal found in Kingston Bay, Jamaica.

Dr. Cyrus Gordon inspects the "Bat Creek Stone." Inscription in ancient Canaanite reads "Promised Land of the Israelites." Found in 1885 at Bat Creek, Tennessee.

Chinese stone anchor found off
San Francisco, of pre-
Columbian origin.

Bronze Roman fibula, for
fastening garments, found on
the Roman shipwreck site in the
Bay of Guanabara.

Greek war galley on a silver coin of the third century B.C.

Phoenician merchant ship of the fifth century B.C. engraved on a stone.

Model of a Phoenician ship of about the thirteenth century B.C.
MODEL FROM THE COLLECTION OF THE COMMERCIAL MUSEUM,
PHILADELPHIA, PENNSYLVANIA.

and filled with air, it exerted additional pulling force, which helped considerably.

Once the tube was extracted, another plug was placed on its bottom, and we swam it ashore atop an inner tube. On the beach both plugs were pulled out and the contents of the tube were carefully shaken out onto a piece of canvas. Then we gingerly separated the sediment, searching for objects from the wreck. Those we found were placed in water inside plastic containers, with tags denoting the location and stratigraphical depth we found them at. The first day, we took seven cores. Five cores produced a number of pieces of wood, several of which were two to three inches thick. They had been cut from larger pieces of wood by the sharp edge of the tube bottom. The two other cores we had started had struck solid objects at a depth of four feet and couldn't penetrate any farther. Using the water jet, we found ballast rock to the solid objects that had stopped the corer.

That night we dined on fried fish speared during the day, as well as beans and rice, delicious and nourishing—and repeated every day. After sunset the mosquitoes and sand fleas were so thick that we had to sleep with our rubber diving suits on to keep from being devoured. During the day, the local people had worked on Alphonso and Coral, scaring them with tales of man-eating sharks in the bay. Twice during the night, Alphonso woke us up, screaming from shark nightmares. It didn't help matters when early the next morning we sighted a large tiger shark hovering near the site. Both Alphonso and Coral shot out of the water, and they refused to dive again. From then on, Judd and I had to dive alone, except for the few times when my wife and Stan Judge were there to lend a hand.

The next day we got eight good cores. In addition to more pieces of wood (which, I later learned, were oak and pine), we found fragments of animal bones (pig and chicken), pieces of charcoal, a striking flint (either for a weapon or to start a fire with), and a small coral-encrusted nail. During the day, several more inquisitive sharks appeared, and one suddenly began butting me with its snout while I was trying to measure the distance between the last core hole and the one we were then making. I smashed him on the head with a crowbar, and he took off.

Our problems weren't confined to the water, however. Before we had arrived, a rumor had started that we were after a large quantity of gold on the wrecks. The mayor of the town and four police officers appeared that afternoon and tried to arrest us—until I produced the permit from the Beach Control Commission and the letters from Seaga. When they realized their mistake and saw that they were losing face with the townspeople who had come with them, they decided instead to arrest Coral and Alphonso, who were brazenly smoking ganja (marijuana) cigarettes right in front of the mayor and policemen. I had to talk fast to keep them out of jail. It was really strange that both Coral and Alphonso considered the Jamaicans who lived on the northern coast to be foreigners and would have nothing to do with them. On several evenings when they went into town for a few beers, they returned with cuts and bruises from scrapping with the locals.

On the third day we struck solid objects at a depth of about nine feet, and three times forced our way through them. We came up with samples of ballast rock that were different from those we had found near the surface. In addition to more wood, bone, and charcoal, we found several coral-encrusted tacks, a few ceramic sherds, a fragment of green glass, and a black bean of the kind called *frijole* in Spain. Although we lost time whenever we had to cut our way through ballast rock (because it entailed resharpening the cutting edge at the bottom of the tube), we managed to get nine good cores this day.

During the next four days we got thirty-four additional cores, each of which yielded wood and other material. We now had enough samples to identify and date the wreck. I didn't want to disturb the wreck anymore, so we stopped using the coring device. Nearly all of the material we had recovered came from a depth of eight to ten feet beneath the seafloor. Only a few pieces of wood were from farther down, and these may have been pushed deeper into the sediment by the coring tube before it cut through them. Judd came up with a system for defining the limits of the wreck that was an improvement on my system of using a metal rod as a probe. We attached one of the hoses from aquanaut unit to a twenty-foot piece of one-inch galvanized water pipe, and it worked beautifully. The air rushing down the pipe enabled the pipe to go down rapidly and without much force, and it was easy to extract When solid objects were encountered, we turned off the air. Tapping the object, we could tell whether it was wood or ballast rock both by feel and from the sound.

Before heading back to Kingston, we spent an additional day diving at the site. All the evidence indicated that the wreck lay at a stratigraphical depth of eight to ten feet below the sea floor, but I was curious about the ballast rock we had found at a depth of only four feet in a small part of the site. My curiosity was satisfied by blowing away a large area of mud covering the rock. I was able to date the artifacts we found among them, including clay pipestems and bottle fragments, as mid-seventeenth century. The absence of wood and ship's fittings indicated that a ship had probably been anchored here and, before taking on a heavy cargo of sugar, rum, or molasses, had jettisoned some of the ship's ballast overboard, a common practice at the time.

An amusing incident occurred during our last evening there. Judd announced that he had had his fill of fish, rice, and beans and offered to take everyone out for a good meal. Walter and the two divers had dates with local girls, so Judd and I went alone. Barefoot and attired in dirty shorts and jerseys, we chose one of the fanciest restaurants on the island, one in nearby Ocho Rios. When the headwaiter refused to seat us because we didn't have jackets and ties, we asked to see the manager, who apologized after we explained our situation and produced two ties and dinner jackets. We brought all talk to a stop as we walked into the packed dining room. The dinner jackets hung lower than the shorts; it looked as though we had forgotten to put our pants on. Several tourists laughed so hard that we fled for the exit, with stomachs growling, especially when we saw the fantastic food being served. We then went to the Playboy Club, where things were a bit more informal. The club was serving a smorgasbord, which we attacked voraciously. Judd went through eleven heaping plates of food before even tackling the dessert.

We left for Kingston the next morning. At one point Judd yelled to the driver to stop and leaped from the cab of the truck. His shorts were on fire. He had pushed the seat down so that it touched the battery terminals underneath, and the seat had caught fire. After applying first aid, we continued on our way.

The waiting game that now began took longer than expected. The material we had recovered had to be sent to experts in England, Spain, and the United States, a process that took almost three months. Most of the ballast rock had come from Central America, though a little of it was from Spain. This didn't surprise me. I knew Columbus had careened his vessels several times during his voyage along the coast of Central America. According to many documents written by persons of various nationalities who had sailed aboard Spanish ships, the Spaniards were very messy and cared little about sanitation. Rather than throw trash overboard, they frequently tossed it (and sometimes even human waste) into the hold among the ballast. Consequently, when Spanish ships were careened, the old fouled ballast was replaced with new.

According to experts at the Corning Glass Museum, the fragment of green glass had been made in Venice and was probably from an hourglass; it definitely dated from the time of Columbus. I knew that the pottery we had found was Spanish, which was confirmed by experts, but it was of a type commonly in use for several centuries and therefore wasn't easy to date. A new method called thermoluminescence, for dating ceramic and other material fired in a kiln, had recently been developed, but it wasn't as helpful as we had hoped. I sent two sherds to the Museum of Applied Science Center for Archaeology at the University of Pennsylvania, which dated the pieces at circa 1637 A.D., plus or minus 150 years. Sherds sent to Oxford University in England were dated at 1475 A.D., plus or minus a century. Both the striking flint and the black bean were thought to have come from Spain.

The fragments of wood were identified as having come from Spain, but the date I received for the first piece of wood that had been dated by the carbon-14 process presented a prob- lem. It was said to be twelve hundred years old, give or take a hundred years. I figured that it might have been a piece of firewood that crewmen found on land, which would furnish a reason for its age. So I sent several more pieces for carbon-14 dating and received the same date. Was there a Viking ship lying beneath the Columbus wreck? I knew carbon-14 dating produced more accurate results for organic material dating in the thousands rather than hundreds of years, but even so, the date shouldn't be off that much. The mystery was solved when I consulted some dendrologists (tree experts). It isn't unusual for an oak tree to reach the age of a thousand years or more, so it was conceivable that an oak tree seven hundred years old had been cut down and used in building one of the ships lost in St. Ann's Bay.

As a final test of the authenticity of our discovery, I sub- mitted the findings to Samuel Eliot Morison and three other experts on Columbus in Spain and Colombia. All of them were convinced that we had found one of Columbus' wrecks. Ironi- cally, while writing this book I received a newspaper clipping reporting that archaeologists from the Institute of Nautical Ar- chaeology at Texas A&M University had "discovered" the two Columbus ships in St. Ann's Bay, Jamaica. Apparently, they forgot about our discovery back in 1968.

8

The Voyage of the Alfie

After completing my projects in Jamaica I moved to Florida to direct salvage operations in Florida and the Bahamas for the Real Eight Corporation. Real Eight was primarily involved in salvaging the galleons of the 1715 Spanish treasure fleet that were lost in a hurricane off the coast of Florida between Cape Canaveral and Vero Beach. It was fascinating, exciting work, but I still couldn't shake my passion for tracking down the great white gods. I devoted all my discretionary time to pre-Columbian contact. The idea of constructing an accurate Phoenician ship and making an authentic ocean crossing in her was always on my mind. I had plenty of time to think about it during the hundred-mile round trip I made each day to get to Fort Pierce, where our salvage vessels were tied up, and I even thought about it when I was underwater.

By this time the Viking ships discovered in Roskilde Fjord, Denmark, had been completely excavated. I made several trips to consult with the archaeologists and conservationists working on the project, but it would take many more years before they would complete the actual reconstruction of the hulks and be able to provide me with plans for constructing a decked-over Norse ship.

I also made three trips to Israel to dive and inspect the findings of the team working under Dr. Elisha Linder on two Phoenician shipwrecks found off Caesarea, but my hopes of finding structural remains were dashed. Like most classical-period Mediterranean shipwreck sites, they yielded an abundance of amphorae and other interesting artifacts but no wooden remains of any kind.

Back in 1961 I had discovered the remains of three Phoenician shipwrecks dating from the eighth to sixth century B.C. in the cove of La Caleta in Cádiz Bay. These had been protected in the anaerobic sediments; the mud coating sealed off the ship remains from oxygen. Without oxygen, there are no sea worms and microorganisms to consume the ship's timbers. Usually these conditions are only encountered in the deep ocean basin or in ports and bays with muddy sediment and fresh water entering these areas from rivers. At La Caleta I had determined from test holes on all three sites that a great amount of the ships' wooden remains still existed and were well preserved, and knew that these shipwrecks could provide most of the data I needed to build an authentic replica of a Phoenician ship.

Spain has become somewhat of a second home to me. I spend a month or more there every year doing archival research and soliciting permission to carry on underwater excavations in Cádiz Bay. My wife, Jenifer, refers to these trips as "Don Quixote chasing after windmills," because I never seem to make progress in obtaining the permission, but I am ever hopeful. This quest is still going on today: in 1991 I made three trips to Spain, all in vain.

After the debacle of the *Long Ship* I intensified my activities in Spain, hoping to be able to excavate one or more of those Phoenician shipwrecks. I kept their existence and locations secret at first. Over the years it became clear that Spain was adamant that none of its undersea patrimony ever leave the country. I was only interested in collecting data on Phoenician ship construction so I could build a replica. I reasoned that if I offered to excavate the Phoenician wrecks for the government, turning over everything I found, the government would be delighted. I submitted a new proposal in which I would even finance the project. I hadn't mentioned my intention of wanting to build and sail a replica Phoenician shipwreck, but the bureaucrats were able to read between the lines. Word leaked to the press, and I was crucified once again. One journalist wrote: "Marx is up to his old tricks. Once again he wants to defame the feats of Columbus and has the nerve to expect Spain to contribute to his folly!"

Not surprisingly, my application was refused. Sadly, since that time two of the three sites have been destroyed by construction of a pier; but as recently as 1990 I was able to establish that one remains intact. Maybe someday my dream will come true and I will be able to excavate my Phoenician shipwreck in La Caleta. Through persistent lobbying and the personal intercession of King Juan Carlos, I have at least been able to persuade the Spaniards to protect what remains in La Caleta. No dredging, landfill, or construction is now permitted in the area, which amounts to 15 percent of the original underwater museum of ancient ships.

In 1968, Metro-Goldwyn-Mayer had two replicas of the Gokstad ship built in Denmark by the same firm that had built the three for Columbia's Viking film. The MGM replicas were for the movie *Alfred the Great,* which was being filmed in Ireland. I worked on the movie for several months as a technical consultant on the scenes involving the ships. Part of the film was made around Galway Bay, where I was astonished to find a large bronze statue of Columbus pointing to the west, with an inscription which read: "From Galway Bay Columbus set sail on his first voyage of discovering America." Someone was apparently drinking too much Irish whiskey when the monument was erected. It was removed several years ago at the request of the Spanish government.

MGM sold me one of the ships for a dollar. There were two conditions: I would have to sail the northern route, and I would have to initiate the voyage around the time the movie was released—which proved to be at a time of the year when the North Atlantic was at its worst. The vessel I had chosen did, at least, have a solid keel, unlike my *Long Ship*. However, she was just as poorly fastened together. I wanted to refasten her using wooden treenails and bronze spikes before sailing for America, but I had neither the time nor the funds for such a costly modification. I had already lost my heart to the sleek vessel. She was so beautiful under sail that I knew I would attempt to reach America in her no matter what.

Before MGM hit me with those special conditions, my original plan had been to duplicate a Phoenician voyage by sailing down to Lisbon, then over the Canaries, and, more or less following in the wake of *Niña II,* on to Yucatán. While I was working on the movie, a fellow underwater archaeologist, Peter Throckmorton, paid me a visit. Peter, who had worked on classical-period shipwrecks for years off Greece and Turkey, was very knowledgeable about early ship construction and sailing capabilities. He gave me a great deal of advice on sailing my vessel. He wanted to come along on the voyage but was committed to excavating a recently discovered Phoenician shipwreck off Turkey. At the time he believed that the wreck would produce wooden remains so that he could provide the data I needed to construct a Phoenician ship replica. Unfortunately, the site yielded too little wood to be of any help in reconstructing the original hull.

Dozens of other historians and archaeologists appeared on the scene to inspect my ship and give advice. They were in agreement with Throckmorton that sailing the northern route would provide a great deal more historical information and that even though this was not the type of vessel most likely used by the Norsemen on ocean voyages, by sailing such a vessel, which was less seaworthy than a decked-over ship, I would prove beyond any doubt that the Vikings could have reached the New World. I reminded them all that Helge Ingstad and his wife had already proved this point and also that twentieth-century climatic conditions in the North Atlantic were harsher than when the Norsemen were making their voyages. They all assured me that no matter what the outcome of the voyage, I would shed more light on the manner in which these ships were sailed and certainly put the Norsemen in the limelight that they deserved. Two scientists from the U.S. Office of Navel Research asked to come along to collect marine specimens and to study the effect of such a hostile environment on the crew. So the die was cast—I would take the northern route.

My plan was to pick up the ship in Ireland and take a shakedown cruise to Bergen, Norway, where the voyage would officially start. At Bergen we would take on Viking-period supplies and provisions. The only nonauthentic items would be photographic gear and the lifesaving equipment MGM insisted on. I spent over fifty hours studying the skies of the North Atlantic in a planetarium in the States and was confident we could sail by the same methods as the Norsemen. From Bergen, using only the sun, moon, and stars as our guide, we would sail for America, with stops at the Faeroe Islands, Iceland, Greenland, Labrador, and Newfoundland (where we would visit the Norse ruins).

Meteorological experts in Europe and the United States told me that the only feasible time to attempt the voyage was between early February and the middle of May, a period that has some of the coldest weather of the year. That was the only time when we would have easterly winds to carry us across the Atlantic. Also, after May, the glaciers begin to break up, making the seas in those areas unnavigable because of icebergs and pack ice. Mindful of the *Titanic*'s fatal encounter with an iceberg, I rushed preparations, planning to sail from Bergen no later than mid-February.

At the end of January, just a few days before I was to fly to Ireland to pick up the ship, which I had named *Alfie,* and take her to Bergen, the first of many problems arose. According to its lawyers in London, MGM couldn't provide me with ownership papers to the ship unless it was first registered. Registering a ship is normally an easy procedure, but registering a replica of a Viking ship is quite another matter; it had never been done. The lawyers in London couldn't seem to make any headway with the British Admiralty. Days of impatient waiting slid into slow weeks and then months. Frustration turned into anxiety as I grew increasingly desperate, aware that every day of waiting reduced *Alfie*'s chances of getting across the Atlantic before the winds changed. Finally, in mid–April, I had had it. I notified MGM that I was heading for Ireland and would sail without the ship's being registered and without ownership papers. Reluctantly, MGM gave me a bill of sale after first clearing itself of any legal connections with the ship.

By this time, I had received nearly two thousand applications from volunteers all over the world. I selected what seemed to be a competent crew with capable alternates. I was pleased that Bill Holmes, the only member of my previous Viking crew I could track down, signed on again despite the harrowing voyage of the *Long Ship*. However, in the four weeks before we sailed the crew began to unravel. Men canceled for various reasons. Some decided on thinking it over that they couldn't give up smoking, or couldn't face the prospect of so much cold, wet weather, and rough seas. Others were dissuaded by wives or girlfriends. Ironically, at the last minute four men who had requested to make the crossing—two scientists from the Smithsonian and the two from the Office of Naval Research—canceled. Just four hours before we left New York, three others deserted. I replaced one with a German photographer named Dietrich Truebe who claimed to be an expert seaman. Another last-minute volunteer was a ninety-five-pound Greenwich Village hippie, ten pounds of whose weight was hair. However, before sailing he said he wanted to consult his astrologer, Madam Bird Feather, and called shortly afterward, saying she felt vibrations of disaster; so he withdrew.

When I finally flew from New York, I had a crew of only

three with me: the German photographer; George Belcher, a strange, rather intense chap who had just returned from a tour of duty in Vietnam; and my tried and true friend Neal Watson, who was worth three men. I had met Neal when he broke the world's record for the deepest dive on compressed air. In addition to being an experienced diver, he was a karate expert and pilot. At the time he was running a detective agency in the Bahamas. In London we were joined by Bill Holmes, who looked perfect for the role; he had just finished playing Saint Paul in a British movie and had an enormous beard and hair down to his shoulders.

I got the shock of my life when we arrived at Lake Athlone in Ireland, where I had left the ship the previous summer. I had made arrangements for a shipwright to change the fastenings and make other modifications and repairs. I had checked with him periodically and been assured work was progressing. I found to my dismay that except for applying a bit of caulking here and there, he had done nothing. Instead of my paying his outrageous bill of almost $2,000, Neal found the shipwright in the local pub and broke a bottle of whiskey over his head— which precipitated a hasty departure on our part.

I had heard that the ice was breaking up around Greenland much earlier than expected. As a consequence we would have to rush to Bergen or the voyage would be impossible that year. The nearest seaport was Limerick, about seventy miles down the Shannon River. There I hoped to find a shipyard in which to make the necessary repairs. Because of rain that had been falling for weeks, we had an exciting and dangerous ride down the river. We passed through one set of rapids at a breathtaking speed of over twenty knots without sail up or the use of two outboard engines I had had mounted on the stern in case we needed help getting down the river. Dietrich Truebe decided, on the basis of this preliminary phase of the voyage, that it was too hair-raising for his taste, and he deserted when we reached Limerick.

Needing more crew just to get to Bergen, I advertised for

volunteers in the major Irish newspapers, but none of the men who responded were suitable. Then a German freighter put into port, and her first officer, Otto Washchkau, fell in love with *Alfie*. So I signed him on as first mate.

Limerick was once a great seaport and was even used by the Vikings. Today, however, there is very little shipping, and I couldn't find a single shipwright. We had no choice but to head for Bergen with the ship as she was. Just trying to leave, however, took another two weeks. First we were told by the harbormaster that because the ship wasn't "exactly what one could call a seaworthy craft," we would have wait while he consulted the Admiralty in London. After a long delay, the Admiralty gave us permission, provided the ship and crew were adequately insured. I took a plane to Lloyd's of London. No soap. Nobody in his right mind would insure us. Through a close friend, I managed to get a forged set of insurance papers, and with them I hurried back to Limerick. Then I learned that the lord mayor had laid on a celebration in honor of our departure. The celebration consumed three precious days and left us with Gaelic hangovers that lasted for several more days.

The festivities were launched with a grand medieval banquet in an old castle, during which my crew managed to seduce most of the delectable serving wenches. When this feast ended around sunrise the next morning, we were whisked off to the cathedral for a High Mass performed by the archbishop, who threw another party after the Mass. Somewhere along the line, Neal and Bill kidnapped three Pan Am stewardesses who had a day's layover in Ireland. Naturally, they missed their plane. The stewardesses threatened to file charges against Neal and Bill, but were soon cajoled into joining the festivities. On the morning we were to sail, the archbishop blessed the ship, with most of the town present, and we christened her with a bottle of tequila and one of Irish whiskey. As we were about to leave, a truck appeared, with the hospitable and generous lord mayor shouting at the top of his lungs. As a present from the port of Limerick, "to get ye safely to America," as he put it, they gave us a hundred gallons of mead (a very potent liquor, made from fermented honey, that the Vikings drank), twenty cases of Irish whiskey, and twenty-five cases of Irish stew in tins.

With expressions of thanks for Limerick's hospitality, we rode the outgoing tide to the sea—and immediately encountered problems. Leaks sprang all over the place. We had one hell of a time patching them. Between our throbbing hangovers and the work at hand, no one slept that first night.

For the next three days, despite contrary winds, rough seas, and a Russian trawler that almost ran *Alfie* down, we made good time. Then the really harrowing events began. Off the northern tip of Scotland we ran into a gale. With only the storm sail up, we were forced to run before it for three days until it finally abated and we found ourselves close to Iceland. Two days later we were off northern Scotland again and were once again struck by a gale. This tempest lasted for eight days and nearly carried us all the way to America. We were west of Iceland when it dissipated. If I had known what the future held, we would definitely have kept on that heading. It was a nightmare. No sooner had we sighted Scotland again than another gale caught us, and back to Iceland we went, where we almost wrecked off the east coast.

By the time we reached what I thought was Scotland again, we had been through hell. Fortunately *Alfie* held together better than the *Long Ship* had. We were too busy fighting the elements to worry about plugging leaks. By now, we had lost twenty-six days being blown back and forth between Scotland and Iceland, and the highest temperature we had encountered was 34 degrees Fahrenheit; most of the time, it was closer to 10 or 15 degrees. Only large doses of the mead (which we blessed the people of Limerick for) kept us from freezing to death in the open vessel. Once, when I tried to open a can of Irish stew with a can opener, the skin on my hand came off and stuck to the can opener.

Things weren't much better when we reached Scotland for the fourth time. Visibility was down to less than a mile when we finally sighted land. Both bitter wind and dark seas were blowing us onto a rocky coast that seemed as barren as the moon. We tried dropping anchor, but the water was too deep even when we were only a few hundred yards from shore. In desperation we cranked the two outboards we had used to get down the river, never really expecting them to start. They saved the ship—and probably our lives, as well.

Finding a bit of sea room, we went down the coast for several miles until we sighted a small partially protected cove and dropped anchor. It was just in the nick of time; we had run out of gasoline for the outboards. The crew were a sorry sight. Everything was soaked, and the ship was a shambles. Neal had fallen off the mast top and sprained his ankle, I had sprained my arm pulling on the halyard trying to raise the sail, and Bill had slipped on some ice and broken his leg. Just a few hundred yards away was the shore, but we didn't have a skiff. We were too exhausted to row *Alfie,* and the freezing water ruled out any thought of swimming ashore.

After a brief perusal as we entered the cove, the villagers, who lived in the twenty-odd cottages encircling it, paid us not the slightest attention. It was as though Viking ships came to that tiny, isolated cove every day. We did everything we could think of to attract their attention. Nothing. For three days we lay in that cove, not even knowing exactly where we were. It was a bizarre, exasperating experience.

With only a Boy Scout compass and a Michelin road map of the British Isles, I couldn't figure our location. I did know that if we headed north and then east, we would eventually round Scotland and could cut across to Norway. We departed from that strange village, and after a three-day sail against contrary winds we were still heading north off the western coast of Scotland when we sighted what turned out to be the port of Tobermory.

After getting everyone patched up by the local doctor, I decided to take a shortcut to Norway—through the Caledonia Canal, which cuts across northern Scotland. Compared to what we had been through recently, it was a calm but memorable trip. It took a day to reach Fort George, a small village on the western end of Loch Ness, where we anchored for the night. Early the next morning we started across the twenty-three-mile-long lake, using the outboard motors (we had to lower our mast to pass under many of the bridges over the canal). A thick blanket of fog lay about ten feet above the surface of the lake. To see where we were going, one of us would periodically crawl onto one of the dragon figureheads for a sighting. When we reached Inverness on the other side of Loch Ness, there was quite a bit of excitement in the town. An unusual number of sightings of the Loch Ness monster had been reported that day, but what they had seen, of course, were our Viking figureheads sticking up above the fog layer.

After a brief stay in port to have the mast stepped and minor repairs made, we started across for Bergen in reasonable weather. Twenty hours later, as we neared the Norwegian coast, gale-force winds struck from the north. We had to run before it with only a small storm sail up, and by the time it abated three days later, we had been blown so far south that we were off England. We entered Scarborough, which had been a Roman and later a Viking seaport. While there, I learned of the voyage Thor Heyerdahl planned to make in his raft, *Ra*.

This development, coupled with advice from the weather experts that it was too late in the season to attempt the northern route, prompted us to head for Lisbon and take the southern crossing. We hoped to catch up with and pass the *Ra*. Twelve hours after leaving Scarborough, we were hit by another gale. *Alfie* developed several leaks so serious that we had to put in to another port, running the ship aground to keep her from sinking. When the tide went out and she was high and dry, we found that several planks near the keel had worked loose. We repaired them, using brass spikes.

Things looked good for the next two days as we made fair progress down the coast. Then another of what seemed like an inexhaustible series of gales caught us, and the situation became critical. Running with a storm sail, we were fighting huge cross seas; sometimes two would strike at the same time from different directions. *Alfie* was twisting so violently that the gunwales began heaving in and out, as they had on her predecessor. She was acting like a drunken snake, making very strange noises. The iron nails holding the planking to the ribs flew out faster than we could replace them. At one point we heard a sharp snap. Two ribs below the waterline had broken in half. While we were trying to cope with this, loud and unfamiliar noises assaulted our freezing ears, and we discovered that whole planks above the waterline on both sides of the ship had worked loose from the ribs as much as six inches. We were, quite literally, falling apart. We quickly passed lines under the keel and all the way around the hull of the ship—holding her together like a soggy Christmas package. To prevent further strain on the hull, I lowered the storm sail, and we threw out a makeshift sea anchor. Then we rode out the storm, which subsided about twelve hours later.

By the time we crawled into the port of Lowestoft, I had reached the conclusion that it was plain suicide to go back out on the high seas with the ship in that condition. We had *Alfie* hauled out of the water, and I hired a bunch of shipwrights to refasten the ship completely with brass spikes. I also had several of the planks and the two ribs replaced, as well as the mainsail, which had been torn to shreds in the last storm. As an added safety precaution, I even bought an emergency radio and a rubber life raft.

After we left Lowestoft, I was sure our luck would change. At first it looked as though the fates were smiling on us. A lovely, stiff twenty-knot breeze enabled us to average twelve knots sailing to Dover. George Belcher deserted there when I sent him ashore to purchase some food, but I didn't have time to try to find a replacement. From the newspapers, I knew that *Ra* had already started across the Atlantic. Leaving Dover for the crossing to France, we again had a tail wind and for the first twelve hours made remarkable time. Then, when we were within sight of Cherbourg, another gale struck. Unfortunately, but in keeping with our rotten luck, the wind came from the south and we were blown back across the English Channel. We had to put into a small fishing port on the Isle of Wight. Two days later, in midchannel, we had a repeat scenario, this time ending up in Weymouth. On our third attempt, after waiting a week for reasonable weather, we made it across and put in to St. Peter Port on the Isle of Guernsey, near the French coast. Guernsey is one of the Channel Islands, owned by Great Britain.

We landed to find most of the townspeople gathered at the wharf. Neal addressed the crowd: "We Vikings have come to rape, pillage, and plunder." As it turned out, he meant it. Early the next morning we were given the option of leaving port immediately or facing thirty days in jail for disturbing the peace and numerous other misdemeanors. We had gotten in three brawls in various pubs the night before, and four men who had the misfortune to tangle with Neal ended up in the hospital. A police launch towed us out of port and left us nursing monumental hangovers and facing thirty-to-thirty-five-knot winds and high seas. Lisbon was more than a thousand miles away, and on the way there, we would have 350 miles of open sea, crossing the Bay of Biscay. I put it to a vote, and everyone agreed that we should go for bust—reach Lisbon or sink trying. I threw my Boy Scout compass and Michelin road map of Europe overboard; we would sail or sink as the Vikings had, without modern aids.

Three and a half days later, we were off Lisbon in record time. We had averaged almost twelve knots, a feat few racing yachts can lay claim to today. It was downhill all the way, or rather more like riding a surfboard, thanks to tail winds of twenty-five to thirty-five knots. At times as we were flying down a huge sea, it seemed that only the keel was touching the water. It was incredibly thrilling, but none of us slept more than a few minutes at a time. We were aware of being in constant danger. One miscalculation on the steerboard and we could easily capsize. I have always loved sailing, but for sheer thrills, nothing has ever equaled this.

We received a great reception from the Portuguese when we entered the port of Lisbon. In fact, it was a little too great. As we were dropping anchor, a tugboat full of the press accidentally rammed us, cracking the sternpost and putting a large hole in the hull at the waterline.

There was so much to do, and all of it quickly, before starting the transatlantic crossing. I felt pressed; *Ra* had already passed the Canaries, and the hurricane season was fast approaching. One of the major tasks was to raise more crew. I figured that eight was the minimum for an ocean crossing. When we arrived, there were only four of us. Then Neal had to rush home to his wife, who was seriously ill, and Otto Washchkau announced one morning as he was being tortured by a wicked hangover that he didn't think the ship could make it. He departed as suddenly as he had come, without even picking up his personal effects. Now, with only Bill Holmes left, I had serious problems.

I appealed for volunteers in the newspapers and even on Portugese television, to no avail. I decided to hire professional seamen, but none were interested, no matter how much I offered to pay. Bill finally talked his younger brother, Dick, into joining us. As ludicrous as it sounds, the three of us sailed the morning after Dick arrived from London. Five hours later and thirty miles south of Lisbon, I knew it was futile. It was virtually impossible for the three of us even to raise and lower the mainsail. The Vikings had used crews of twenty or more. So, with broken hearts, we returned to Lisbon.

I spent the next twenty-four hours making four hundred dollars' worth of phone calls in a vain effort to raise a crew, calling to places as far away as California. After another wasted week in port, we finally recruited two crew members—Trevor Whitehouse, a hundred-and-twenty-pound Englishman who had never been on a sailing ship, and Manuel Santos, a Portugese draft-dodger with similar qualifications. Within minutes of leaving Lisbon, both of them were wretchedly seasick, and they remained so for days.

We had a good northerly breeze during the first three days and made excellent time toward the Canaries. Then, when we were about a hundred miles from Lanzarote Island, a nightmarish gale came out of the southwest. It struck so suddenly that before we could get the mainsail down, the mast had cracked along its entire length. The large fish-shaped block that holds the mast in place also cracked. There was nothing to repair—both parts had to be replaced before the sail could be used again. While trying to put up a jury rig so we could run before the storm wind, I fell on the wet deck and slipped a disk in my back, which put me definitively out of action. Poor *Alfie* wallowed around on the stormy seas for three days until a Spanish fishing boat appeared and towed us to Cádiz.

Once more the Spaniards were jubilant because I had failed to discredit Columbus by crossing the Atlantic in a Viking ship. Soon after this came news that *Ra* had also sunk before reaching Barbados. Lying in traction in the Cádiz hospital, I made the decision to end the voyage. The ship needed extensive repairs (which I didn't have the money for), and the doctor said I wouldn't be able to walk—let alone sail a Viking ship—for several weeks. It was already the end of July, and it would be sheer stupidity to cross the Atlantic during the hurricane season. Old *Alfie* had been through hell; it was time for her to go into retirement. My back injury was more serious than the doctors in Cádiz could handle, so I was sent to Madrid. Meanwhile *Alfie* was tied up at a dock in Cádiz and the crew were at the mercy of some Spaniards who enjoyed throwing garbage and rocks at them and onto the ship.

While I was in the hospital in Madrid the Spanish press had a banner time lambasting me for trying to discredit the accomplishments of Columbus. One newspaper went so far as to suggest that I be thrown out of the country even before my back was in good shape. My temper got the best of me and I challenged the reporter who wrote that article to a duel with old Spanish swords in the Buen Retiro Park in central Madrid. As soon as I was able to walk again I announced the day of the duel, and the press played it up big. I even went out and purchased two seventeenth-century swords for the event. With great fanfare I arrived in complete Viking regalia to a jeering crowd of hundreds, including members of the press and television from all over Europe. My only supporters were a handful of Scandinavians—tourists and others living in Spain—and a few friends. The duel itself was a nonevent; the reporter, who had said he would face me, lost face by not turning up.

On the same day the saga of *Alfie* started up again. The captain of the port of Cádiz ordered the vessel and crew to leave Spanish waters immediately. Bill and Dick couldn't reach me, so they repaired the mast as well as they could and set sail for the coast of Africa. As soon as I heard about this I rushed to Tangiers, where they were supposed to arrive the following day. By the fifth day they still hadn't arrived. I initiated an air and sea rescue operation, and even the Spaniards assisted in the search—all to no avail. For me this was the most nerveracking part of the entire expedition. A strong east wind, known as a levanter in that part of the world, prevented *Alfie* from reaching the coast of Africa. Instead, Bill and Dick were blown far out into the Atlantic, something that happened to many ancient mariners over the centuries. They later estimated they had almost reached the Azores when the winds abated and they began making their way back to the Mediterranean. It's really amazing that they were never spotted by either planes or vessels. After nineteen days, *Alfie* finally reached the coast near Cádiz, but having been booted out of port there once, Bill and Dick continued to the east until reaching Gibraltar. The hapless mariners had no charts and were headed into the off-limits naval port by mistake when a sudden gust of wind slammed them against the end of the mole, tearing a gaping hole in the side of the ship. Within minutes *Alfie* sank. The crew swam safely ashore, but *Alfie* had come to her final resting place.

I failed to cross the Atlantic Ocean both on the northern route, following in the wake of the Norsemen, and on the southern route used by the Phoenicians and other early Mediterranean mariners, but I consider both Viking voyages to have been valuable. I learned a great deal about Viking ships and important aspects of Norse voyages. By the end of the second voyage, I had logged nearly seven thousand miles sailing Viking ships, testing them under practically every sea and weather condition and experiencing some of the worst storms imaginable. I am convinced that a properly built Viking ship could sail around the world with no problem.

Our most important discovery was the unforeseen impressive speed of this class of vessel. The Norsemen did not measure distances when relating their voyages in the sagas. Rather, they measured in time: "After so many days' sail from [one place], we reached [another place]." The speed of Viking ships has been an area of controversy for years. Some historians believe the Viking ships could average about four knots, or roughly a hundred miles a day, while others believe that six knots is a more realistic figure. Using this rough estimate, plus descriptions of the places the Vikings reached on the North American continent, some historians claim that the farthest south the Norsemen went was Newfoundland, while others think they got as far as Chesapeake Bay. With the speed we averaged between Guernsey and Lisbon, they might have reached Florida or Mexico.

Another widespread misconception we disproved was that these ships weren't seaworthy under poor conditions at sea. Most experts agreed that because they were open-built, like a large canoe, the waves would break over the gunwales and they would fill with water and sink in rough weather. After going through some of the roughest seas in the world and countless gales, I can honestly say that isn't so. Except for spray, we did not take a single sea over the side. Still another interesting discovery was how close to the wind these ships could sail. Most armchair historians believed that the Viking ships could sail only with a following wind, but we found that with light winds and the aid of whisker poles to spread the sail, we could sail our ship as close as 70 degrees to the wind, although she naturally had a bit of drift because of her shallow draft. With stronger winds, which meant rougher seas to plow into, this figure decreased proportionately to the wind's velocity.

On balance, these insights into Norse seafaring made up for the disappointments, the aches, the freezing, and the soaking.

9

The Sunken Continent
of Atlantis

The possible existence of the sunken continent of Atlantis, whose golden spires once lighted the whole world, as Plato wrote, has tantalized men for more than two thousand years. One of the great mysteries of the past is the apparent suddenness with which highly developed prehistoric cultures disappeared, leaving no clues to the fate that befell them. Scholars and scientists theorize that these civilizations were abruptly terminated by geophysical events involving earthquakes, volcanoes, floods, tidal waves, sunspots, and the submergence and emergence of land. Some of the civilizations—that of Atlantis, for example—are generally thought to have been mythical. But Atlantis has its fervent believers.

I first got involved in the Atlantis controversy in 1962, while working in the Archivo de las Indias in Seville. A noted historian from the University of Vienna approached me, claiming to have proof that Atlantis existed in the shallow waters off Cádiz. I was skeptical and declined his request to conduct an underwater survey of the area. But several weeks later, he returned with letters from high-ranking government officials in Madrid asking that I help him; so, as an act of goodwill, I consented. A secretive man, the historian never really told me what proof he had, not that it mattered; I didn't find any sign of a sunken continent, the earthly paradise of antiquity.

The Spanish government provided a boat, the necessary equipment, and six good divers. Since the depth of water ranged from 75 to 250 feet, I planned to conduct a sonar survey of the area and locate positive targets that the divers would then inspect visually. We used side-scan sonar, which indicates the presence of any objects protruding above the seafloor, and sub-bottom-profiling sonar, which indicates the presence of solid objects buried in sediment below the seafloor. It took twelve days to cover an area of six square miles. The sonar located thirteen "possibles," an unlucky number, as it turned out. It took us three days to dive and identify the first twelve anomalies, which turned out to be seven rock outcroppings, three fishing vessels, a tanker sunk during World War II, and a Dutch warship of the eighteenth century.

On the morning of the fourth diving day, I had a funny feeling in the pit of my stomach, a premonition that we would have trouble. Our thirteenth target was the deepest of all. It lay in 245 feet of water. The sea was exceptionally rough that day, and as I prepared to make the dive the captain of the ship ordered me to stay on board. He said that considering the depth, he couldn't take responsibility for the life of a civilian. He wanted instead to sent down his two best divers. Of course I was upset, but I complied with his order.

Both divers were to make what is called a "bounce dive" —to go down quickly, spend only a few minutes at the assigned depth, then surface to thirty feet and undergo decompression there, and again at the twenty-foot and ten-foot levels. Two other navy divers were stationed at the thirty-foot level to meet them on their ascent and aid them if necessary. About ten minutes into the dive, one of the safety divers surfaced and said there was no sign of the two deep divers. They were only two minutes overdue, so he went back down, only to surface five minutes later with the same alarm. Over the protests of the captain, I quickly grabbed my scuba tank and started down. At two hundred feet I saw the remains of a large steel-hulled vessel and headed for it. About twenty feet lower, as I was swimming along the deck of the ship, I came upon one of the divers. He was entangled in some steel cables. He was still alive, so I took a big gulp of air and stuck the regulator from my scuba tank in his mouth while removing the cables that were wrapped around his tank and head. On the way to the surface, he perked up a bit, and we shared the same air source until reaching fifty feet and getting fresh tanks from the safety divers.

After spending twenty minutes decompressing, we surfaced and learned that the other diver had not come up. Surely he was dead by now. His air would have run out long before. The diver I had rescued said that the last time he saw his companion, he was apparently suffering from "raptures of the deep," or nitrogen narcosis, and was swimming away from the shipwreck.

Making two dives to that depth in such a short period of time is extremely hazardous, and I was reluctant to risk our lives by going down after him. However, none of the other navy divers had been down to this depth before, and the chap I had rescued was still too shaken from his close call, so I had to go down alone. Before jumping in, I arranged for safety divers to meet me at one hundred feet, and we worked out a detailed decompression schedule, starting with a stop at sixty feet for twenty minutes and including a total of almost three hours of decompression before surfacing. One thing I certainly didn't want was a dreaded case of the bends.

Going down, I carried a line to attach to the diver's body in the event that I found him. All went well at first. After two minutes on the bottom, I found him and tied the line to him. I jerked the line three times to signal the men in the boat to pull him up and then started up, pulling myself hand over hand on the same line. At 180 feet, the line suddenly became taut. I knew it had snagged on the wreck, and I made the mistake of descending again to unsnag it. This went off without a hitch, and I headed toward the surface. All was well until I reached the sixty-foot stop, where I began to feel faint. My body began to tingle all over. This signals the first stages of the bends, and I knew I was in trouble. At the fifty-foot stop, I blacked out, and the divers rushed me to the surface.

Still unconscious, I was taken from the deck of the boat by helicopter to the U.S. Navy base at Rota on the far side of the Gulf of Cádiz. There I came to, only to find that I was totally paralyzed. Thanks to the quick action of the U.S. Navy doctors, my life and mobility were saved. They packed me in ice and flew me to the U.S. Air Force base in Wiesbaden, West Germany, which was the nearest place with a recompression chamber. After ninety-six miserable, claustrophobic hours in that hot chamber, I emerged in a weakened condition from the ordeal, cured and very thankful.

This event should have sated my curiosity about Atlantis, but only six months later my avid curiosity led me to another search for the sunken continent. When we had been in Las Palmas, Grand Canary Island, on the *Niña II* voyage, the director of the island's museum had told me that a fisherman had reported finding a "sunken city" off the southern side of the island. The director thought it might have some connection with the Atlantis theory. Expecting another wild goose chase, I dived to the site and was amazed to find the remains of more than fifty stone buildings in the middle of a large bay at a depth of sixty feet. Although it wasn't Atlantis, it was a remarkable find, and I hope to return someday and carry out further exploration. From the materials I recovered and the historical research done later, the buildings appear to be the remains of a fishing village that was submerged by an earthquake in 1607.

In 1968 I really caught the Atlantis bug. In August, while

searching for shipwrecks on the Little Bahama Bank north of Grand Bahama Island, I made two important discoveries. On a shallow sandbar about three miles north of Memory Rock, in fifteen feet of water, I found over fifty fluted marble columns. At first I assumed that they were part of the cargo of a shipwreck, but when I didn't find any signs of a wreck, ballast, or other type of cargo, I was mystified. How did they get there? I finally surmised that a ship had run aground there and that to lighten the ship and get it off the bottom, the columns had been jettisoned. They may have been aboard a ship carrying British Loyalists to the Bahamas during the American Revolution. The Bahamas served as a refuge then and a century later after the Civil War, when a number of Confederate planters relocated in the Bahamas in an ultimately unsuccessful attempt to raise cotton. They took with them slaves, equipment, and even dismantled homes and building components.

Then two weeks later, about ten miles to the south, near Sandy Cay, I located several hundred round marble balls, two to four feet in diameter. Again there was no shipwreck or other material. This time, the water depth of fifty feet precluded the possibility that a ship had run aground and jettisoned the heavy balls. The water was too deep. Now I was really baffled! How did those balls get there, and even more interesting, what were they used for? Prior to the seventeenth century, stone balls were used as cannon projectiles, but they were never more than a foot in diameter.

I chipped off samples of marble from the columns and balls and sent them to several geologists. I knew that a date couldn't be obtained from marble, but I hoped that the place of origin could be determined. All I could learn was that the marble wasn't of North American origin—that it was most likely from somewhere in the western Mediterranean. Had it been brought over by Phoenicians or some other culture that had reached the New World long before Columbus? I decided to turn over my findings to someone more qualified to study the matter. First I consulted scientists at the Smithsonian Institution, but they weren't interested. Then I met Dr. Manson Valentine, curator of the Science Museum in Miami, who had devoted his life to seeking explanations of mysterious phenomena, and soon after that I met the Frenchman Dimitri Rebikoff, who is a well-known inventor of underwater photographic products and an amateur underwater archaeologist. I discovered that both men were involved with a number of interesting underwater sites in the Bahamas. They had recently formed the Marine Archaeological Research Society (MARS), and they invited me to become part of their group.

While flying over the Grand Bahama Bank in 1967, Rebikoff had sighted a rectangular object about a quarter of a mile long at a depth of about three fathoms (eighteen feet), which, from his more than twenty years of experience, he identified as definitely man-made. Several weeks later, he returned with Dr. Valentine to investigate further and photograph this strange site, but they found it covered over by shifting sands, something common in the area. On subsequent flights in that general area, Rebikoff and Valentine discovered many other suspicious bottom patterns around the chain of islands extending from Bimini south for about sixty miles, but lack of time and money prevented further investigation by diving.

During July 1968, Robert Brush, a pilot flying between Miami and Nassau, reported sighting a square structure in shallow water off the northern tip of Andros Island in the Bahamas, not far from where Rebikoff had made his original sighting. He passed this information on to Rebikoff and Valentine, but before they could mount an underwater investigation of the site, the press learned of it and various articles appeared, stating that a sunken temple of Atlantis had been discovered. A few months earlier, the son of Edgar Cayce, the clairvoyant, had published a book in which he wrote that in 1933 his father had predicted that a temple of the sunken continent of Atlantis would rise out of the sea in the area of Bimini in 1968. Naturally, many of his followers associated this discovery with Cayce's prediction, and the press was only too happy to agree with them.

Valentine and Rebikoff made a preliminary exploration of

the site and discovered that the structure *was* man-made; that it measured sixty by one hundred feet, with walls three feet thick; and that the limestone blocks of which the walls were constructed were laid with an accuracy not to be expected of recent inhabitants of the area. Nor was there any reason to believe that it was the work of the Lucayo Indians, who lived in the area when Columbus first visited it; they weren't stone-builders. Nevertheless, many "experts" jumped on the bandwagon, with the opinion that the structure was probably a pen used by modern inhabitants of the Bahamas for storing turtles, sponges, or conch shells.

Although Valentine does believe in the existence of Atlantis and has publicly said that this structure may be associated with Atlantis, further investigation convinced him that the site belongs to the Mayan civilization or to some other American Indian culture. By a strange coincidence, the site duplicates the floor plan of the Mayan Temple of the Turtles at Uxmal in Yucatán, even to the extent that both sites have their east end and southwest corner partitioned off. Some scientists agree with Valentine that because of the relative water level over the site, the site is certainly pre-Columbian.

On subsequent expeditions to this area, Valentine and Rebikoff located several other submerged man-made structures. One day when Rebikoff was showing me these sites from the air, we discovered another large, rectangular, man-made structure near the others.

One of the sites Valentine discovered is close to a small sandy key where he found hundreds of cut stone disks about eight inches in diameter, lying in a heap on the beach, no doubt thrown there by storms. From these disks he followed two parallel ranks of identical disks into the undergrowth. The disks were partly buried in the sand in straight lines that made several abrupt, right-angle turns and appeared to delineate definite boundaries, perhaps that of a ceremonial court. The top half of the disks, which were protruding from the sand, were so weatherworn that there is little doubt that they have been there for centuries.

On September 2, 1968, while searching for other submerged sites off Bimini, Valentine and his associates were taken to an area near the northern shore of Bimini by a local fisherman who said he had seen many "square stones" on the sea floor at a depth of three fathoms. There Valentine was astonished to find two extensive parallel walls of rectangular and polygonal flat stones of varying thickness and size. They had obviously been cut by men and were accurately aligned to form a convincing structural pattern. These stones had evidently lain submerged for a long time; their top edges had been rounded off by weathering, giving them the appearance of giant loaves of bread. The main orientation of the site was parallel to the coast for about half a mile, and the tops of the massive blocks, which protruded some three to four feet above the sandy sea floor, were in a pattern that averaged seventeen feet in thickness.

Before visiting the sites Rebikoff and Valentine were investigating, I researched vanished cities and found that whereas some had suffered a cataclysmic fate, others took centuries to disappear beneath the sea. For example, only three thousand years ago, there was a land bridge between the British Isles and the European continent; today the English Channel flows over vast forests covered by the sea. In the Mediterranean alone there are more than 180 known sites of sunken ancient cities, the majority of which were covered by a rise in the sea level of the world. Rebikoff, who spent years investigating these phenomena, found that the level of most the world's oceans has risen sixteen feet in the past two thousand years as polar ice melted as a result of the general warming of the earth since the last Ice Age.

These worldwide changes in sea level caused large landmasses in the Western Hemisphere to be inundated. Many early-sixteenth-century maps of the New World show various islands in the Atlantic and Caribbean that no longer exist. While some of them may never have existed, there is evidence that some did. Many early Spanish navigators mentioned sailing past a large, low-lying island about two hundred miles west of the Cayman Islands, which are shown on the early maps. Later mariners did not see this island, and it was eventually named Isla Misteriosa, or Mysterious Island. Modern maps show a Misteriosa Bank in this same area, with depths as shallow as four fathoms (twenty-four feet). No doubt this is the site of the island that disappeared beneath the sea. In recent years divers have discovered intact sunken Mayan temples on the coast of Yucatán, and I think other submerged archaeological sites— possibly even complete cities of ancient civilizations—will be found elsewhere in the Western Hemisphere.

Some traces of ancient civilizations may eventually be discovered right off the coast of the United States. In 1959 the U.S. Coast and Geodetic Survey conducted hydrographic surveys off the Florida Keys. The surveyors found sinkholes as large as a half mile in diameter at depths of nine hundred feet about fourteen miles off the Keys. These sinkholes are presumed to have been freshwater lakes in an area that subsided beneath the sea.

According to the *Dictionary of Anthropology*, Atlantis is "a hypothetical land in the Atlantic Ocean where civilization is alleged to have begun." Many scholars are convinced that it is a mythical land; but others are equally convinced that it did exist. Troy, the sacrifice of maidens in the Sacred Cenote of Chichén Itźa, and King Arthur and his Knights of the Round Table were also believed to be mythical until recent archaeological evidence showed a kernel of truth lies at the heart of stories about them.

The earliest written reference to Atlantis is found in two dialogues of Plato, which date to around 335 B.C. In a discussion between Solon and certain Egyptian priests, Plato introduces Atlantis, whose disappearance they put at about twelve thousand years ago. Plato wrote:

> . . . and there is an island situated in front of the Straits [of Gibraltar] which are by you called the Pillars of Hercules; the island was larger than Libya [Africa] and Asia put together,

*and was the way to the other islands, and from these you might
pass to the whole of the opposite continent which surrounds
the true ocean, for this sea which is within the Straits of
Hercules [the Mediterranean] is only a harbor, having a narrow entrance, but the other is a real sea, and the surrounding
land may be most truly called a boundless continent. Now in
this Island of Atlantis there was a great and wonderful empire.
. . . But afterward there occurred violent earthquakes and
floods; and in a single day and night of misfortune all the
warlike men in a body sank into the earth, and the island of
Atlantis in like manner disappeared in the depths of the sea.*

Since Plato's time, hundreds of books and articles have
been written about Atlantis. But the important fact is that many
scholars have compared his writings with historical and archaeological data and have substantiated his narrative. The earliest-
known maps that are still in existence place Atlantis in the
Atlantic Ocean, but later maps, published before Columbus's
discovery of the New World, show a massive landmass in the
Atlantic, calling it Antillia. Some scholars believe that the present islands of the Caribbean, which the early Spanish explorers
first called the Antilles, are remnants of Atlantis, higher points
of the sunken continent.

We need not rely on the misty surmises of these controversial myths or legends; we can look at more recent geological
evidence. Most geologists believe that a continent did at one
time exist between the European and American continents. The
question still being debated is the precise period in geological
history when this "Atlantean" continent existed.

The bed of the Atlantic is the most unstable part of the
earth's surface. It would have taken only a relatively small
warping of the earth's crust—only an eight-thousandth of the
earth's diameter—for a considerable portion of the ocean floor
to rise above the water and another large landmass to sink
beneath the sea. Scientific evidence that this did indeed happen
has come to light only recently. In the past decade, we have

witnessed the emergence of two islands—one off the Azores and the other off Iceland—because of volcanic action.

In August 1964 two French naval officers, Captain Georges Houot and Lieutenant Gerard de Froberville, reported an amazing discovery. While diving in the research submarine *Archimedes* at a depth of five miles off the northern coast of Puerto Rico, they found a gigantic stairway hewn from solid rock on a sloping seafloor, obviously man-made. Two years later, the research vessel *Anton Bruun* was engaged in oceanographic investigations off the coast of Peru under the direction of Dr. Robert J. Menzies of Duke University. Their deep-sea underwater cameras unexpectedly focused on what is believed to be the site of an ancient civilization. On a muddy plain at a depth of six thousand feet, they found elaborately carved columns with some sort of inscriptions on them. Nearby, the sonic depth recorder detected strange "lumps" on the otherwise level bottom. These were thought to be ruins of ancient buildings. "Although the idea of a sunken city in the Pacific seems incredible," Dr. Menzies said, "the evidence so far suggests one of the most exciting discoveries of the century."

Soon after I met Rebikoff, we made several flights in his plane to the Bahamas to investigate the sites that had been found. Flying with him was an adventure in itself. On one flight, which originated in West Palm Beach and ended three hours later on a rather sour note, I survived two near midair collisions, a serious fire, and an emergency landing. I chose to return to the States on a scheduled airline. On another flight with Rebikoff, between Fort Lauderdale and Nassau, over the Gulf Stream, one of the plane's two engines quit. Losing altitude, we had to jettison our expensive diving and photographic gear in order to stay airborne.

We received the backing of several universities and the promise of funds from the National Geographic Society to make a survey of each site. We planned to submit detailed reports to various experts for analysis and evaluation. I flew to Bimini with Rebikoff and Andy Pruna, a professional diver who had just left the U.S. Navy Sealab III Project and joined Rebikoff's underwater equipment firm. Upon arrival we were surprised to learn that only three weeks earlier, two divers were reported to have discovered two stone statues, as well as fragments of a carved column, and spirited them away in a yacht to the States. Such stories are always floating around, but this time we located over a dozen people who swore they had seen the artifacts.

While Andy, who is an excellent draftsman and cartographer, made drawings and measurements of the site, Rebikoff and I did an extensive survey. Everything he and Valentine had said I found to be true. Our first goal was to ascertain that none of the blocks was attached to the seafloor. In doing so, we made two further discoveries that substantiated their early findings. By fanning away the sand on the sides of the blocks, we discovered that the buried part of the blocks was square-cut and did not appear to be attached to the seafloor in any way, but instead was lying on top of other massive, square-cut blocks.

Our first day of diving came to an abrupt halt with the appearance of a twelve-foot mako shark. The remora fish on the shark, which itself measured over three feet, tried to attach itself to Andy's back while he was sitting on the bottom, drawing. Boarding our small boat, we found the reason for the shark's sudden appearance. Anchored only a hundred yards away was a yacht owned by the late congressman Adam Clayton Powell, who had a home on Bimini. The people fishing from his boat were using chum to attract fish and had inadvertently attracted the mako shark.

A well-known expert on prehistoric architecture, who asked to remain anonymous, studied the photographs and Andy's mosaic drawings. He said that the construction used on this site is known as "Cyclopean," which was the type used by the earliest civilizations of man. Cyclopean architecture was used not only in Europe and Asia, but by early American civilizations.

The Bimini area has always had a bit of mystery about it.

It is the site of the legendary Fountain of Youth sought by Ponce de León. Forty years ago, there were reports of stones with carvings being found on land, but the location is unknown. Neither the Spaniards nor any other Europeans built anything on or near Bimini; this at least rules out the possibility that the site belonged to modern man.

As soon as we returned to Florida, we applied to the Bahamian government for excavation permits for the Bimini and Andros Island sites. Unknown to us at the time, another group, dominated by Edgar Cayce psychics, had applied for the same permits. The press played up the discoveries. Tabloid headlines claimed that the sunken continent of Atlantis had been discovered. Quite a number of people got in the act, which inevitably complicated our work. Eager as we were to return to the sites, months dragged by with no word from Nassau about our request for permits. Valentine and I agreed that it would be prudent to wait for government permission before doing anything, but Rebikoff was terribly impatient and made frequent trips to the sites. During one, he reported seeing a number of marble columns that some amateur divers had found in only four feet of water near Entrance Point on North Bimini Island, and we later saw these columns ourselves.

In early November 1970 I was surprised to read in the newspapers that North American Rockwell Corporation, which has substantial landholdings on Bimini, had been granted exclusive exploration rights on all underwater ruins in the Bimini area. Included in this agreement with the Bahamian government was a plan to construct an underwater restaurant and bar near the sunken walls. When he heard about this, Rebikoff rushed to Nassau, demanding an explanation; but none was forthcoming. Nor would the authorities tell him whether they would grant us the permit to explore the sunken buildings off Andros Island. Two months later, the Rockwell Corporation got an exclusive permit for the Andros area.

Around this time, two interesting discoveries were made. A Pan Am pilot phoned me one day to say that he had found still another large wall off Bimini—this one in sixty feet of water—that had a large archway extending through the middle of it. Three days later a charter-boat captain named Pat Delaney, working out of Bimini, reported that he had discovered a large, steep, pyramidal structure with a rectangular base in sixty feet of water. He claimed that a psychic with an excellent reputation for finding oil for petroleum companies had rented his boat and from a psychic impression had located the sunken pyramid. Both the pilot and Delaney refused to reveal their location unless we paid them an outrageous sum of money. Rebikoff and I made several trips to Bimini but failed to find either the new wall or the pyramid. When I gave up, sure that both were hoaxes, Rebikoff kept searching. During one trip he found an underwater freshwater spring, or well, pouring out of the seafloor. It was enclosed by a stone wall close to the two parallel walls we had already surveyed.

As an archaeologist, I considered that my main objective was to identify and date these sites through careful and systematic excavation, with the help of other experts. I didn't put much stock in the Atlantis theory, but I did think the sites might be tied in with some pre-Columbian culture, and this, in itself, made them interesting. From dealings I had with representatives of the Rockwell Corporation, I gathered that the company wasn't eager to prove or disprove the authenticity of the Atlantis theory. Soon after Rockwell obtained the lease for the Bimini area, it hired a geologist who had experience in the area. After a brief trip to Bimini, during which he didn't even go in the water, he announced that the walls were not man-made and that the columns were probably from a shipwreck. Unhappy with this report, the Rockwell people engaged scientists from the Marine Laboratory of the University of Miami. One of these, Dr. John Gifford, a geologist, made a thorough survey of one of the walls and reported that the blocks were "something of a geological enigma; none of the evidence conclusively rules out the possibility of human intervention in their formation."

As a result of Gifford's encouraging report, Rockwell decided to mount a major expedition to uncover one of the walls, with astronaut Edgar Mitchell as the leader of the expedition. About twenty-five people were invited to participate, including Rebikoff and a number of psychics from the Edgar Cayce Foundation. Until just three days before the expedition was to begin, I thought I was to be in charge of the actual excavation of the wall; then my invitation was withdrawn on the pretext that there wasn't enough room on the boat. However, I discovered that in fact the Rockwell people were afraid I would publish an unfavorable account of the excavation that would make their stockholders unhappy.

I was determined to see what went on and persuaded a friend, Art Hartman, to take me over in his boat while the Rockwell expedition was in progress. We found their salvage vessel, the *Venture,* anchored over one of the walls where just a month earlier Rebikoff had reported sighting sixteen-foot-high pillars holding up some of the massive fifteen-ton blocks. We anchored alongside the Rockwell vessel despite shrill warnings that we would be arrested for diving in an area in which they had exclusive excavation rights. We weren't worried, because we had permission from the Bahamian government to dive there, although not to excavate.

In any case, nature had already done the excavation. The bottom was clear of sand. We could see that *the wall wasn't a wall at all.* The stone blocks, which were three to four feet thick, rested on the hardpan seafloor. If anything, the site resembled a road or causeway similar to many I've seen in Yucatán and elsewhere. When challenged about the sixteen-foot-high columns he'd reported seeing, Rebikoff said he had actually seen them on another wall, which, unfortunately, had been covered over by sand. The most important information gleaned from this expedition was that none of the blocks was attached to the sea bottom, proving that they are not natural formations.

Before leaving Bimini, I talked to some of the island's

fishermen, asking if they knew of any other underwater walls or ruins near the island. One showed me a bronze coin he said he had found on the beach near where most of the walls and columns were found. The coin, which is not necessarily connected with the ruins, was Phoenician, dating from the fifth century B.C.

Although Rebikoff and others are still convinced the walls are man-made, I am sure they are the work of Mother Nature, because I have since seen very similar underwater formations in other areas of the Bahamas, off the coast of Yucatán, and near the Dry Tortugas Islands, west of Key West. As for the marble columns and Phoenician coin, the columns were probably dropped off a ship that ran aground trying to enter the port, and the coin was probably a plant arranged by someone who wanted to convince me that the site was the real McCoy.

The buildings off northern Andros Island are another matter. They are certainly worth further investigation. I made a brief trip to that site shortly after the Rockwell expedition. A friend flew me there in his small amphibious plane, and we spent several hours exploring with snorkeling gear. Alongside the largest building I dug down more than seven feet, but did not reach the bottom of the wall. Walls made of square-cut stone of this height and covered as they are with a mortarlike substance would never have been built as turtle pens by the modern-day inhabitants of the Bahamas, nor were they in an area where the Spaniards or other Europeans had settlements. Even more tantalizing was a ceramic face of a man that I found in the sand there. I also found a carved piece of marble and more than a dozen ceramic sherds—none of which appear to be New World in origin, according to the experts I have consulted. I hope to have time one day to investigate the site further.

On a small cay near this submerged structure off Andros, Valentine had reported finding hundreds of wheel-like stones with holes in their centers, ranging from two to five feet in diameter. I visited the cay and verified their existence. On a reef nearby, I found several more of these perfectly cut stones buried deep in the coral, which indicated that they have been there a long time. In appearance, the stones are similar to the stone currency used for centuries by the natives of Yap Island in the Pacific.

One of these days, the sites around Andros Island will be thoroughly investigated and important archaeological evidence will be uncovered. Who knows—perhaps proof will emerge that the area was settled in antiquity by people from the other side of the Atlantic who reached these clear, warm waters long before Columbus.

10

Back to the Land of the Great White Gods

In March of 1971 I was involved in what may eventually prove to be the greatest treasure discovery of all time. During the past five centuries there have been many fruitless searches for Montezuma's fabulous treasure. Judging from the results of an expedition I participated in, however, I am convinced that the Aztec emperor's treasure has now been found and that it will eventually be recovered. The mystery surrounding the disappearance of the treasure is fascinating in itself.

In 1519, Hernán Cortés and his soldiers disembarked from their galleons on the beach near the tropical port of Veracruz to begin their conquest of Mexico. Their goal was the accumulation of great wealth. But few if any of the sea-weary Spaniards had any idea of the incredible treasure they were to see when they eventually reached Tenochtitlán, Montezuma's capital, a city of canals on an island in Lake Texcoco, which has since been drained and is the site of present-day Mexico City.

Montezuma believed that the white god, Quetzalcoatl,

would come once again to the land, in accordance with ancient Aztec prophecies, and that Cortés was indeed the white god whose return had been prophesied. On hearing of Cortés's landing, Montezuma sent the Spaniards many valuable gifts, including gold, silver, and jewelry with precious stones. Excited by the gifts, Cortés drove his men relentlessly on a grueling march over the mountains to the capital, fighting hostile Indian tribes along the way. When news reached the emperor of the atrocities committed by the approaching Spaniards, he began to have second thoughts about their divinity. He dispatched messengers with large amounts of treasure to pacify Cortés and asked him not to enter the city. When Montezuma saw that the strange-looking men were determined to enter Tenochtitlán, he reluctantly permitted them to enter unmolested.

The Spaniards were astonished at the beauty and high degree of development of the city. They were agog at the lavish amounts of precious metals and other treasure decorating the Aztec temples and shrines. They soon learned that this was only a small part of the treasure stored in the city. Sensing their insatiable greed for wealth, Montezuma had had most of the royal treasure hidden before the Spaniards arrived. In the dark of night soon after they reached the city, Cortés and several of his men broke into a treasure storehouse. One of the conquistadores later wrote: "I took it for certain that there could not be another such store of wealth in the whole world." Tons of golden idols, ingots, and jewelry, much of it tribute exacted from tribes that paid allegiance to the Aztec and collected over a span of centuries, were stacked in piles. There were also thousands of finely wrought pieces made from gold, silver, and precious stones. They resealed the building and returned to their quarters, vowing that even at the risk of their lives, they would attempt to gain the fantastic treasure they had seen, as well as more that they knew was hidden elsewhere in the city.

Several days later the Spaniards seized Montezuma and

held him prisoner, demanding a huge ransom for his release. The treasure house the Spaniards had previously broken into was turned over to them, but the insatiable Cortés wasn't satisfied and demanded still more, which the Aztec were reluctant to deliver. Not long afterward, while Cortés was out of the city, some of his soldiers, disobeying his orders to respect the Aztec, attacked and massacred priests and worshipers at a sacred temple. Incensed over the desecration of their temple, the proud Aztec rebelled en masse, and Cortés rushed back to the city to find his men fighting against overwhelming odds.

During an attack on the building where Montezuma was being held hostage, the emperor was accidentally stoned by one of his own people, and he died soon after, which made the plight of the Spaniards even more perilous. Forced to flee, they were able to take only a small part of the treasure they had already amassed, and they lost much of this as they fought their way out of the city.

After weeks of fierce fighting, Cortés and what remained of his army reached the coast near where they had first landed. They spent several months there, licking their wounds and training friendly tribes in European combat. When reinforcements from Cuba arrived, Cortés and his men returned to Tenochtitlán to recover the lost treasure. The conquistadores laid siege to the city for three months. Tenochtitlán, one of the world's most sophisticated and beautiful cities, fell on August 13, 1521. The frenzied Spaniards, heedless of anything but treasure, sacked the city, but not a single piece was found.

Cuauhtemoc, the new emperor of the Aztec, and his aides were subjected to torture, but refused to reveal the location of the treasure. They were put to death, carrying the secret with them. Hundreds of other Aztec were also killed. Although the Spaniards did learn that the treasure had been thrown into a lake, they were never able to discover which one of the region's myriad lakes. Over the years they used divers and in some cases even drained whole lakes in a vain effort to find the treasure.

In 1954, when skin diving was still in its infancy, Pablo

Bush Romero and some of his diving buddies began using their skills for historical and archaelogical pursuits. Pablo, who had been fascinated by the legend of Montezuma's treasure since childhood, persuaded his friends to help him hunt for it, and over a period of years they made hundreds of dives in various lakes within a large radius of Mexico City. In 1959, Pablo founded CEDAM, the Club de Exploraciones Deportivos Aquaticas de México, Mexico's first diving club. He then had a larger number of divers to aid him in the search, which by now had become something of an obsession with him.

After systematically exploring and eliminating many of the lakes in which the treasure might be hidden, Pablo resorted to logic. He knew that Cuauhtemoc had come from the town of Izcateoban before being named to succeed Montezuma as emperor. Pablo theorized that he probably would have tried to have the treasure hidden near his native town. Since the treasure was known to have been thrown in a lake, Pablo at first assumed that this was done because the Spaniards were closing in too rapidly. Near the road that once connected Tenochtitlán and Izcateoban were numerous lakes, but all of them had been thoroughly explored without finding any trace of treasure.

Flying over the area between the two ancient cities, Pablo noticed two small lakes in the crater of the Toluca volcano that had not been marked on the maps of the area he had used in his earlier explorations. At first he disregarded the possibility of the treasure's being in the two lakes. At an elevation of 13,828 feet, they are the highest lakes in the world, and Pablo thought it would have been impossible for the Aztec to carry the treasure to such a height. Soon, however, as a result of research, he changed his mind. He learned that the volcano had been called Xinantécatl by the Aztec and that it was sacred to them. The larger lake was called the Lake of the Sun and the other the Lake of the Moon. The Aztec believed they were the home of their rain god, Tlaloc. Did the Aztec make offerings to the rain god in these two lakes, as the Maya did at the Sacred Cenote of Chichén Itzá in Yucatán? Had the Aztec cast the royal treasure into the lakes as an offering to their rain god, combining the need to hide it with a religious sacrifice?

Pablo discovered that a number of experienced divers had made dives in both lakes. On almost every occasion, there had been near-fatal accidents. After surfacing from their dives, some divers lost consciousness from anoxia, or lack of oxygen. Little was known about scuba diving at high altitudes in those days, and it is a miracle that no lives were lost. Questioning Raúl Echeverría, one of the first to dive in the lakes, Pablo was glad to hear that he had found several large pieces of copal, a ceremonial incense used by the Aztec and Maya as offerings to their rain god. Pablo knew he was on the right track; the presence of copal showed that the Aztec had made offerings in the lakes. It had been the discovery of copal that convinced Edward Thompson, the American who in 1905 had recovered several million dollars' worth of treasure from the Sacred Cenote of Chichén Itzá, that the legend about the treasure in the *cenote* was true.

Pablo knew something would have to be done about the hazards of high-altitude diving before a search of the two lakes could be made. For seven months, extensive tests were performed under the supervision of doctors from the Mexican navy and Dr. Miguel Guzmán, one of the early divers in the lakes. A polygraph was taken up to the lakes, and Dr. Guzmán, Raúl Echeverría, and other CEDAM divers were wired to it during their dives. From the pulmonary-ventilation and cardiographic data obtained from these experimental dives, the doctors were able to determine the cause of the accidents and find a way to prevent them. The surface air at the high-altitude lakes contains 25 percent less oxygen than at sea level, but underwater the diver breathes normally, since the compressed air in his tanks contains sufficient oxygen. As a result, the diver surfacing in these lakes goes from the equivalent of sea level to an altitude of almost fourteen thousand feet in only a few seconds. To overcome this problem, Dr. Guzmán and the others recommended that a diver ascend and breathe very slowly upon surfacing. When a diver is severely chilled by the cold water and can't control his breathing rate, however, anoxia cannot be avoided and he must quickly be supplied with pure oxygen on the surface.

Another potential source of trouble at such an altitude is decompression sickness, the dreaded bends. Although the maximum depth of the lakes is only sixty feet, the difference in air pressure between the compressed air in the diver's tank and the atmospheric air at the surface makes a sixty-foot dive the equivalent of a hundred-foot dive at sea level, so decompression stops must be scheduled accordingly.

While the medical tests were going on, Echeverría made an interesting discovery. At a depth of only a few feet, near one edge of the Lake of the Sun, he found the mechanisms of several dozen old pocket watches. On subsequent dives, he and other CEDAM divers discovered more mechanisms, as well as a gold ring and several tin boxes with "Monte de Piedad de Madrid" inscribed on them. Pablo soon discovered their origin. Near the end of the Spanish Civil War, a yacht, the *Vita,* carrying Spanish Republican officials and loot they had taken from safety deposit boxes in Madrid, reached Mexico. Using some of their treasure to obtain Mexican citizenship, the Spaniards settled near Mexico City. The exact amount of money and treasure they brought was never revealed, but Franco claimed it was in the millions of dollars. Mexico refused to surrender either the fugitives or the loot, and the two countries broke diplomatic relations. It seems that the safety deposit boxes and watch mechanisms (stripped of their gold cases) were thrown in the lake in an attempt to cover up the theft.

CEDAM members made many dives and found hundreds of other copal fragments and many wooden and ceramic artifacts, including two ceramic heads of Tlaloc. In certain sections of both lakes, the mud bottom is over fifteen feet deep. The divers were able to dig down only a few feet by hand and recover the lighter artifacts of copal, ceramic, and wood. Heavy objects such as gold had settled on the hard bottom under the mud. Pablo decided the next step was to make a thorough electronic metal-detection survey of the lakes to determine whether the treasure was really there and, if so, in which of the two lakes, as well as to pinpoint its location. He asked me to undertake the job for him. I jumped at the chance to participate in this expedition, lured by the possibility that some pre-Columbian Old World artifacts might also lie on the bottom of these volcanic mountain lakes.

Since I heartily dislike diving in cold water, I planned to eliminate the need for diving by using a metal detector that could be towed and operated from a boat. I arrived in Mexico City to learn that the detector, which I had shipped via air freight, had been lost in transit. I knew from more previous experience than I care to think about that it might take days for it to be found. I had another expedition scheduled to start in Yucatán in a few days' time and reasoned that I had no recourse but to use the hand-held underwater metal detector I had brought with me. It would do the job, but it would mean diving in the frigid lakes. I consulted Raúl Echeverría, who told me that the best months for diving were July and August, when the water was warmer—relatively warmer, that is, reaching 40 or 45 degrees Fahrenheit. Since I already had other commitments for those months, I was determined to do the job right away. Raúl reluctantly agreed to dive with me and talked two other CEDAM divers into coming along as safety divers.

Pablo was leading another archaeological expedition at the time, so he had made arrangements with Alfonso Romero, the vice president of CEDAM, to provide logistical support for the survey of the two lakes. Within a few hours of my arrival, Alfonso had me over the site in a small plane. Below me lay a majestic and awesome sight. The jagged, snow-covered peaks of the extinct volcano towered above precipitous, barren cliffs that encircled the crater and lakes. The water was an opaque jade. There was no sign of vegetation; the entire area looked forbidding. Down in the valley, five miles from the volcano, archaeologists were excavating a newly discovered Aztec site called Tenango del Valle.

The following morning we set off for the lakes in jeeps. A

narrow dirt road strewn with fallen boulders led to the crater. The air temperature was a brisk 34 degrees, and powerful gusts of wind blew, buffeting us from all directions. The desolate shore around the lakes was covered with ice crystals, and the water temperature was 28 degrees. Sections of both lakes were covered with surface ice. To make matters worse, I was having great difficulty breathing at that altitude and would gladly have called the dive off. But pride prevented me from doing so.

My friends suggested that we wait a few hours until we were better acclimated to the dense air and the sun rose above the surrounding mountain peaks. I was only too happy to wait. Within an hour, however, everyone was having difficulty breathing and we were afflicted by severe headaches, which were alleviated somewhat by gulps of pure oxygen.

By noon the air temperature had risen somewhat, raising the surface temperature and melting some of the ice on the shore. We decided to make our first dive in the Lake of the Sun, which had yielded most of the artifacts that had been recovered from the lakes. Right from the start, everything went awry. I discovered that I had left my rubber diving boots and gloves behind and that my rubber suit was torn in several places. Two of the diving regulators failed, even though they had been checked that morning, and the valve on one of the air tanks had a bad leak. While I was adjusting the controls on the metal detector, Raúl entered the water, and minutes later he emerged with a deep cut on his hand. He had been probing in the mud for artifacts and had cut his hand on a broken beer bottle. With Raúl out of action, our two safety divers, Genaro Hurtado and Oscar Bush, decided to accompany me. Alfonso Romero would follow our bubbles in a small boat so that he would be on the spot if any of us surfaced in trouble.

In the water I soon began suffering from the intensely cold water, which entered my rubber suit through the torn places. Within five minutes my hands were so numb I could barely grasp the detector. Nearby, Genaro and Oscar, digging in the mud, located several chunks of copal, one of which had been molded in the shape of the two volcano peaks. After only ten minutes I was so cold and breathing was so difficult that I decided to surface. I pushed myself off the muddy bottom, but to my astonishment I didn't have the strength to kick my way to the surface. In a state of near panic, I began crawling on all fours toward shore. It seemed like an eternity before I reached it. Seconds after emerging from the water, I blacked out, and Raúl rushed to my aid with the emergency oxygen bottle. I came out of it in a few minutes, but had to continue breathing oxygen for over an hour.

We quit for the day and headed home, but our problems weren't over. Our headaches and breathing difficulties disappeared after we descended the mountain, but when we had to climb over a ten-thousand-foot mountain range before reaching Mexico City, Raúl blacked out at the wheel of the jeep. If his wife hadn't reacted quickly and grabbed the wheel, we would have had a serious accident.

The next day I returned to the lakes with the same group, plus an additional ten divers. This time I was better prepared. Wearing not one but two good rubber suits and equipped with good rubber gloves and boots, I made three hour-long dives that day and three on the following two days. With the divers working in teams of two, alternating between holding the metal detector and rubbing the numb parts of their bodies, we completed the metal-detection survey in three days and without further serious complications. A doctor was standing by each day, and we used a new system to prevent the divers from being affected by the lack of oxygen when they surfaced. Each time a diver neared the surface, a small bottle of pure oxygen was lowered to him, and he switched from his scuba tanks to the oxygen bottle. On the surface he continued breathing the pure oxygen until the doctor felt he could cope with the rarefied air.

That first day we concentrated on the Lake of the Moon, which was the smaller one. Twice we got good readings on the metal detectors, indicating the presence of metal under the mud, and each time we were able to dig down and locate the sources, because they were buried only a few feet deep. Our hopes were dashed when they proved to be a fishing-tackle box and a geologist's pick.

We began the survey of the Lake of the Sun after stringing colored lines across the bottom of the lake in a grid pattern. Our only discoveries during a long cold day on the bottom were several beer cans, which were fairly close to the surface of the mud bottom. We were a bit worried, because we had surveyed all of the areas bordering the lake that we estimated were within the maximum range heavy objects could be thrown into the lake from shore. In an attempt to cheer everyone up (and make sure they returned the next day), I said that maybe the Aztec had boats on the lakes and had dumped the treasure in the middle of the lake.

The next day was unproductive. When it began to get dark, most of the divers were already preparing to go home. Raúl and I went into the lake to complete the survey. Only an area about the size of a tennis court remained to be surveyed. After only a few minutes, Raúl motioned to me, and I swam over and looked at his metal detector. At first I thought it had gone on the blink. After testing it, I realized that Raúl had found a large mass of metal right in the middle of the lake in the deepest part. We surfaced and took bearings. Then two other divers went down with ten-foot-long metal rods, but they were unable to reach the bottom of the mud deposit.

Raúl and I were very excited by the discovery and decided to make another dive despite the protestations of the doctor. Using longer metal probes, we soon established that the mud was some twenty feet deep in this area. Without proper excavation equipment, there was little likelihood of finding any of the treasure. We decided to dig a hole by hand, on the off chance that we might uncover something. At a depth of only two feet in the mud, we started hitting a bonanza: two jade axheads, four obsidian spear points, and two ten-inch-high figurines of Tlaloc, the rain god. Working frantically, and forgetting about the cold that had numbed our bodies and senses, we soon discovered two more jade axheads, eleven ceramic figurines of Tlaloc, and seven small gold bells. About this time, Raúl ran out of air and had to surface. I stayed on the bottom alone, breathing as slowly as possible. Just as I was exhausting my air supply, I saw a glint in the dark water. Quickly I grabbed it and rushed for the surface, grasping a beautiful ten-inch jade birdlike figurine. The doctor insisted I go right back down, where I had to remain, teeth chattering and limbs trembling, at a depth of twenty feet to begin the thirty-minute decompression sequence.

That night in Mexico City we were euphoric. We met with Pablo and made plans to go after the treasure the next day, using an airlift to remove the mud. But getting a boat large enough to hold an air compressor and other necessary equipment up to the lake turned out to be next to impossible. Instead, we took up a dozen fifty-five-gallon drums and lumber and built a barge, which took three days. CEDAM had obtained a permit to explore the lake from the Mexican government, and we thought we had kept our discovery secret—but word of our planned excavation leaked out, and the same authorities who had issued our permit suddenly announced that it didn't cover any actual excavation. They told Pablo we would have to apply for an excavation permit. Until it was issued, we could do no more diving in either lake. I waited around for a week, champing at the bit to get back to the treasure on that lake bottom. Finally, when it appeared that the permit wouldn't be issued in the foreseeable future, I returned to Florida, with the intention of coming back as soon as Pablo and his team had the permit.

That was years ago, and to date the permit still has not been issued, nor has Pablo ever been given an explanation why not. I learned from several sources that politics are involved. Some members of CEDAM are apparently in disfavor with the top cultural people in Mexico, who have prevented the issue of not only this permit but all others that CEDAM has requested over the years. Since the original shipwreck permit I had back in the mid-fifties, the Mexican government has never issued another to anyone for any type of underwater exploration. Sooner or later, however, the site will be excavated and Montezuma's treasure may be recovered.

A month after the Toluca volcano expedition I headed back to Yucatán again, this time with my adventurous old comrade Milt Machlin, who was then the editor of *Argosy* magazine. Machlin had recently returned from New Guinea, where he had made a documentary about the Cargo Cult natives. Since Machlin is also an adherent of the theory of pre-Columbian Old World contact with the Americas, he is the perfect traveling companion. In Mexico City I had heard rumors about the recent discovery of a large Egyptian statue on a sisal plantation near the village of Tihosuco in the center of the Yucatán Peninsula.

Before heading for Yucatán I had contacted a number of Mexican archaeologists about this find. They said it was a fake, although none of them had even seen a photograph of it. The life-size statue of a man looked Egyptian. The Indians who found it had painted it white. Scraping away the paint on one spot, we discovered it was granite, a type of stone unknown in Yucatán or in any area for hundreds of miles around. I sent photographs to various experts. The Smithsonian was interested and sent an archaeologist down to examine the statue, but when he arrived it had disappeared without a trace, and the villagers offered no explanation.

While making further inquiries about the statue in the village of Tihosuco, we made a very interesting discovery. While exploring the ruins of a sixteenth-century church in a relatively isolated area, we noticed that a large stone lintel over the main entrance of the church had an inscription carved into it. Expecting the inscription to be in Spanish or Latin, I was amazed to find upon closer inspection that it was in some strange writing that I knew was not Mayan hieroglyphics. The great white gods were whispering in my ear again to pursue the enigmatic writing. Dr. Cyrus Gordon identified the script from photographs as belonging to some ancient form of Mediterranean writing—most likely Phoenician. Other experts would only agree that it was not the writings of any New World culture and most likely was from the early Mediterranean period.

One of the elders of the village informed us that the church had been constructed on top of some very old buildings that, tradition had it, had been erected long before the Maya appeared in this area. Stories handed down for generations told of white men coming long before and living in this area for many years, departing when the Maya arrived. The gnarled old Indian also claimed that beneath the ruins of the church there was a hidden cavern that contained many "old things left by the foreign visitors, including old books."

What was supposed to be a week's trip to Yucatán ended up being a month. Milt and I hired twenty laborers to start digging a tunnel, and despite numerous nearly fatal cave-ins, we eventually broke through the wall of an enormous cavern. The workmen all fled, claiming that evil spirits would kill them, so Machlin and I went at it alone. Armed with flashlights and machetes, in case we ran into poisonous snakes or evil spirits, we entered the enormous room, where we discovered thousands of earthenware pottery sherds, charcoal from fires, and two human skeletons.

Our spirit of adventure was really soaring at the time. However, after many hours of braving the foul air and finding nothing more, we gave up the search. We took a sample of the charcoal and some of the sherds to an archaeologist in Mérida for analysis. Months later we were informed that the samples had been "accidentally lost."

A month later I returned to Cozumel with my wife, Jenifer. Friends had written that some puzzling ruins had been uncovered in the center of the island. Unfortunately, we were a bit late: a bulldozer had just cut through the largest ruin on this site. It lay in the path of a new road across the island. The other ruins had been dismantled, and their stones were being used in the construction of a new hotel. Ceramic sherds and some human bones were scattered over a wide area, and we began searching through the debris. Jenifer spotted an object embedded in one side of the pathetic rubble that remained from the main ruin. Gingerly, we extracted what turned out to be a bronze axhead. This was a rare and exciting find, since although bronze was used by the Inca and several other indigenous New World peoples, it was never used by the Maya. Chemical analysis showed that the copper used in the axhead came from somewhere in the western Mediterranean—the ancient home of the Phoenicians. Before leaving the island we also saw several hundred beads made from amber, another material never located in this region but widely traded by the Phoenicians. We also heard that several gold figurines had been unearthed from this site, but we weren't able to locate the people who allegedly had them.

We had barely returned home to Florida when the great white gods beckoned again. I decided to follow up something I had first heard about many years before. Once again I persuaded Milt Machlin to come along on another expedition to Yucatán. It proved to be the most fascinating one yet. As preposterous as it may sound, we found Maya in a remote area who believed that Queen Victoria, who died in 1901, was still on the British throne. We met Indians in various isolated villages who believed not only that Queen Victoria was still alive but that she would eventually help them to secede from Mexico and become a part of Great Britain.

The explanation for this time warp lies in the history of Yucatán. Although the rest of Mexico was conquered fairly rapidly by the Spaniards, Yucatán wasn't defeated until 1546, after nineteen years of brutal conflict. During the next three centuries there were several minor revolts in Yucatán, which were quickly suppressed. Catholicism was forced on the Indians by the Spanish missionaries, but a large percentage of the indigenous population clung to their ancient pagan religion. Even today, many Indians still practice a synthesis of the two religions. As was the practice in the places conquered by the Spaniards, the Maya were treated little better than animals by the white masters and their *mestizo* cohorts. After Mexico gained its independence from Spain in 1821, the condition of the Indians worsened. Exorbitant taxes were imposed by civil and church authorities. Many priests charged so much for administering the sacraments of baptism and marriage that the devout Indians were perpetually destitute.

In 1847, after three centuries of white domination, the Maya revolted and the brutal but little-known Caste War began. During the early years of the war, it seemed that the government forces would be annihilated or at least driven from the peninsula. The Mexican government sent in large numbers of troops and even employed American mercenaries. Then the Indians resorted to guerrilla warfare. The vast amount of plunder they had obtained from the towns they captured bought guns and supplies from the English in nearby British Honduras.

During the first eight years of the war, more than 300,000 lives were lost on both sides. The Mexicans were in control of the northwest section of the peninsula around Mérida, but the rest of the peninsula was in the hands of the rebel Indians. Realizing that they weren't making any headway fighting an offensive war against the Indians, the Mexicans went on the defensive. Throughout the remainder of the century, the Indians continued making raids against the settlements held by the Mexicans, usually for alcohol, food, and prisoners (who lived out the rest of their lives as slaves in Indian villages).

Several years after the war began, a band of Indian warriors was being pursued by a superior force of Mexican soldiers. Taking refuge one night in a cave, they discovered a large, crudely made wooden cross. Their leader, who was a good ventriloquist, impersonated "God's voice," and his men believed that God was speaking to them through the cross. The voice advised them to stop their flight and turn and attack. The next morning they ambushed the Mexican soldiers and massacred them.

This was the foundation of the Speaking Cross cult, which became an element of the Indians' syncretic religion. Soon after this, a town named Chan Santa Cruz was founded near the cave. It became the religious and military center of the rebels. A massive stone church was constructed, which still stands today, and the miraculous cross was placed over the altar. Beneath the altar there was a hidden chamber with excellent acoustical properties. During religious services, a priest impersonated "God's voice." The entire war effort was directed through the voice of the Speaking Cross.

The church was lavishly decorated with statues and other religious items that the Indians had stripped from churches and cathedrals on the peninsula. Many of their leaders became priests in the cult, wearing sumptuous religious vestments also obtained in their raids. They developed their own society and maintained a more or less independent nation. A strong trade in chicle and mahogany was maintained with British Honduras, and repeated, abortive attempts were made to have the area they controlled annexed to British Honduras. At the time that the Mexicans discontinued their offensive war, there were more than 100,000 Indians living in the twenty-thousand-square-mile area, but by 1900 repeated epidemics of smallpox, cholera, and whooping cough reduced their numbers to less than ten thousand.

The Mexican government, which had been biding its time for half a century, decided to go on the offensive again. An army under the command of General Arturo Bravo was sent to obliterate the Indian stronghold. After winning a series of minor skirmishes with the Indians, the army entered and took possession of Chan Santa Cruz on May 5, 1901, without any resistance. The population had already fled. Mexican soldiers were then dispatched throughout the captured territory—then called Quintana Roo—and hundreds of the Indians were slaughtered. Even today the Mexicans are so violently hated by many Indians that it is suicide for a Mexican to enter some of the remote jungle villages.

A few of the survivors of the war with General Bravo are still living. They and their descendants numbered about five thousand at the time Machlin and I went to Yucatán. They shunned all contact with the outside world, especially with Mexicans. Before escaping from Chan Santa Cruz, the rebels had stripped their church of all religious items, including the Speaking Cross. Fearing that the Mexicans would discover and destroy any new religious center they might create, the Indians resolved to establish three separate centers, on the premise that at least one would survive.

The three places selected were Champon, Chancah, and Tixcacal Guardia. Their locations were kept so secret that it was not until fairly recently that their existence became known to outsiders. A church was built at each place. The Speaking Cross was converted into three smaller crosses, one for each church, and the statues and other religious items rescued from the church in Chan Santa Cruz were divided up among them.

The old religion is still practiced by some five to eight thousand faithful. During times of religious festivals, some Indians come from as far as a hundred miles away to attend ceremonies at each of the villages. Men from the various villages in the territory are sent for a week at a time to stand around-the-clock guard duty at the churches.

Very few outsiders have ever been in any of the three villages, and none has been permitted even to approach their churches. A few of the devoted American Maryknoll missionaries who do so much to help the people of Yucatán have visited the villages, but they have made little progress in converting the Indians to Catholicism.

Quite by accident, I was one of the first outsiders to enter one of the villages. In 1958, while living on Cozumel Island, I was alone on a week-long hunting and exploring trip in the Quintana Roo jungle and, not for the first time, got lost. Sighting smoke from a treetop, I made my way into the settlement of Champon, nearly crazed with thirst. I was relieved of my rifle and pistol by a welcoming committee of six armed Indians and tied to a tree. I attempted to explain in Spanish that I was lost, but no one understood me. They spoke only Mayan.

Soon afterward, I was approached by a very distinguished-looking elderly man. He ordered me untied and took me to his thatched hut, where he gave me food and water. Speaking fluent Spanish, he told me that he was the chief of a large number of Indians and that I had entered one of their important religious centers where no outsiders had ever been permitted. He said that the high priest of the church wanted me killed but that he had interceded in my behalf. The chief said he was called Tatich by his subjects, but his real name was Juan Baptista Vega. He had been born on Cozumel Island in 1888. In 1897 he went on a boat trip with his father and two other men, one of whom was a Spaniard, to search for a buried treasure on the coast of Quintana Roo. Shortly after landing on the coast near the ruins of Tulum, the party was attacked by Indians and the three adults were hacked to pieces with machetes. His life was spared because of his youth and because the Indians discovered he could read and write, making him an asset in questioning prisoners. Within a few years he was named secretary to Florentino Quituk, who was the Tatich of the Indians. After the deaths of Quituk and several of his successors, Vega became Tatich in 1955.

I was fascinated by the man and his story. We talked for several hours, and I learned a great deal about his life and the people he led. What aroused my interest the most was the mention of two "holy books" that he said were kept in the church there. The oldest book was written shortly after the conquest. It was made from tree bark coated with chalky stuff. Half of the pages consisted of Mayan hieroglyphics and the other half of Mayan written in Latin characters, which he said was very difficult to read because much of the writing was faded and the language hard to understand. The second book he called the Book of God. It was written in a language resembling modern Mayan and dealt with religion and prophecies. The Tatich told me he read parts of the book to the congregation during the two masses said each day in his church. He said he was the only one capable of reading in the village.

After our talk he recommended that I leave the village, because the high priest was very unhappy about my presence, and the Tatich feared for my life. He gave me food and water and assigned two armed guards to escort me. They stayed with me for the three days it took to reach the coast where my boat was anchored.

During the conquest the Spaniards, who had no feeling for the fruits of New World civilizations, destroyed nearly all of the ancient Mayan books. Miraculously, three of these manuscript books in hieroglyphics (codices) have survived. One is in Madrid, one is in Paris, and the third is in Moscow. With the exception of the hieroglyphics denoting some of the ancient gods, dates, and numerals, none of the codices has been deciphered.

There is another type of book, called Chilam Balam, examples of which have survived. But they postdate the conquest and are written in Mayan with Latin characters. They contain various segments of the history of the ancient Maya of Yucatán, preserved over the years by oral tradition and compiled during the second half of the fifteenth century by literate Indians, possibly at the instigation of Spanish scholars. Both of the books in the church at Champon are probably of the Chilam Balam type and would be of great historical and anthropological interest. However, the one with both Latin characters and hieroglyphics might be of immense importance in deciphering the ancient hieroglyphics of the Maya, which not only exist in the three codices but are inscribed on thousands of archaeological artifacts such as stelae, wall frescoes, and ceramic objects.

I mentioned my discovery to several archaeologists, but I couldn't persuade them to attempt to see and photograph these books. Some of the Maryknoll missionaries showed more interest. In 1960, Father Bernard Nagle went to Champon but failed to accomplish any more than I had, although he was able to determine that British visitors would be the only outsiders welcome there. He passed this information on to Pablo Bush Romero, who organized a CEDAM expedition into Champon to try and see the books. The expedition members were Americans who couldn't be mistaken for Mexican. They made the rough trip to Champon, taking a picture of Queen Victoria with them for the villagers. They persuaded Vega to let them see the books, but when they approached the church, they were stopped by the high priest and armed guards who threatened to shoot them. The Americans made several mistakes that Milt and I later discovered, so they didn't get to see the books. They frightened the villagers, who weren't accustomed to seeing outsiders, by coming to the village with a large group. They also identified themselves as Americans rather than British.

They found Vega dying from a stomach hernia and a tumor in his mouth. Upon learning of this, Pablo arranged for a helicopter to airlift Vega to civilization and a hospital. It took a great deal of persuasion to convince the old man to leave his people and village, but he finally agreed. He was treated in a hospital in Mexico City and returned, cured, to his village, where he died in 1969.

For years I had been contemplating making another attempt to see the ancient books in Champon, but everyone I talked to thought it was too dangerous. I mentioned my plan to Milt, a man who loves to tackle the impossible. He jumped at the idea and offered to go with me. Our goal was not only to see the old books but to visit all three religious centers, get into each church if possible, attend the religious ceremonies, and come out alive with a photographic record of everything we saw.

Thoroughly researching every aspect of our planned expedition, we waited six months for the end of the rainy season. When we arrived in Mérida, Yucatán, we were met by Pablo Bush Romero, who spent several days filling us in on everything about the area that he had learned from the Americans he had sent into Champon in 1962. We also obtained valuable information from the Maryknoll missionaries, who knew the area. One of them, Father Walter Winrich, had recently been to Champon. He reported that our chance of seeing the books now was even slimmer than when Vega had been alive. The high priest totally controlled the villagers; his orders were to shoot anyone even approaching the church. Father Winrich suggested that we forget about Champon and instead visit Chancah and Tixcacal, where we might receive a better reception. He further suggested that we take gifts such as small bells, mirrors, combs, and brightly colored cloth—a good suggestion, for the gifts were eagerly received in each of the villages we visited.

Our plan entailed going into each place with only one guide who could speak both Mayan and Spanish fluently, carrying no firearms, and posing as Englishmen. Milt had gotten an assignment from an English newspaper to cover our expedition for it, so we figured it would not be amiss if we wore small British flags on our jungle jackets.

We made Carrillo Puerto (the new name for Chan Santa Cruz) our base of operations. There we were fortunate in obtaining the services of an excellent guide and translator named Julian Xix (pronounced Shish). Julian was the sexton of the Catholic church in Carrillo Puerto and was widely known and respected throughout the territory. Several people told us that if he hadn't taken up with the Catholic missionaries, he might have been the person to succeed Vega as the Tatich of the Maya. He had been to all three of the Mayan religious centers but not inside the churches.

Our first objective was Chancah, which was about twenty miles from our base. The night before we started out, the governor's representative in Carrillo Puerto came to us and begged us to forget about the expedition and go home. It would save him a lot of worry, he said, and save us our lives.

The following morning, after a breakfast of cold tortillas and beans washed down with warm Pepsi-Cola, we left before sunrise. We reached Chancah just as the sun appeared over the high trees surrounding the village. We had explained in detail to Julian that we must let the people know we meant no harm, that we merely wished to photograph the holy books. Since many unsophisticated peoples are afraid that the camera will steal their souls, we knew it would be difficult to get permission to photograph the books. But Julian, we quickly discovered, was a born diplomat.

The village consisted of thirty-six thatched huts clustered around the church, which was the focus of community life. The church was about 120 feet long and 55 feet wide, with stucco walls and a thatched roof. Adjacent to it was the guard shack, where three armed guards were on duty. Julian took us directly to the guard shack. He knew one of the guards and, without our understanding what he was saying, convinced them that we were ambassadors sent by the queen of England and that the queen was eager for news about their church. The guards decided to unlock the church and let us in to see and even agreed to let us photograph it. But just as one of them was unlocking the massive church door, an old woman with bright blue eyes and wearing several gold necklaces, one of which contained two large red stones like rubies, ran up and pushed the guard aside and started screaming at him. She was the wife of the high priest and would not allow anyone to enter the church without her husband's permission. She said her husband was away working in his cornfield and insisted we would have to await his return.

We had heard that a few miles away there was a lake. We decided to go there and skin-dive, rather than sit around in the village all day waiting for the high priest. Several of the villagers acted as guides, including the son of the priest. After spending several hours exploring the lake and discovering the remains of an ancient Mayan temple that had fallen into it, we came out to find Julian very excited. While we were diving, it seems, the Indians had told him that vicious alligators as large as eighteen feet long had recently been captured in the lake. During our dive we had run into several baby gators, and I was damn glad we hadn't met any of their parents.

We hiked back to the village. I remarked that this was the day the Apollo 14 astronauts were landing on the moon. Julian translated what I had said to the high priest's son, whose mood suddenly shifted from calm to rage. He said that surely I was trying to make a fool out of him in trying to tell him such a lie. Neither he nor any of the other villagers had heard of the flights to the moon.

Back in the village, we found the people very suspicious of us. Julian soon ascertained that they suspected us of being spies for the Mexican government. To break the ice, he went into great detail about our being representatives of the English queen, and we began passing out our gifts. They were afraid of our various cameras, and it was difficult getting the first picture; but after a Polaroid picture was taken and shown to the people, everyone wanted one of his own. Milt went through several rolls of Polaroid film. On the last roll, he encountered problems. The emulsion on the film had been affected by the intense heat of the jungle. He used up all but the last photograph on the roll. All were duds, so he stopped, saving that last one for an emergency.

Late in the afternoon the high priest returned. He was a short, compact man with a scowl that seemed permanently etched on his broad face. At first he refused to speak with us, but Julian spoke to him at length, and he finally agreed to let us inside the church if—and this was the catch—we took a photograph of him and his wife that he could see immediately. Milt explained through Julian that we had only one Polaroid photograph left and that it probably wouldn't come out. The priest was adamant. No photograph, no holy books. He said that if the photograph didn't come out, it would be a sign from God that we should not be permitted inside the church. By a miracle (or just plain fool's luck), the photograph came out, and for the first time we saw his face break into a broad smile. We then gave him the small bells and candles we had brought and said we wanted him to officiate at a Mass for the queen of England. He agreed, and we headed for the church.

Passing the guard shack, we were halted by a command

from an old man inside. He was introduced as the chief of the village. He said he was 107 years old and had fought in the Caste War. Julian spent another hour convincing him of our good intentions. The hardest part was making him believe that Queen Victoria had died in 1901 and that a new queen ruled Great Britain. He told us of many injustices inflicted on his people by the Mexicans and begged us to convince the new queen to send his people arms so they could wage war against the Mexicans and become an independent nation or a part of Great Britain. We heard this same request in the other villages when we visited them. Finally he said we could have our Mass for the queen if we promised to send him a photograph of Queen Elizabeth and tell her everything he had told us.

Our candles were lit. We knelt for the Mass in front of a large stage with a closed drape on it. When the drape was opened, we could scarcely believe our eyes. There were twenty-eight statues of various saints, ranging from six to ten feet high. All of them appeared to be several hundred years old, and many were ornamented with elaborate gold crowns and other gold and gem-set jewelry of great beauty. Several of the saints wore no crowns. In their place they sported modern panama hats. In the center of the stage was wooden cross about twenty feet high, and around the outside of the stage were about thirty small wooden crosses, all nearly identical, partly covered with brightly colored cloth. (Later we were told that one of them was the one made from the original Speaking Cross and that no one except the high priest knew which it was.) There were also seven tabernacles, several of which were richly ornamented with gold leaf. Scattered about between the statues were many timeworn, but still gorgeous, church vestments of silk and brocade. These items had been taken from various churches during the Caste War. It was an incredible experience. I felt I had somehow stepped back into history. The Mass lasted about half an hour, by which time our knees were really aching, but we didn't budge. It didn't even remotely resemble a Catholic Mass. The priest and several of his assistants prayed in Mayan without a pause and occasionally sang a few lines in high-pitched voices.

They refused to permit us to photograph the interior of the church, for fear that the saints would punish them. After the Mass was over we saw that at the rear of the church there were three old bronze church bells, one dating from 1578, as well as a large drum the Indians had captured from the Mexican army.

Soon after we left the church, we noticed some of the men carrying buckets of water into the church and asked what they were doing. We were told that the high priest was conducting a purification ceremony in the church. We were the first out-siders ever to enter the church, and he didn't want to be pun-ished by God or the saints.

After resting for a day, we decided to tackle Tixcacal Guar-dia. Julian suggested that we go to the town of Señor first. He knew an old man there who had much influence with the high priest in Tixcacal. Julian thought it would be helpful if he would accompany us to the sacred town. The old man in Señor turned out to be a ninety-seven-year-old Chinese who had been captured as a boy by the rebel Indians while working with some Englishmen who were selling guns to the Indians. He was one of the most skilled *curanderos,* or healers, in the area and was widely respected. As soon as he saw the British flag on my shirt, he came up to me, pointing at the flag and pulling my hair. He called us "Englishmen" and agreed to go with us. We replenished our supplies, bought fresh film, and set off.

Tixcacal Guardia was similar to Chancah. As soon as we entered the place, Julian went to work, telling the people that the queen had sent us and that we had come in peace. This information was quickly relayed to the high priest, who sent word that we must wait for a formal escort into the village, as befitted representatives of the queen. After about half an hour the high priest and two other priests, as well as the captain of the guard, appeared with seven armed guards. The high priest was one of the grimmest-looking men I had ever seen. We weren't sure just what kind of reception awaited us. After the long speeches, which were demanded by protocol, we were given oral messages for the queen of England. We then gave the high priest three small bells. He took them in his hand, testing each one. Then, satisfied with their tone, he broke into a friendly grin and passed them on to the other two priests, who went through the same ritual. The high priest apologized for not giving us a proper salute with firearms; his people, he said, might soon have to make war with the Mexicans, and they would need every bullet they had.

Then we were marched to the church between the guards. We stopped at the door to remove our shoes, which was the custom at all of their churches. The church was smaller than the one at Chancah. At the rear were three old bronze bells and two drums. Each of us gave thirteen candles for the Mass (a lucky number to these people). We knelt before a large table of burning candles placed in front of a small altar. The inside of the church wasn't as richly decorated as the one at Chancah, but the Mass took its toll on our knees, because though otherwise the same it was twice as long. These men permitted us to take all the pictures we wished, even during the Mass.

After the Mass we asked if they had any ancient books. To our astonishment, they said they had one and would show it to us. The high priest opened the door of the only tabernacle on the altar and took out the book, which was wrapped in a yellow cloth. He placed it on a table that was covered with an old religious vestment and gave us permission to inspect and photograph it. The book, written in 1848, was copied from a much older document, which Julian had difficulty reading, since it was in archaic Mayan. However, he was able to determine that it pertained to religious matters and predictions about the future of the people.

The high priest invited us to a tasty lunch of boiled chicken, tortillas, and hot peppers. Then we headed back to Carrillo Puerto, after expressing thanks for the hospitality we had been shown.

We next went to Champon, the third religious center. Originally we had expected a two- or three-day walk to the village, but a road that passed within fourteen kilometers of the village had recently been cut through the jungle. The road builders had originally planned the road to cut right through the village, but the high priest and other leaders, quite naturally, refused to allow it. When they persisted in trying to build the road through Champon, several engineers who were surveying the terrain were fired on by villagers from Champon, and the route was changed, so we had a four-and-a-half-hour hike over rugged rocky terrain. We saw plenty of interesting animals—snakes, deer, armadillos, and wild boar—but no jaguar, which was just as well, since we carried only machetes. I had made a little better time than Milt and Julian, and when I was about a kilometer from the village, I was stopped by four armed guards, who escorted me into the village. Fortunately, I was unarmed; I later learned that they had orders to shoot any armed person approaching the village.

Milt and Julian soon arrived, and we gave our usual speech, passed out the gifts, and took Polaroid pictures. Several of the older villagers remembered me, mentioning the fact that I was now quite a bit heavier. The same high priest I had crossed swords with years before was still there, but after hearing that we had come from the queen of England, he was friendly. He explained about his people shooting at the road surveyors, saying that this had probably precipitated a war between his people and the Mexican government. A week earlier, the government had sent word that every firearm in the Indian villages must be turned in to army or police officials no later than the very day we were there, and that if this was not done, the army would be sent in to take them by force if necessary. He explained that their firearms were an essential part of their life. They were not only used to guard their church, but also to acquire wild game and fowl and protect themselves against wild animals such as jaguars, which were plentiful in the area. Milt and I quickly realized that this was no place for us to be if the army arrived. We might be shot as spies or foreign agitators, since we were wearing the British flag and posing as ambassadors from the queen. We had originally planned to spend the night there but decided instead to get out before dark.

The church was encircled by a barricade about six feet high, made of rocks. The high priest declared they would fight to the death before letting any Mexican soldiers inside the holy building. Not surprisingly, the interior of the church was almost an exact duplicate of the one at Tixcacal Guardia. In the rear there were the drums and bronze church bells, but in addition there were two old bugles, a violin, and a small iron cannon with part of its muzzle missing.

Although the Mass was supposed to be offered in honor of the queen, it must also have been to ask God for victory against the Mexican army, because it lasted about two hours, and every male in the village—about fifty men and boys—took part. Women, it seems, are never permitted in the churches. This Mass differed somewhat from the other two we had witnessed in that there was a great deal of bell ringing, wailing, and singing. Again, we were permitted to photograph anything we wished.

At the end of the Mass we inquired about the two old books. At first they claimed that none existed but then said that they wanted to have a discussion in private. We were waiting outside the church and could hear plenty of arguing going on inside. After about an hour we were summoned inside and the high priest said that we could see the books—provided that we have the queen first send them two cases of rifles and shotguns. We explained that this wasn't possible because England and Mexico were at peace and we had to remain neutral. The high priest then became so agitated that to calm him down and before our welcome was withdrawn, we agreed to go to the queen and request the weapons and bring them to the village as soon as possible.

There were two trails from Champon back to the road. We decided to split up, so that if we met soldiers, we wouldn't

all be taken. Milt and Julian took one trail and I took off alone
on the other. On the way, I almost stepped on a four-foot
rattlesnake. Startled, I fell, and my left foot got caught in some
rocks. I ended up flat on my back, unable to move. I can't
remember ever being so scared. I remained motionless, scarcely
breathing, as the snake slithered across my knees, hissing, flick-
ing its tongue, and rattling its tail. It was a miracle it didn't
strike. I had twisted my ankle and was in pain, but I made the
rest of the hike out in record time. Milt and Julian had a rough
time getting out themselves. In most places the trail was overgrown, and they got lost several times. Milt's boots were full
of blood from various blisters that had burst.

As soon as we reached Carrillo Puerto we went to see the
two missionaries and tell them about the impending war. We
asked if they could do anything to stop it and help the Indians.
That night they met with the army commander. He agreed not
to move until they had talked to the governor the next day
down in Chetumal. The governor was sympathetic to the Indians and ordered the army to forget about the shooting incident and let the Indians keep their weapons. I like to think we
were instrumental in preventing bloodshed among the Indians,
who only wanted to be left in peace.

From several sources we had heard that a man in the village
of Yaxley had some ancient documents and maps written on
animal skin, and we decided that they would be worth seeing.
Milt was barely able to walk because of his swollen feet and
blisters, so Julian and I went.

Reaching Yaxley after a four-hour hike, we discovered
that the man we had come to see was at his corn patch several
hours' walk away. The village was keeping watch over a ten-
year-old girl who had been bitten by a venomous fer-de-lance
snake and was dying. So Julian and I went in search of the man
who, the villagers said, had the documents and maps we hoped
to see. We found his wife at the corn patch. She told us that her
husband was somewhere deeper in the jungle, collecting chicle.
We scoured the area and finally had to call it quits because of

darkness and trek out to the road. By the time we reached our car, we had covered over thirty miles and had been walking for over eleven hours.

By this time we had already accomplished a great deal more than we had hoped for, and urgent commitments back in the States dictated our return to the rat race. We planned a return trip and felt certain that next time we would get to photograph the two ancient books at Champon.

Milt and I were to regret publicizing the existence of the two books at Champon, because someone else, not content with photographing them, somehow got one of the manuscripts. Three months after returning to the United States, just as we were making plans to return to Yucatán, an eleven-page fragment of a Mayan codex turned up in an exhibition in New York City, causing a lot of excitement among scholars. It dealt with the religious and astrological philosophy of the Mayan culture. Secrecy surrounded the manuscript. A *New York Times* article said that those in charge of the exhibition "declined any comment on the name of the owner, his nationality, or even the exact year or location of the discovery." Fearing the worst, I caught the first plane for Mérida—a move that almost put me in jail. A friend who met me at the airport warned me that the Mexican authorities believed that Milt and I had found the codex, smuggled it out of the country, and sold it for two million dollars.

I rented a car and rushed to Carrillo Puerto. There I contacted Julian and found that matters were even worse than I could have imagined. Not only were the Mexican authorities after me, but the Mayans of the three religious centers as well. About a month after we left, someone had gotten into the church and stolen both books undetected. Unfortunately, but not surprisingly, the Indians thought Milt and I were behind the theft. Heeding Julian's advice, I left town. I was very angry at whoever had robbed the Indians of the thing most sacred to them and deeply depressed that I couldn't tell the villagers that we had not committed the theft. The identity of the culprit or culprits has never been discovered, but Milt and I were eventually cleared of any involvement by the Mexican authorities. Months of investigation yielded only the disturbing information that the codex had been cut up into many parts and that the eleven-page fragment that ended up in New York had been purchased by a Texan for two million dollars.

11

The Land of Phoenicia

There are few places in the world that encompass such a wide span of history as present-day Lebanon. This beautiful but tortured country where Europe, Asia, and Africa meet has been the crossroads of civilization since earliest times. For seven thousand years it has been the stage where Chaldeans, Babylonians, Assyrians, Egyptians, Phoenicians, Hittites, Persians, Greeks, Romans, Arabs, Turks, and Christian Crusaders fought and settled. Even today this tiny mountainous country that stretches along the rocky shore of the eastern Mediterranean is riven by civil strife between Christians and Moslems and is subject to attack from Israel.

Of all the peoples who have figured in the history of Lebanon, no one populated the land as long, or brought the country as much fame and glory, as the Phoenicians, the Semitic seagoing people who established themselves in harbor towns like Tyre, Sidon, Byblos, and Acre and later pushed westward to found Carthage and Utica on the north Africa coast. I have been fascinated by the Phoenicians since I was a child, when I first read that it was in Phoenicia that the alphabet we use today was developed and then disseminated by seaborne traders. They were unrivaled in antiquity as master mariners and consummate traders. Known as the Sea People, they ventured where others dared not go, sailing into the unknown to trade with Spain and Great Britain to the north, and with tribes along the coasts of North Africa, and venturing south to barter on the coast of West Africa. As I have explained in chapter 2, they are more likely than other Mediterranean peoples to have reached the shores of the New World because of the far-ranging nature of their sea trade.

Therefore, the idea of constructing a replica Phoenician ship and sailing it to the Americas was always on my mind, no matter what I was doing. By the early 1970s I had decided that since I couldn't excavate the Phoenician shipwrecks in Cádiz Bay to gather the data required to construct a replica, and since Peter Throckmorton had found scant wooden remains on his Phoenician site in Turkey, I should search the Lebanon coast for Phoenician wrecks with remnants of their wooden hulls.

UNESCO agreed to sponsor an expedition, and Emir Maurice Chehab, Lebanon's director general of antiquities, offered his full cooperation in the undertaking. We declined the government's offer of military protection, although some of our underwater explorations were planned for the southern coast of Lebanon, which was then under the control of the PLO and other Palestinian organizations. Our initial goal was to make preliminary explorations of the ports of Byblos, Sidon, and Tyre to determine if there were sufficient amounts of sediment on the seafloor of these ancient ports to conceal and preserve the remains of Phoenician shipwrecks.

Interestingly, just a few days before I was to fly to Lebanon in January 1973, with Milt Machlin and Jack Kelley, a diving friend from Tulsa, the *New York Times* carried a story about a Phoenician wreck, dating from about the fifth century B.C., that had been discovered off the coast of Israel near the port of

Shavei Zion, quite close to the Lebanese border. My old friend Dr. Elisha Linder was at it again. This find excited the archaeological world because part of the cargo consisted of figurines of Tanit, the goddess of fertility and the principal female deity of the Phoenician world. Made of red clay, they ranged in size from six to fifteen inches. Previously, archaeologists excavating at Carthage in Tunisia had found drawings and symbols of the goddess and impressions of her on bronze coins. However, this was the first time that figurines of Tanit had ever been found. I called Dr. Linder, ready to switch our itinerary and head for Israel, but he told me that the cargo had been found on a hard rocky bottom and that no traces of the ship had survived. Linder said, "You old pirate, with your luck you'll probably find a better Phoenician shipwreck in Lebanon and really make me furious." How right he turned out to be.

I headed for Lebanon all fired up and excited as a kid at Christmas. We spent several days in Beirut, which was then still a very beautiful, sophisticated city. Under the tutelage of Dr. Chehab, we spent many hours studying the Phoenician artifacts in the National Museum before going to Byblos, where we were to begin work.

According to tradition, Byblos is the oldest continually inhabited town in the world. Recent excavations have revealed the existence of a Neolithic culture dating back to 5000 B.C. Long before the Greeks and Romans arrived, Byblos, under the Phoenicians, was a powerful independent city-state with its own kings and culture and a flourishing trade. During the third millennium B.C. it was the most important seaport in the Mediterranean until eclipsed by the Phoenician seaports of Tyre and Sidon. Today very little of its former glory can be seen. Byblos is a sleepy little fishing port with several small restaurants for weekend visitors, who come to see the massive Roman ruins that are the town's most impressive sight. Unfortunately the Romans built on Greek ruins, which in turn covered the site of the Phoenician city. Wherever we walked we found traces of the past in the form of ceramic sherds of all periods of history.

Although the coast here is rocky, earthquakes over the centuries have toppled many of the ancient buildings into the sea and caused soil to slide into the sea. Underneath all the debris there was a good chance that remains of wrecks could be found. Dr. Chehab arranged for us to meet a hotel owner named Pepe Abed, who has the most extensive private museum in the country. His collection contains many priceless artifacts, including Greek and Roman statues that he discovered underwater or bought from fishermen. He had recently acquired a highly unusual piece—a gold ring with a reversible setting, showing a Phoenician king and his son on one side and his queen and daughter on the other. Along the beach, local boys find coins—copper, bronze, and sometimes silver and gold—which they sell to tourists.

The water was a chilly 45 degrees Fahrenheit, but the excitement of diving in such a place kept us from minding the temperature. I'll never forget my first look at the seafloor off Byblos. It was like an underwater museum. Scattered over the bottom were large numbers of immense marble columns and worked building stones, covering thousands of years of history. Many were carved with beautiful designs. Even more exciting was our discovery of the cargo of a Phoenician shipwreck dating to the eighth century B.C., consisting of amphorae and other ceramic objects. However, we found no wood of the ship's hull. During the four days we spent surveying the site we recovered eight Phoenician stone anchors, many ceramic artifacts and sherds covering a span of three thousand years, and the lower torso of a Roman man in terra-cotta.

We then went to Sidon, founded around 1400 B.C. and second only to Tyre in the heyday of the Phoenicians. This city has been destroyed many times by earthquakes and invaders, and very little of the fabled ancient town can be seen today. Like Tyre, Sidon has borne the brunt of Israeli bombings over the past few decades. The most impressive building still standing, a sea fortress built by the Crusaders at the port entrance, dates back only to the twelfth century.

After Byblos we had a high level of anticipation as we began our first dive. However, we found Sidon to be quite a letdown. The seafloor was covered with tons of modern trash, and it was almost impossible to find any traces of antiquity without first removing layers of debris. In addition, a large portion of the seabed was covered with thousands of projectiles and bombs, all of them still explosive. During World War II, before a fleet of Vichy French warships surrendered to the British, they jettisoned their munitions overboard at their anchorage off Sidon. Nevertheless, we were fortunate in finding the cargo of a second Phoenician ship, a cargo of amphorae, but no traces of the ship itself.

Tyre, founded by the Phoenicians in 2750 B.C., was one of the most celebrated cities in the ancient world and the most important commercial center in the eastern Mediterranean. Tyre enjoyed a flourishing maritime trade and established colonies all over the Mediterranean and Atlantic coasts. The city was renowned for its glass industries and purple dye from the murex shell; "Phoenicia" is the Greek translation of "Canaan," "Land of the purple [traders]."

Originally Tyre consisted of a mainland settlement and a highly defensible island city a short distance offshore. In 332 B.C., Alexander the Great stopped with his army at Tyre's mainland settlement and was offered full hospitality by the inhabitants. However, those living on the island refused to welcome the Macedonian emperor. They believed themselves invincible because of a 150-foot wall that surrounded the city and a large fleet of galleys that formed a barrier to the entrance of its two harbors. Incensed by this breach of courtesy, Alexander laid siege to the island for seven months. A fleet of 250 vessels was assembled to blockade the city by sea, and during a number of encounters ships were lost by both sides.

This is the first recorded time that divers were used in warfare. Both sides employed them. The Macedonians, after reducing the fighting spirit of the defenders, used divers to destroy the boom defenses of the harbors, which Tyrian divers then rebuilt. According to legend, Alexander himself descended in a diving bell to inspect the destruction of the defenses. After failing to capture the city by sea, the Macedonians built a causeway connecting the island to the mainland and made use of it to breach the city walls. Once inside, Alexander's men massacred more than eleven thousand inhabitants and sold thirty thousand others into slavery. Before departing they set the city afire and razed it.

Although Tyre was rebuilt, it never regained its former glory. Carthage, on the African coast, soon replaced it as the most important Phoenician seaport in the Mediterranean. Many believe that some portion of the island city is now sunken under the sea and covered by sand. When we dove around the island we found that, as at Byblos, the seafloor is littered with hundreds of columns and massive building stones. The ancient jetties and moles of the two harbors are also visible underwater at an average depth of six fathoms. Excavations on land during the past thirty years have uncovered remains of Crusader, Arab, Byzantine, and Graeco-Roman towns, but the archaeologists have not yet reached the level of the underlying Phoenician city. One of the largest hippodromes of the Roman period has recently been uncovered; built during the second century A.D., it lay buried under twenty feet of windswept sand.

Arriving at Tyre, we were shocked to see a clamshell dredge being used to deepen the modern harbor, one of the two harbors in use in ancient times, on the north side of the town. As bucket after bucket of mud was brought up, we spotted many artifacts, including a couple of miraculously intact Roman amphorae. When one of the Lebanese archaeologists who had been assigned to work with us tried to take possession of several important objects, a number of the workmen launched into a furious argument; violence was averted only by the fortuitous arrival of several police officers.

We were soon to discover that the modern inhabitants of Tyre feel that anything coming out of the sea rightfully belongs to them, not to the government. The illegal sale of ancient artifacts is one of the town's main businesses. Several dozen sponge divers work out of the port and are known to make more from the sale of antiquities than from sponges. They took great offense at our coming there to find anything that might deprive them of a source of income. Most of the fishermen felt the same way, and it was with difficulty that we were finally able to rent a small boat.

It was only after plying the fisherman whose boat we rented with a staggering amount of the local brandy that we got him to take us to an area where he had snagged and raised several amphorae in his nets. He placed us right on top of a Roman amphora wreck dating from the first century A.D. Unfortunately, he had also shown others the site, probably the sponge divers. Where once there were thousands of intact amphorae, there are now only thousands of sherds, because the coral growth in which the amphorae were lodged was dynamited by someone trying to dislodge them. We mapped the site for the government archaeologists and then dug into the mass of broken amphorae, managing to find two that were still whole. Nearby we found another area containing lots of Roman ceramic oil lamps, plates, small jars, and ointment bottles, all of which appear to have been lost when a small boat capsized.

Half of the town's inhabitants were waiting as we came ashore with our finds that first day. They were clearly unhappy, and our poor fisherman guide bore the brunt of angry remarks for having shown us a good area and having helped us to find artifacts. However, he continued with us for the next three days. He took us to a number of sites that he swore had yielded ancient artifacts, but we found only several Phoenician stone anchors, which have no value to the local people. We realized that he had been deliberately taking us to areas where he was certain nothing would be found in order to keep his good standing in the community.

When we reported this to Emir Maurice Chehab, he arranged for one of the men on his excavation team who had a small boat to work with us. Our first goal was to survey a large area near the southern harbor where Dr. Chehab believed a number of vessels had been lost during the siege of Alexander the Great. After a visual search that produced a few pieces of pottery and one large lead Roman anchor stock, Jack Kelley and I used long metal probes to locate solid objects buried under the deep sand. In four areas we located what we felt certain were shipwrecks, but lack of excavation equipment prevented us from verifying these finds.

We then began searching visually again, this time closer to shore inside the southern harbor, and we made one exciting find after another. The bottom was nearly covered with a paving of artifacts. We recovered some samples for study by Dr. Chehab and his staff. When the local sea dogs learned that we were recovering more important objects without their help, they resorted to drastic action. Many of the fishermen use dynamite to kill fish, and we soon found that some of them were always near whenever we were on the bottom; they were soon dropping dynamite to discourage us. When we moved on to a new site, so did they.

To cover larger areas we hung on lines and were towed behind our boat, which was always shadowed by at least a couple of fishing boats. In two days of searching in this manner we found four more shipwreck sites: a Phoenician wreck from the fourth century B.C., two Greek wrecks from the third and second centuries B.C., and a Byzantine wreck dating around 600 A.D. The Phoenician and Greek wrecks were on rocky bottoms with no surviving traces of the ships that carried cargoes of amphorae. Like the Roman wreck we had found our first day at Tyre, all three of these had been dynamited and plundered, but we still brought up an interesting collection of artifacts from them. The Byzantine wreck was on a sandy bottom, and by digging in the sand we recovered part of her cargo of brightly colored plates and bowls, ceramic jugs, and several mortars of basalt.

We started off our last day at Tyre using the metal probes

to determine the depth of sand and mud in the center of the southern harbor. The day began badly but ended happily. After about two hours on the numbing cold bottom, I accidentally touched a venomous scorpion fish. I immediately felt severe nausea and had to surface. While I was recuperating in the boat, Kelley surfaced. He reported that his probe had struck something solid six feet beneath the sand. By this time he was out of air and too cold to go back down, so I went back in, although I was still dizzy and on the verge of vomiting. I loosened Kelley's probe, which felt as if it had been stuck in wood. Digging by hand in loose, powdery sand is no easy task, and after an hour I had only succeeded in digging a small hole about three feet deep.

Kelley then rejoined me, and we finally reached a depth of four feet, where we uncovered several Phoenician amphorae, which the expedition's Lebanese archaeologists quickly dated to the fifth century B.C. While widening the hole and uncovering more amphorae, I suddenly spotted three clay figurines, ranging from five to thirteen inches in length. Nearby I found two more. I brought them to the surface, and the two archaeologists were ecstatic. Their excitement increased when Kelley came up with two more, making a total of seven figurines found. Our air was almost depleted and the sun was already fading on the horizon, so I made one last brief dive. Forcing my hand as far down in the deepest part of the hole we had dug as if it were a drill, I felt hard wood, which to me was far more important than anything else we had found during our stay in Lebanon. Only a complete excavation of this site will reveal if we found only a small section of the hull or a greater part of the wooden remains of a Phoenician ship that once plied the Mediterranean. It is a shame that because of the incessant state of war that exists in the area, no one has been able to carry out a thorough excavation of this promising site.

Amazingly, the statuettes we found are identical to those found at Shavei Zion in Israel. The two sites are only about fifteen miles apart. The figurines represent the goddess Tanit with her right hand raised in a gesture of blessing and her left hand either over her breast or holding a baby, and two of them show her pregnant.

Our expedition was more than we had bargained for. We had come to Lebanon to study the feasibility of locating Phoenician shipwrecks and in just three weeks had found more Phoenician shipwreck sites than had been found throughout the entire Mediterranean to date. During our last night in Beirut I never slept. There was no way I could leave without knowing if there was enough wood on that Phoenician shipwreck to enable me to reconstruct a replica. Machlin and Kelley left in the morning for New York without me.

I went to see a surprised Dr. Chehab at the National Museum and told him that I was returning to Tyre to explore the Phoenician shipwreck site further. He explained that he and his assistants were about to leave for a conference in Paris and I would have to go alone. I was concerned about the high level of anti-American feeling in the area and was able to find a UNESCO representative to accompany me. I also hired a university student as a translator.

The mood of the people along Tyre's waterfront was clearly menacing. I couldn't find a boat for hire despite the translator's heroic efforts to explain that I only wanted to examine the Phoenician wreck to determine its construction. It seemed the people were enraged at our having found the Tanit figurines for the National Museum. They felt they had been robbed, and their demeanor so unnerved my companions that they left for Beirut after a couple of hours.

I had no choice but to work from shore, using a snorkel to swim out to the site and then scuba equipment, which I dragged behind me, to explore on the site. When I got to the shore closest to the wreck, however, I was shocked to find half a dozen small fishing boats on the site. I made my way out, dreading an encounter but determined to explore the ship's hull area. I saw about twenty divers on the bottom. Some wore hard-hat helmet rigs, and all of them were digging into the mud retrieving artifacts. They smashed all the intact amphorae they found and even disregarded intact bowls and plates in their frenzy to find as many figurines as possible.

At first they seemed unaware of my presence. Taking advantage of their preoccupation, I began digging into the mud to expose as much of the hull as possible. It was one of the most memorable dives of my life. I was using a double-tank scuba arrangement that gave me over two hours of bottom time. During that period I was able to uncover an area of two by four meters of one side of the Phoenician ship. There were timbers, and I was surprised to see they were of pine, not the cedar the Bible (our best source of information on the subject) describes as being the chief wood used in Phoenician ship construction. I found ribs, too, made of oak. Interestingly, pine and oak were the principal woods used in the Spanish and Portuguese ships of the colonial period that I have done so much work on. This in itself was quite an important discovery. I had been concerned about finding cedar to build my Phoenician ship replica. The few remaining cedar trees in Lebanon are national monuments, and elsewhere in the Mediterranean region cedars have disappeared.

I finally ran out of air and had to surface. One of the boatmen recognized me, and all hell broke loose. He rowed over and began beating me on the head with an oar, after screaming to other boats that I was there stealing their treasures. Unable to swim very fast with my scuba equipment on, I dropped my tanks and weight belt and broke a world's record heading for the shore, with the boatmen in hot pursuit. Once ashore I found that someone had made off with my clothes and shoes. Fortunately, my money and passport were locked in my hotel room. Running barefooted in my dripping rubber suit, I headed for the local police station, with several fishermen chasing me. Instead of getting a bit of sympathy, I was informed that I was being arrested for plundering an archaeological site. By this time, Dr. Chehab and his team had left for Paris, and I had no documentation authorizing me to make any underwater explorations. For a while things looked pretty bleak. The police even refused to permit me to return to my hotel room for my clothes or to make a phone call. I then told them a little white lie and said I was on the staff of UNESCO and asked permission to call my office in Beirut, a request they debated for a couple of hours before relenting. I called UNESCO and reached someone in authority, who first berated the police chief and then sent a man down from Beirut to escort me back.

This might have been the end of the matter. But I couldn't let it rest. Dr. Chehab was convinced of the extraordinary archaeological significance of this site, and the following year he arranged for me to return with a minimum of problems. I agreed to be interrogated by several intelligence officers of the PLO. After I convinced them I didn't work for the CIA, they introduced me to several of Tyre's leading citizens, whom I then had to persuade of the importance of my work. They in turn ordered the fishermen to give me a free hand at whatever I wanted to do.

This time I came prepared with a Zodiac rubber boat so I wouldn't have to rely on the local fishermen. Dr. Chehab also promised to provide several local sport divers to assist me, but at the last moment they thought better of assisting an American in this troubled area. Before leaving Beirut I visited several antique shops and was disheartened to see dozens of the Tanit figurines on sale. One of the antique dealers informed me that Pepe Abed had had a team of divers completely dig out the wreck using high-pressure water jets. The same man suggested that I should meet a grave robber in Tyre who had recently discovered a stone at a nearby Phoenician site that depicted a ship. So after I got clearance from all concerned to work the site further, my first stop was to visit this chap. He had found a stone with a Phoenician ship engraved on it, but even more important was the fact that this ship had a small foresail in addition to its mainsail. It had been unknown up to this point whether the ancients had used a foresail, which allows a vessel to sail much better and be more easily steered. This discovery underscored the celebrated maritime abilities of the Phoenicians.

Seeing and photographing the inscribed stone was enough to make the expedition worthwhile, but I still needed to know much more about Phoenician ships. What I saw upon reaching the bottom where the Phoenician shipwreck had lain broke my heart. Nothing remained but a giant hole with thousands of broken pieces of ceramic and parts of shattered Tanit figurines.

The fishermen and Pepe Abed's divers had destroyed my best chance of reconstructing an ancient Phoenician ship replica. I was crestfallen, but I was not going to give up. If one Phoenician wreck lay buried in this port, there had to be more. The best way to find one would be to utilize a sub-bottom-profiling sonar device, the way we had at the sunken city of Port Royal and on the Columbus shipwreck site in Jamaica. There were none in Lebanon, so my thoughts turned to Dr. Edgerton, but he was on a several-month-long cruise aboard a Russian oceanographic vessel. I spent a staggering amount on long-distance phone calls trying to rent a unit, but none was available. Consequently, I had to resort to low-tech methods.

Armed with a metal probe about twelve feet long, I began a systematic search of the bottom. Each time I struck something solid only a few feet deep, I dug a test hole with my hands and investigated the spot. I mapped the deeper buried targets for further investigation. Using this method I located three buried Roman wrecks, which I quickly reburied to conceal them from plunderers and Pepe Abed's divers. Five weeks of tedious work produced many Phoenician amphorae and other artifacts, but no intact shipwrecks, at least not in the depths of shallow sediment that I was able to uncover. I am convinced that other Phoenician shipwrecks are buried deeper in the sediment, and it is my hope that if peace ever comes to Lebanon, I can participate in a project to find and excavate one.

Several nights before I was going to leave Tyre, all hell broke loose, and I thought that World War III had commenced.

It seemed that the local fishermen had been providing boats to infiltrate PLO saboteurs into nearby Israel. That night the Israelis launched a retaliatory strike against the fishermen. From rubber Zodiacs, identical to the type I was using, Israeli frogmen came ashore and dynamited or set afire every single wooden boat in the harbor at Tyre. They also took my Zodiac away with them. During a heavy exchange of gunfire between the invaders and local PLO units, about twenty Lebanese were killed and about a hundred were wounded. The Israelis claimed to have suffered no casualties.

At first light next morning I was unceremoniously grabbed from my hotel bed by several PLO soldiers, who kept shouting that I was an Israeli spy and would be shot immediately. Circumstantial evidence weighed against me, and I thought my goose was cooked. Five years earlier the Real Eight Corporation, which I worked, had bought Rebikoff Underwater Products, a company that manufactured very sophisticated underwater vehicles. Rebikoff sold them to many of the world's navies, including Israel's. In 1969, while I was working on a Spanish shipwreck in the Florida Keys, Real Eight asked me to train a team of Israeli frogmen in the use of the Pegasus, the most elaborate of the underwater vehicles. I didn't remember that during the training I had been photographed with this Israeli frogman team, but the PLO intelligence officer who grilled me actually had a copy of the photos. They were convinced that I was an Israeli spy and that my work at Tyre was actually to map the waters for the Israeli raid that had just happened a few hours earlier. I could hardly blame them.

What a jam the great white gods had gotten me into! I was sure I was facing a few torture sessions, no doubt to be followed by a bullet in the head. Nothing I said, not even the Catholic medallion around my neck, could sway their conviction that I was an Israeli spy.

Once again, however, the good luck I have been blessed with throughout my life came to my aid. Little more than an hour after I had been seized, slapped around a bit, and interrogated, I was on my way to Beirut in a Mercedes with a beautiful dark-haired woman as my escort. She refused to say who she was or how she had happened to come to my rescue. Much later I learned she had been sent by a mutual friend, Mirna Bustani, one of the wealthiest and most powerful women in the country and the daughter of a former president of Lebanon. I am eternally grateful to Mirna and the mysterious beauty for liberating me from the grasp of those PLO guerrillas, most of whom had lost close friends and relatives in the lightning-fast Israeli raid.

As I flew across the Atlantic on the way home, after obtaining a new passport, I kept thinking what my next move would be. I knew enough to stay away from Lebanon for a while, but I thought I eventually could resume work there. Of course, I had no idea how conditions in Lebanon would deteriorate, making any underwater archaeological projects impossible.

I was still determined to find a Phoenician wreck and thought that I might as well search in Israel's waters. Dr. Linder agreed and offered the assistance of the Israeli Maritime Society, warning me that if I worked in his country it would only confirm the PLO's suspicions about me and subsequently I wouldn't be able to work in Lebanon or other nearby Arab countries. I decided to accept this risk. The Israelis were very helpful. The entire academic establishment and the Israeli navy were willing to assist me. Dr. Ben Eli, the director of the Haifa Maritime Museum, was ordered by the prime minister to offer me the complete facilities of his staff, and the Israeli Tourist Board provided free lodging and other services. They were eager to have me construct a Phoenician ship in Israel and initiate my planned transatlantic voyage from there.

Project Tanit, or "Westward Ho," as the press dubbed the endeavor, got underway in September 1975 and continued until May of the following year. We set up base at the Center of Maritime Studies at the University of Haifa. Teams of university students were assigned the tasks of determining what victuals were used on Phoenician ships, how sails and cordage were made, what games were played on shipboard, and hundreds of other aspects of Phoenician voyages. We even went so far as trying to determine the recipe for making the type of nourishing beer drunk by the Phoenicians. However, the project's main goal was to find a relatively intact Phoenician hull so a replica ship could be properly constructed.

Ancient Israel, unlike Spain and most other Mediterranean countries, had no natural harbors. This makes finding a ship-wreck more difficult. The Romans constructed harbors at Cae-sarea and other places along the coast, and the Phoenicians may have done the same, but we didn't know where. It would have been ideal to find a Phoenician shipwreck in an anaerobic mud environment so that it would be better preserved. But there are no places like that on the coast of Israel, and we had to search in the open seas. This was a slow, painstaking process, and I knew there was little likelihood of finding an intact wreck or even one that would furnish us with additional data on Phoe-nician ship construction.

Divers from as far away as Australia had read about Project Tanit and volunteered to work on the project. We needed all the help we could get and selected several qualified sport divers to join our team. We spent thousands of hours combing the seas up to depths of 150 feet. In the end we did find dozens of shipwrecks, including five more Phoenician wrecks, but none, sadly, with any wooden remains. There was always a great deal of excitement going on, sometimes more than I bargained for.

One morning we were about two miles offshore. Our Zodiac was anchored over a shipwreck we were investigating. I heard the high-speed pitch of a fast-approaching vessel and surfaced to check it out. An Israeli frigate was bearing down on the rubber boat at full speed. I waved frantically, to no avail. I realized that the frigate's crew apparently hadn't seen me and swiftly headed for the bottom. Seconds later all our diving equipment, such as extra scuba tanks and cameras, and the Zodiac's outboard engine came raining down on us. By the time we surfaced the vessel was heading away back toward Haifa. "My God," I told my bewildered divers, "this place is more dangerous than Lebanon." It turned out that the Israeli navy had assumed that the rubber boat had been used by Palestinian infiltrators and then abandoned, so the frigate destroyed it and then headed back to port. Swimming to shore was no picnic, because there was an offshore wind blowing and the seas were relatively high. On another occasion we happened to be in the wrong place at the wrong time. While checking out another location, we came under an artillery barrage.

After we had exhausted all hope of finding a good Phoenician shipwreck in Israel's waters, Project Tanit came to an end. It was at times like this that I wished I had never heard of the great white gods.

Two years later, in 1979, I came very close to accomplishing what I had failed to do in Lebanon and Israel. Close friends, Jean-Yves and Maria Luísa Blot, who are underwater archaeologists living in Portugal, wrote me that many Phoenician artifacts were coming up in the nets of fishermen in the small port of Portimão on the coast of Portugal's Algarve province. By the time I appeared on the scene they had a nice collection of Phoenician ceramic sherds and several stone anchors and had already determined where two Phoenician wrecks lay. Several hours of diving in the muddy harbor convinced me that we had another site like La Caleta in Spain. The mud in which both Phoenician shipwrecks lay was anaerobic, leading us to think they might be in a fair state of preservation. I went to Lisbon to apply for an archaeological excavation permit and found the bureaucrats there at least as difficult to deal with as those in Spain. Don Quixote was now chasing windmills in Portugal.

During the ensuing three years, I was unable, despite the support of UNESCO, to persuade the government to give me permission to work on the wreck sites. I was caught in a Catch-22 situation. Portugal had no legislation relevant to shipwrecks, and the bureaucrats were adamant that before the government could issue a permit a law would have to be passed. To date, such a law is still in the works, and most likely it won't be passed in my lifetime. It didn't matter in the end. In late 1982, dredging operations commenced in the port of Portimão and all traces of both Phoenician ships were obliterated along with my dream.

12

Romans in Brazil

I n the summer of 1976, I was off the western coast of Australia participating in the exploration of an early-seventeenth-century Dutch shipwreck. I was having a wonderful time. The wreck site, located off a particularly barren and beautiful stretch of shore, was fascinating, and I thoroughly enjoyed the Australians I was working with. But when Jenifer called and told me that a Greek shipwreck had purportedly been found in Brazil, I immediately arranged for a helicopter lift to civilization and headed home. The great white gods beckoned me.

Jenifer said that a Brazilian friend, Commander Max Guedes, director of the Maritime Museum in Rio de Janeiro, had sent me several newspaper and weekly magazine articles that reported that a Greek shipwreck had been discovered in the Bay of Guanabara, about nine miles from the center of Rio de Janeiro. The basis for the claim was the identification of two clay jars recovered from the site. The amphorae, according to archaeologists, were of fifth-century-B.C. Greek origin. I jumped at the opportunity to follow up on the find.

The Paraíba Stone, an artifact found in northern Brazil in 1872, had been identified by Dr. Cyrus Gordon and others as being Phoenician. I had long thought there was little doubt that the Phoenicians had been the first to reach the New World from the east. Now it appeared there might be a further indication that other early Mediterranean mariners had followed in their wake. During the forty hours it took to fly home from Australia I began rehashing everything I could remember about pre-Columbian contact with Brazil.

My mind went back to 1954, when I represented the U.S. Marine Corps and won the International Underwater Spearfishing Championship. That year the tournament was held just off the shore of Rio de Janeiro, near an impressive headland called Gavea Rock. I remembered that near its top are a number of ancient inscriptions, which our hosts told us were believed to be either Phoenician or Greek. Someone had joked that one of us might be lucky enough during the tournament to find an ancient shipwreck loaded with gold. The other contestants had a good laugh, but I had taken the matter a bit more seriously.

At the conclusion of the tournament I had gone to the National Museum and met with the director. He confirmed the existence of the inscriptions and went on to tell me that there were hundreds of such stones all over the country. He said they had been studied and proved to be authentic. Most were considered to be Phoenician but others were identified as being Roman, Greek, or Norse. He produced a stack of books, but they were written in Portuguese and other European languages that I could not read at the time. I could see from hundreds of photographs, however, that this was something that I should study in the future.

I began researching, over the years amassing thousands of pages of notes and photocopies of documents about pre-Columbian contact, and I discovered that there were more books written about pre-Columbian contact with Brazil than with any other place in the Western Hemisphere. The one day that I had been able to spend in the "hidden" archive in Seville, the Archivo Colombino, which held the records about Columbus and his descendants' perpetual suits against the government, I found documents that speculated that King Solomon had discovered Brazil. I have come across this theory in numerous old books and documents. Brazilwood has been found in Egyptian tombs, which lends a little support to this belief. In the National Library in Madrid I found a Genovese chart dated 1367 that shows the coast of Brazil, labeled "Bracir." A notation on this chart states that this land was discovered by King Solomon —most likely using Phoenician mariners for the undertaking.

Under the guidance of Dr. Armando Cortesão, I located a wealth of documents in Portuguese archives and libraries that shed more light on this subject. I learned that dozens of the first Portuguese explorers and settlers who reached Brazil reported finding evidence there of earlier Old World contact. In 1545 the archbishop of Salvador, which was the capital of Brazil until 1763, reported that several large elephant heads made of stone with Egyptian inscriptions had been discovered and that a Greek inscription had been found that stated a fleet of "Alexander of Macedonia" had arrived at that place. These discoveries were confirmed by a number of learned Jesuits who also saw these objects.

Another Jesuit reported that in 1641 gold prospectors had located some strange buildings in the area that is now the state of Minas Gerais. They brought back to Salvador several strange ceramic pots and three bronze figurines with undecipherable inscriptions on them. These objects were sent to the Jesuit headquarters in Rome and three years later, after careful study, were declared to be Phoenician.

A find in 1754 created a stir all over Europe. Missionaries reported finding a large abandoned city in ruins about "three days sail up the Amazon River." They described the city as having massive stone walls and many temples and palaces. Since stone was not used by any of the Indians of Brazil in any construction prior to the arrival of the European, there were numerous suggestions about who might have built such a city. Drawings of the stone buildings and copies of inscriptions found on them were sent to Lisbon and Rome. Scholars concluded that Phoenicians were most likely the founders of the mysterious city. Interest died down, but in 1840 there was a brief flurry of excitement when it was refound. However, there was no further mention of it, and its location remains a tantalizing mystery despite a large-scale expedition led by the German explorer Herman Kruse in 1940, which spent six months searching for the lost city.

In Brazil rarely a year goes by that something doesn't appear in the press about new evidence linking the Old World to Brazil during pre-Columbian times. With five such claims, 1975 was a banner year. Several hundred silver and bronze Roman coins were unearthed near Recife. This was followed by the discovery of some Greek gold coins on Santa Catalina Island. Like the first find, they may have been part of a collector's hoard buried in more recent times. A Roman statue was discovered near Rio de Janeiro; however, I was later able to determine that it had been brought over from Europe in the 1820s.

Two of the discoveries made news around the world. In June of 1975, Brazil's National Indian Foundation announced that a tribe of white, blond-haired, and blue-eyed Indians had been found in a remote region of the Amazon. Anthropologist Raimundo Alves, leader of the expedition that discovered them, reported that the hundred-plus people in this tribe all had very similar features. Dr. Helio Rocha, the director of the foundation, whom I contacted in 1980, said that "the tribe's features could only be explained by the presence of white men in remote times who came to Brazil." I suggested these people could be descendants of more recent arrivals in Brazil, but he said there is no record of exploration by Europeans in that extremely remote area.

The most intriguing discovery occurred just a few days before Christmas of 1975, although I didn't learn of it until 1982. Two divers searching for placer gold nuggets in the Urubu River in the state of São Paulo located an ancient shipwreck at a depth of eighteen meters. Newspapers reported they had picked up a number of amphorae and sections of the hull with intricate carvings on them, which had survived in a remarkable state of preservation because of the freshwater environment. These items, sold for a pittance, ended up in the hands of an antique dealer in São Paulo. He took them to a local museum for identification. The curator realized what significance the finds had and notified the director of IPHAN, the Brazilian Historical and Artistic Institute in Rio de Janeiro.

An archaeologist, Dr. Roldão Pires Brandão, was sent to investigate. Brandão identified the amphorae as Phoenician. On shore close to the wreck site he located and excavated a cave burial. Among the bones he found two gold rings, which various experts have identified as Phoenician. Then, in spite of the riveting nature of the discoveries, the entire matter was officially laid to rest. When I learned about it I was tremendously excited and went to see Dr. Brandão. He was not particularly welcoming when I told him what my interest was, and when I requested a copy of his findings he became quite hostile. "Cabral discovered Brazil, and let's leave it like that," he said. I asked him why, if that was how he felt, he had announced the find in the press. He refused to respond and walked away. He also refused my request for the names of the divers who had discovered the shipwreck.

The director of IPHAN, to whom I then turned, was just as noncommittal. "We have so many finds in Brazil of this nature that I can't remember that incident at all," he said. He too had been extensively quoted at the time declaring the shipwreck and burial to be Phoenician, yet only seven years later he couldn't remember anything, or so I was supposed to believe.

Politics had once again reared its ugly head to thwart the great white gods. Officially, credit for the discovery of Brazil is generally given to the Portuguese explorer Pedro Alvares Cabral, a friend of Vasco da Gama's. In 1500, Cabral sailed on an expedition to the East Indies at the behest of King Manuel I of Portugal. In attempting to reach the Indian Ocean, he was becalmed off the coast of Africa and strong currents bore him to the coast of Brazil, which he claimed for Portugal before heading back eastward.

The Spanish, however, claim Vicente Yáñez Pinzón discovered Brazil. Pinzón, commander of the *Niña* on Columbus's first voyage to the New World, sailed from Spain in 1499 with his own fleet and reached the Brazilian coast, discovering the mouth of the Amazon River and then continuing further south, several months before Cabral appeared on the scene. In recent years, documents have turned up suggesting that a Frenchman named Cousins may have beaten them both and reached Brazil in 1488. But whether it was a Portuguese, Spanish, or French mariner who first reached Brazil in the Age of Discovery, I believe the Phoenicians had beaten them all across more than 1,000 years before.

As soon as I got home from Australia, I called my old friend Commander Guedes at the Maritime Museum in Rio and asked him about the Greek amphorae he had written to me about. I was ready to leave for Brazil the following day, but Max told me he thought the amphorae had most likely been brought over from the Mediterranean by one of the many European divers who work in Brazil's offshore oil fields. "Probably," he said, "one of these divers found them on a shipwreck in the Mediterranean, came over on a yacht, and flung them overboard when his wife said she didn't want those dust catchers in her home." This sounded like a sensible explanation, and I let the matter die for the moment, since I had obligations to fulfill elsewhere.

In May 1979, I was able to go to Brazil. I formed a Brazilian company, Fenicia Pesquisas Arqueologicas Ltda. (Phoenician Archaeological Explorations), and for three years spent six to eight months annually working around Salvador, formerly Bahía, on the east coast south of Recife and north of Rio de Janeiro. For centuries, Portugal's most important New World seaport was São Salvador de Bahía de Todos los Santos, better known as Bahía or Salvador. It was a major entrepôt of the lucrative trade in Brazilian sugar and African slaves, as well as a port of call for Portugal's richly laden East Indiamen. The floor of the vast bay, over a hundred square miles in area, is littered with the remains of more than three hundred vessels that sank during the colonial period. We located and excavated over a dozen sixteenth- and seventeenth-century shipwrecks, recovering an amazing amount of artifacts. There were so many that after the Maritime Museum in Rio was filled, the government converted an ancient fort in the harbor of Bahía into a museum to display the remaining artifacts and treasures.

Whenever bad weather, which could last for a couple of weeks, prevented diving operations in Bahía, I traveled all over the country chasing down information on anything relating to the great white gods. Then in March 1981, an event occurred right in Bahía that I wish I had never learned about. A local diver named Ze Lauro brought me a rather strange glazed platter, unlike anything I had ever seen before. He claimed he had found it on a shipwreck in the bay. He said there were many large earthenware "vases" about a meter high. They sounded like amphorae, and certainly they were unlike any storage vessels used in Brazil either during the colonial period or more recently. He refused to show me the location, but I did persuade him to send the ceramic platter to the Maritime Museum in Rio de Janeiro. Commander Guedes turned it over to several archaeologists at IPHAN, and the matter was forgotten for several months.

One day I received an urgent summons to Brazilian Navy headquarters in Rio. When I arrived I found that a press conference was underway, with Admiral Maximilian Fonseca, the head of the Brazilian Navy, officiating. The platter was the focus of attention. I listened at the back of the room as the admiral told the assembled media people that twenty-five international experts had identified the object as of Phoenician manufacture. Then he held the platter up, displaying some scratch marks on the back, and said, in all seriousness, "It gives the date of 1256 B.C., written right here."

I couldn't believe such nonsense. He never explained how a plate could be dated B.C., nor did the press pick up on it. When he spotted me he pointed me out to the press, saying that I had also dated the plate and would be excavating the Phoenician shipwreck in the near future, which under the circumstances I had difficulty denying. This find made news around the world, but instead of quoting the admiral who made these claims, which I found had no scientific backing, the news accounts gave me all of this unwanted publicity. After a press conference I discovered that no experts had even seen the platter. I asked to take it to the United States and Europe for study. Not only was this request denied, but the platter disappeared, perhaps in response to protestations from the Portuguese government that occurred several days after the news was released. To my further disappointment, upon returning to Bahía I learned that Ze Lauro had been killed in a knife fight with another diver and the location of the "vase" shipwreck was lost again.

A month later I was summoned back to Rio, this time by the director of IPHAN, who wanted me to examine a "Phoenician amphora" that had been confiscated from a diver who had been arrested when he sold it. I assumed it was from Ze Lauro's site, even though Bahía is almost fifteen hundred miles north of Rio. But I never had the chance to see it, because when I went to the police office where it was supposed to be, the police who had confiscated the amphora claimed they couldn't find it. To compensate me for making the long trip to Rio, the director invited me to his home for dinner. I noticed he had a Roman amphora covered with barnacles and other marine growth. I asked him if he had picked it up on a trip to the Mediterranean, and he told me that it was one of two "Greek" amphorae that a diver named Roberto Teixiera had picked up from the bottom of the Bay of Guanabara in 1976. The great white gods were whispering in my ears again! I persuaded him to let me borrow this amphora and also the other one, which was stored in a shed on his farm, for further study. I took them to the only oceanographic institutions in Brazil: one to the Naval Oceanographic Institute in Rio and the other to the oceanographic institute in the state of Rio Grande. I requested that they study the encrustations on the amphorae.

In the meantime, I had to go on the other side of the Atlantic to the Cape Verde Islands, which lie south of the Canaries near the coast of Africa. This was a UNESCO-sponsored project in which I was asked to explore a shipwreck site found by fishermen. This shipwreck was very interesting. It turned out to be a late-fifteenth-century Portuguese caravel, lost only several decades after the islands had first been discovered by the Portuguese, but I discovered something else that set my adrenaline flowing.

I was stranded on Ilha do Sal (Salt Island), the northernmost of the Cape Verdes, for several days when my flight was canceled, and I decided to make the best of the time by exploring the island. Salt pans cover most of the island, which has been a major source of salt ever since the Portuguese first arrived, and most likely for a much longer time. Walking along many stretches of beach I found thousands of pottery sherds that were Phoenician and Roman—debris either discarded when ancient ships visited this island or washed in from shipwrecks close off the shore. The Phoenicians were the first to use salt in bartering with various African tribes for gold dust and ivory, and the Romans followed in this trade along the west coast of Africa.

It was always assumed that the salt was obtained from sources along the southern coast of Spain or Portugal, but now it appeared that Salt Island might have been one of these sources. I knew that I had made a significant discovery. Most of the hundreds of accidental crossings of the Atlantic recorded during the past century originated with vessels sailing in the vicinity of the Cape Verde Islands, and most of these ships—like Cabral's in 1500—ended up in Brazil. Phoenician and Roman ships stopping at Salt Island could have been blown across to Brazil just as easily as modern sailing vessels.

When I got back to Brazil I checked with the oceano-graphic institutes and was not surprised to hear that the marine growth on the Roman amphorae was not from the Mediterra-nean, but rather from the Bay of Guanabara, proving that they hadn't been recently brought from the Mediterranean and dumped in the bay. I asked them to reexamine the jars and make certain that there was no underlayer of Mediterranean marine growth. They informed me that it was all from the Bay of Guanabara and had taken hundreds of years to grow. Later on I sent sherds from this site to Dr. Walton Smith of the University of Miami's Oceanographic Institute and to Dr. Ruth Turner of the Museum of Comparative Zoology of Harvard University; both confirmed the results.

Dr. Eliezer de Carvalho of the Oceanographic Institute in Rio Grande had carbon-14 dating done on the marine growth and stated it showed that some of it dated around 2,000 years old, plus or minus 140 years. Thermoluminescence testing, used on anything fired in an oven, such as ceramics or bricks, is an even more accurate dating process. An IPHAN archaeol-ogist sent another sherd to the Institute of Archaeology of the University of London, which responded with a date of 2,000 years plus or minus a century. This certainly ruled out the possibility that the amphorae had been found in the Mediterra-nean or were copies made at a later date.

When I told Commander Guedes that I wanted to investi-gate the discovery of the amphorae further, he suggested that I let the matter rest, because, he said, "it will cause you nothing but trouble." I should have taken his advice. Instead I initiated one of the most tedious searches of my life. I wanted to find Roberto Teixiera, the original discoverer of the Guanabara am-phorae. I thought it would be easy, but there were over two hundred Roberto Teixieras listed in the Rio de Janeiro tele-phone directory. I called them all, without success, and enlisted several assistants to call the more than 2,350 other Teixieras listed in the directory. After weeks of frustration we located a distant cousin who told us Roberto was now a commercial diver working in the oil fields. We contacted the offices of dozens of oil exploration firms without locating him. I then began an odyssey lasting several months, starting at the southern ports of Brazil and working northward. This time my luck took a long time to materialize. I did find Roberto Teixiera in Natal, over two thousand miles north of Rio de Janeiro and the last place I had intended to search.

At first he was very reluctant to talk with me because I was associated with the Brazilian navy, which had jailed him some years before. However, after he downed most of the bottle of scotch I'd brought him, he spilled the beans. He had found the intact amphorae, actually eight of them, while spearfishing around a rock somewhere in the middle of the bay. He said there were thousands of sherds on the bottom. He had sold six intact amphorae to tourists before being arrested with the remaining two. We talked at length and reached an agreement. He would show me the site and work with me, in return for which I would give him 100 percent of all profits made from the venture, as well as full credit for being the original discoverer.

Unable to take time from his job, he said a close friend of his in Rio would show me the site. He and this friend, Raul Cerqueira, had gone back to the site one night about two years after his initial find, and Raul had shot a movie using underwater lights.

I rushed back to Rio de Janeiro and met Raul, president of the Brazilian Professional Divers Union, who was happy to assist me. He had two large sections of amphorae. They had the necks, useful in identification and dating. He also lent me a hundred feet of 16mm motion-picture film of the site. Viewing the film was one of the most thrilling moments of my life. Hundreds of broken amphorae lay scattered all over the mud-covered bottom among rocks and coral growth. I must have looked at it a dozen times before taking the next step, which was to show it to marine biologists in Brazil. My main objective was to determine where the film had been shot—in the Bay of Guanabara or the Mediterranean. The experts assured me it was the Bay of Guanabara from the identification of fish and other marine life. Before Raul could take me to the site I needed permission from the navy, which entailed a wait of several months.

With a minimum of fanfare, Raul and I went out to dive on the site. But he was unable to locate the spot. He said that there had been several navigation buoys in the area that no longer existed. In fact, we went out daily for two weeks, and I was beginning to believe that the whole deal might be a hoax. When Raul was no longer able to continue the search, I resorted to my old method of talking to local fishermen. Like divers, fishermen are more talkative after a few drinks, but it took many bottles of *caçasa,* a strong cane liquor, and many conversations before I met a fisherman who told me he fished around a rock that stuck up from the bottom of the bay.

He told me that many times he pulled up large "macumba jars" in his nets, especially in an area about a hundred meters off the rock. Each time he brought up an intact jar, he broke it with a hammer and flung the sherds back into the water so his nets wouldn't bring it up again. Macumba is the type of voodoo practiced in Brazil, and offerings, usually of money, jewelry, and perfume, to the macumba gods are placed in ceramic jars and thrown into the sea. These jars are usually less than a foot high, but he was describing jars three times that size. I showed him a photograph of one of Teixiera's amphorae and he excitedly said it was identical to those he had been finding.

The fisherman told me that only a few months before he had shown this site to a local diver, who recovered many intact "macumba jars." Before the day was out I had located this diver. He turned out to be the one who had been arrested the year before for selling the "Phoenician amphorae" that had disappeared from police custody. He showed me twelve others of the fourteen he had found after I promised to keep his finds a secret. He claimed to have found two life-size marble legs on the site, which he had already sold to someone he refused to identify.

This diver, in turn, sent me to visit a grizzled old fisherman who said that over fifty years earlier he had recovered a life-size bronze statue that he and his brother cut up in pieces and sold for scrap. There is no keeping things quiet in Brazil, and after the papers reported that I was working in Guanabara Bay, another fisherman appeared at the Maritime Museum with a Roman bronze fibula—used to fasten garments. None of these people, including Teixeira and Raul, had anything to be gained from inventing their finds, so once again I felt that I was on my way to making the discovery of a lifetime.

The following morning, I went to dive the site with the fisherman as my guide. Many things had changed since Teixeira and Raul had been there. Dredging activities associated with the construction of a nearby oil refinery made the water so dirty that on good days the best visibility was only three feet. The rock was a large basalt pinnacle rising to within a meter of the surface. Today a beacon is mounted on it to warn ships en route to the oil refinery of the navigation hazard. This rock, called Xaréu for a type of mackerel that schools around it, slopes away to a base approximately one hundred meters in diameter at a depth of fifteen meters. Many other rocks, some over five meters high, surround the main spire. On three sides of the base, the bottom drops off to twenty-five meters; the harbor floor consists of coarse sand on top of one to two meters of soft mud, underlain by mud of a harder consistency up to fifteen meters deep.

Within seconds of starting my descent down the face of the rock I found several ceramic sherds, embedded in crevices, that I recognized as being from Roman amphorae. But on the bottom all I saw was mud and more mud. Where were the thousands of broken amphorae I had seen in Raul's film? I soon realized that the surface deposit of sand and one to two meters of soft mud was the result of recent dredging operations and was covering the wreck site. Digging frantically by hand, I began uncovering dozens of other sherds and filled a bag with them before my air ran out.

I was well aware of the significance of this site. It was the most important I had ever dived on, and I was tempted to keep on exploring. But I knew that I needed to stop and make sure that the site was handled in a way that would be above reproach so that whatever information it yielded would be accepted by archaeologists and historians. During the ride back to shore I kept saying to myself, "Marx, all your life you have been convinced that Mediterranean mariners came to the New World before Columbus, and now here is the proof. You know there will be people who will suggest that you planted the evidence."

It would have been much better if I hadn't been involved, since I do have a bias, but I was involved, and it was too thrilling to walk away from. On the way back to Rio, I mentally planned the international team I would put together to work on this unique site. I went right away to Max Guedes with the sherds I had collected, thinking he would be as excited as I was. To my great disappointment he was dismayed rather than overjoyed. Again he reiterated his earlier statement about this find causing us all a great deal of trouble. I begged him to issue me an archaeological excavation permit. He reluctantly promised he would but said he had to talk to his superiors first.

I then contacted over twenty underwater archaeologists, historians, and other experts from both sides of the Atlantic, inviting them to participate in excavating the Roman sherd site. Knowing what effect this would have on the Spaniards and Portuguese, I included several scholars from each of these countries.

My intention was to keep the find a secret until we had further evidence, but word leaked out, and the find made a sensation around the world. The Brazilians still classified the site as Phoenician or Greek, but I was able to convince the rest of the world it was Roman. Suddenly I was contacted by experts from around the world offering their assistance and telling me about other finds I hadn't known of. A Jesuit in Argentina sent me information about the discovery in 1897 of a cave full of Roman amphorae. Another priest, a Dominican, also from Argentina, informed me that some Roman artifacts had been recovered by a farmer plowing a field about twenty years before and that the artifacts were stored at the University of Cordova in Argentina. I also heard from lots of people in both North and South America who claimed to have found all sorts of ancient coins.

I hadn't anticipated the next development, which was a major battle between IPHAN and the Brazilian navy. IPHAN demanded the right to supervise the excavation. I thought this was a good idea to have Brazil's chief archaeologists involved in the project, but the navy, which felt the site was on their turf, was adamantly opposed. Finally the president of Brazil intervened, giving the navy the rights. On March 2, 1982, my archaeological permit was finally issued. It contained a major flaw. No foreigners could be involved but me, and I would have to use navy divers as my assistants. The navy wanted all of the glory for itself. This meant no international observers to monitor the work, no international historians and archaeologists. I couldn't even use my diving team, which was still working on the colonial-period shipwrecks up in Bahía. I had really looked forward to international cooperation on this project, which was of global significance. It was essential that the Guanabara Bay project be carried out under the strictest of archaeological standards, and I planned to use new technology to solve certain problems the site presented. For example, once the bottom sediment was stirred up, underwater visibility would be nil, so I wanted to construct some sort of large underwater igloo of clear plastic to place over sections of the site. The water inside it could be pumped to the surface, filtered, and sent back down again. We would then be able to work in relatively clear water, taking necessary measurements, making drawings, and photographing everything *in situ*.

Several more months flew by before I could continue the preliminary survey while the navy selected a team of divers to work on the project with me. Six notably unenthusiastic navy divers were assigned to the project, but after one dive on the site I was back to diving alone. None of them disagreed when their senior officer decided the water was too murky to work safely. They hung around for several days drinking beer and after that never even showed up again. The replacements the navy was to furnish never materialized.

During a period of several months I logged over two hundred hours exploring and mapping the site, recovering several hundred more sherds, including the necks and handles of at least twelve amphorae and the top half of one amphora and the bottom half of another. I also located ceramic sherds of smaller jugs and plates, as well as a circular stone with a hole in the center resembling a grinding wheel, which may have been used as a small anchor. Almost all of these finds were exposed and cemented to the rocky peak by marine growth. I didn't plan to dig into the sediment until I could follow acceptable archaeological guidelines, because it was critical not to jeopardize the validity of any data that would emerge.

I was going home to Florida at Christmas, but before leaving I really wanted to know as much about the site as possible. The National Geographic Society helped me persuade the navy to allow one foreign expert, Dr. Harold Edgerton, to help me. Doc came down in December 1982 and conducted a three-day search with his sub-bottom-profiling sonar in an attempt to locate wooden remains of the ancient amphora carrier, if such a ship existed in the first place. In his report Dr. Edgerton wrote:

> *Two buried targets were located below the seafloor which produced sonar records such as can be expected to result from the disintegration of ancient wooden ships. If these two targets are indeed part of a Roman sailing ship it would appear that after hitting the dangerous high pinnacle of rock, the ship broke into two or more pieces. The largest piece (target one) drifted off to the north-northeast before submerging, which could be expected since the prevailing wind blows from the southwest. The smaller section (target two), which might be the stern of the ship, slipped off the pinnacle top and slid down the south*

side of the rock [where most of the finds were made]. The scatter pattern of the amphorae sherds suggests that this occurred. The fact that intact amphorae have been found on the surface of the seafloor over the top of both buried targets indicates that the targets may possibly be a Roman ship. However, there is always the possibility that both targets are more recent shipwrecks and that the amphorae were deposited over the targets by tidal currents or when snagged in fishing nets. A proper excavation of the site may resolve the matter.

The navy held a press conference upon receiving Dr. Edgerton's report, and the following day, when it made front-page news, my troubles started. I was underwater at the time using a long metal probe, confirming that wooden remains did in fact exist where the sonar had shown the targets. The American consulate in Rio was picketed by over a hundred protesters, brandishing placards reading "Cabral Sí, Marx No." A week later at a Christmas party in Rio I was singled out by the Brazilian minister of education, who tersely informed me, "Every plaza in Brazil has a statue of Cabral, the real discoverer of Brazil, and we are not going to replace these with monuments to some anonymous Italian pizza vendor just because you have invented a Roman shipwreck where none exists." Heading home the next day, I had a bad taste in my mouth.

While I was still in Florida, the Portuguese and Spanish governments expressed great concern to the Brazilian government over the possibility that the Roman wreck discovery would displace Columbus and Cabral as discoverers of the New World and Brazil. I couldn't believe that petty nationalistic jealousies about who first reached the shores of Brazil could stand in the way of such an incredibly important find. However, I greatly underestimated the comic-opera potential of this whole affair.

In a new twist of the plot, the Italian ambassador notified the government that since a Roman ship had been discovered, it proved that the Romans were the first to discover Brazil. A huge number of Brazilians are of Italian descent; many of them are immigrants. Consequently, he demanded that the Brazilian government extend immediate citizenship to all Italian immigrants. As descendants of the Romans, they should enjoy the same freedom from the long, tedious citizenship procedure that Portuguese immigrants are granted as descendants of Cabral. The Brazilians countered by claiming that the wreck was not Roman but Phoenician, and the local press has continued to refer to it as a Phoenician wreck.

When I returned to Rio after Christmas, university students were still picketing the United States consulate with the same placards saying "Cabral Sí! Marx No!" No sooner had I landed at the Rio airport than immigration officials told me to report at once to the office of Admiral Fonseca. After he greeted me he launched into a tirade telling me I was the cause of a lot of trouble. He announced that I had to sign a prepared statement declaring that I had made a serious error in my findings and now admitted the shipwreck was Phoenician, not Roman. No amount of pleading, followed by threats, could force me to sign this document.

As I walked out of the admiral's office, leaving him screaming in fury, I knew the end had come. I felt a sense of unreality. How could this be happening? I rushed over to the Maritime Museum seeking the intervention of Max Guedes, but he was away on a convenient leave of absence and couldn't be reached. The following day I was notified that my archaeological permit had been rescinded. A few days later my work permit was canceled as well. Even without a permit I was determined to take one last look at the Roman shipwreck site. A naval patrol boat was anchored over the site with instructions to arrest me if I went into the water. The final blow came some days later when naval authorities ordered a large dredge boat to cover the entire site with tons of mud "to prevent others from plundering it."

For more than a year I tried every means possible, with help from scholars around the world, to persuade the Brazilians to reinstate my permit and let me get back to work on the site. When they refused, I urged them to let someone else do the project, but they were dead set against any further excavation or investigation. I was told that the whole subject was just too controversial and that Brazil would not benefit from continuing the project. However, the Brazilian press kept the matter alive for years afterward. Stories appeared in a Rio paper about a man who claimed to have manufactured the amphorae. Allegedly he had thrown them into the water "so they could grow barnacles to look authentic." However, when confronted, the paper was unable to produce the "amphora maker."

Then a retired naval officer was quoted to the effect that in 1966 he and I had found a complete Roman shipwreck off the coast of Italy. The Italian government, the officer said, had paid us to transport wreckage and artifacts from Italy to Brazil, where we planted them in the Bay of Guanabara. When I produced my passport covering this period of time, which showed that I was in neither Italy nor Brazil in 1966 (actually I was in Jamaica working seven days a week excavating Port Royal at the time), the Brazilian press refused to print my rebuttal. Just a few years ago, in 1988, another naval officer accused me in the press of "finding and smuggling out tons of gold" that he claimed I had discovered on some shipwreck in Brazil. All of this would have been funny if it hadn't been so sad.

Experts with impeccable credentials confirmed that the amphorae and other materials I had recovered were Roman, dating between the second century B.C. and third century A.D. The world's leading expert on identification and dating of amphorae is Dr. Elizabeth Will of the Department of Classics at the University of Massachusetts. She first dated them as belonging to the second century B.C. and then after a great deal more study changed the date to the third century A.D. Most other authorities agree with the earlier date of the second century B.C. Dr. Will stated that the amphorae were "apparently manufactured at Kouass, the ancient port of Zilis (Dchar Jedid), on the Atlantic coast of Morocco, southwest of Tangier." The archaeologist who had conducted excavations at Kouass, Dr. Michel Ponsich, agreed with Dr. Will on the origin of the amphorae. Fabric studies of the clay body were conducted, comparing the clay used in the manufacture of the amphorae on the Guanabara site and those found at Kouass, and they were identical.

Records exist of Romans circumnavigating Africa, but are lacking for any voyages made across the Atlantic. This is not surprising, because if a ship was lost and no one returned home there was no one to write about the voyage. Dr. Lionel Casson, a leading expert on ancient navigation, says that he sees no reason why a Roman vessel caught by storm off Morocco could not be blown across the Atlantic. It is conceivable that a Roman vessel was near the Cape Verde Islands seeking a cargo of salt, or returning after loading a cargo of salt, when stress of storm or contrary currents in a calm forced it upon the coast of Brazil. Some of the crew must have been alive when the ship sank, because entering Guanabara Bay is very like threading a needle, and the ship needed someone at the tiller.

One thing is certain: there is a Roman shipwreck in Guanabara Bay. How it got there or what happened to its crew may forever remain a mystery, but it is the most conclusive proof I have ever seen that the great white gods reached the New World long before Columbus and Cabral. I trust that Brazil will heed its responsibility and eventually permit study of the site. I have no doubt that further compelling evidence will turn up in the future to shed new light on pre-Columbian contact with the New World. Somehow, I don't think Christopher Columbus would be affronted at having to share the credit for having touched on American shores with Old World mariners of antiquity.

In ancient times, to go to sea on an extended voyage was to brave not only forbidding physical elements but also the terrifying monsters and sea demons that were believed by all mariners to populate the unfamiliar seas. Life aboard ship was never easy and often appallingly arduous. Mariners faced savage storms and deadly calms, shipwreck, and disease. Epidemics could run through a ship killing every last man. Scurvy and dysentery routinely decimated crews. Pirates infested the seas from the earliest days of sail, and seafarers captured by pirates could expect to be cast adrift, sold as galley slaves, pressed into pirate service, or killed outright. Men sailing from their home ports knew they might never return.

Yet, over the centuries, thousands of intrepid men set sail for hazy lands beyond the known world in search of golden frontiers, or seeking opportunity that was denied them at home. The extraordinary achievement was not to have been first on a distant shore but to have successfully crossed the vast uncharted Atlantic. Brothers in daring and fortitude, they each discovered America. Dark-eyed Phoenicians, Latin-speaking mariners of the Roman Empire, tow-haired Vikings from the icy north, Cabral the Portuguese, Pinzón the Spaniard, Christopher Columbus the Genovese Jew, and others whose stories the future may yet reveal: I salute you all.

Epilogue

As I sit at my desk completing this book, there is less than a year left before 1992, when the world will be hearing a great deal about Christopher Columbus and his discovery, or more accurately his rediscovery, of the New World. Spain's major contribution to celebrating the five hundredth anniversary, or quincentennial, is the construction of replicas of Columbus's ships, the *Santa María, Pinta* and *Niña*—the latter about the twice the size of the *Niña II*, which I sailed across the Atlantic. Funded by over eleven million dollars in donations, Spanish naval engineers spent seven years planning and constructing the caravels, which have completed their sea trials. The Spanish government invited me to sail aboard one of the ships as an officer. I have wished them well but declined, because I would prefer a voyage replicating fifteenth-century conditions.

These ships will be marvelous ambassadors of goodwill and will focus attention on the Age of Discovery. However, they will not sail as authentically as we did on the *Niña II*.

Modern power tools were used in their construction, and they are outfitted with radios, radar, and other modern navigation tools, as well as refrigerators and toilet facilities. They have auxiliary engines to use in emergencies and to enter and leave ports. After crossing the Atlantic following in Columbus's wake, these vessels will spend two and a half years visiting more than fifty ports in the Western Hemisphere.

Spain will host Expo 92, the World's Fair, in Seville. Millions are expected to visit this massive exhibition, which was initially scheduled for Chicago. In fact, in 1981 the City of Chicago approached me to oversee construction of replicas of the three Columbus caravels in Spain. The idea was to sail the caravels to America and have them on display at the fair in Chicago. Three years later, after a great deal of work and expense on my part, the government changed in Chicago and the new city leaders decided that the expense of having a world's fair was too much of a burden and dropped the entire project, including construction of the three caravel replicas. However, by this time I was so fired up about making an ocean crossing in 1992 that I decided on another voyage, one that would have a much greater impact on history.

As a youngster I had been obsessed with the idea of someday constructing a Viking ship and making a voyage in her. I grew up to attempt just that, not once but twice. For years I had also dreamed about constructing a Manila galleon replica and crossing the Pacific. I knew that like the Phoenician ships, very little information existed on how these massive ships were constructed.

Sadly, all of the historical documentation and construction plans regarding Manila galleons were stored in the National Archives of the Philippines in Manila, which was destroyed during World War II, when the United States was trying to dislodge the Japanese from Manila. Only three rather crude paintings depicting Manila galleons exist, and that is not enough to make a replica.

I saw my opportunity when a representative of the Marcos

government contacted me in August 1985 and explained that the Philippines wanted to reconstruct a Manila galleon as its contribution to the quincentennial celebrations. After a series of negotiations I agreed to undertake the project if I was given permission to locate and excavate one or more Manila galleon shipwrecks in Philippine waters and to obtain archaeological data on their construction in order to build an authentic replica. My company, Phoenician Explorations, agreed to finance the entire undertaking, and I was granted an area of 18,500 square miles in which to explore for these shipwrecks.

Manila galleons were the largest and richest ships to sail the high seas during the colonial period. Starting in 1565 and ending in 1815, these colossal argosies sailed across the Pacific each year from Acapulco, Mexico, with their holds crammed with silver specie to Manila, where the money was used to purchase all sorts of exotic Far Eastern treasures such as silks, porcelains, spices, rare woods, pearls, gemstones, and objects made of gold, silver, jade, and ivory.

The voyage back to Acapulco took six months on the average, and there was generally a great loss of life from storms, thirst, starvation, disease, and exposure to the cold in the northern latitudes, as the ships, buffeted by contrary winds and currents, sometimes had to sail far north before making their way down the west coast of America to Mexico. Over the years more than 130 of these famous ships had been lost, and about three-fourths of these lay in the area I had selected for my search. None had ever been found in modern times, so finding one was an adventure in itself.

Six months after my project started, I had located two good targets, and then the Marcos government was overthrown. The new government under Corazon Aquino wasn't as interested in the project as the previous government had been. Despite this setback, I continued my work, eventually locating a total of six Manila galleons over a period of three long and difficult years. We had to brave numerous typhoons and were hampered by myriad logistical and communications problems because of the remoteness of the areas we worked in. Our gravest problem, however, was dealing with the New People's Army, the communist insurgents who had total control over the areas we were working in.

The Aquino government declined to give us any protection, and we were unable to start excavating any of the shipwrecks. In desperation I sought an audience with President Aquino and voiced my grievances. She refused my request of military assistance and, in fact, told me she thought it would be best if I abandoned the entire project. She clearly stated, as quoted earlier, that her government did not want to enhance Spain's prestige in any way. Her people had been slaves under the Spaniards for four centuries; the Manila galleons had been used to steal her nation's riches, so the last thing she wanted was for me to open old wounds by making this voyage.

By this time my team and I had endured a host of frustrations and had been fired on seven times by the NPA. I was in no mood to see if we had nine lives, so I regretfully ended the Philippine project. The sad part was that on several of the Manila galleon shipwrecks we had discovered there were sufficient wooden remains to enable us to design an authentic replica.

I concluded that my contribution to the quincentennial celebration of Columbus's voyage of discovery should be writing this book. My aim is not to denigrate Columbus in any way, nor to belittle his achievements, although I am sure that there will be some Spaniards with a parochial view of history who will be up in arms when it is published. I like to think that Columbus himself, master mariner, student of history, and seeker of new worlds, would be fascinated by the growing body of evidence that indicates others from the Old World preceded him. After all, to him goes the credit or the blame, depending on one's perspective, for the New World's development (or exploitation, again depending on one's point of view). I myself am by no means finished with my own quest for knowledge about the great white gods.

Index